Cash
Management

Cash Management

Corporate Strategies For Profit

MARY C. DRISCOLL

A Wiley-Interscience Publication

JOHN WILEY & SONS
New York • Chichester • Brisbane • Toronto • Singapore

Library of Congress Cataloging in Publication Data:

Driscoll, Mary C., 1954–
  Cash management.

  (A Wiley-Interscience publication)
  Bibliography: p.
  Includes index.
  1. Cash management.   I. Title. II. Series.

HG4028.C45D74 1983   658.1'5244   83-10239
ISBN 0-471-87409-4

Printed in the United States of America

10 9 8 7 6 5 4 3 2 1

To E. Paul Harris and Jack B. Rochester

The engine which drives Enterprise is not Thrift, but Profit.

John Maynard Keynes

Preface

Traditionally, the cash manager in large American corporations supervised daily liquidity. This involved depositing receipts, paying current bills, compensating banks, and avoiding short-term cash deficits. The cash manager was the treasury department's traffic cop, directing the orderly flow of cash in and out of the company. He or she prevented collisions between daily cash needs and inadequate bank balances. Temporarily idle funds were often parked at the bank and used to defray the cost of credit services.

In the years following World War II, corporations experienced unchecked growth. Interest rates were low and predictable. Senior financial officers focused on expansion and basic enterprise that generated risk-adjusted rates of return greater than the cost of finance. Because interest rates were relatively low, the cash manager was not evaluated on how much he could earn for the company through investing interim excess balances. The value of daily cash surpluses simply did not warrant energetic schemes for capturing the earning potential of every corporate dollar. In fact, the first lockbox was regarded as an anomaly.

Today, the cash manager's job is radically different from what it was even ten years ago. Economic uncertainty and interest rate volatility, trademarks of the 1970s, caused corporations to reconsider the role of the person responsible for the mechanics of cashflows. Treasury departments with their computing power, independent of corporate mainframes, also transformed the cash manager's objectives. Today, the cash manager engineers the time value of cashflows that are considered just as important as any other corporate resource. He or she plans and directs corporate payment systems with a view toward making company cashflows ultimately productive. Indeed, cash managers are now judged by how well they capture the earnings potential of cash.

The people who work in cash management departments at major corporations have also changed. They embrace computers, which reduce the number of mundane chores that once occupied most of the day. As a result, contemporary cash managers spend more time measuring system performance and deciding how to refine strategies. They plan how to best use cashflows and the information that moves them.

Cash managers now identify their work as a profession, not merely an ill-defined part of the treasury function or a stepping stone to the treasurer's chair. Eager to share ideas and expand skills, the new breed of cash manager belongs to local and national professional associations. Cash managers with a group perspective want to help shape banking regulations that affect corporate payment practices.

The push is on for formally recognized training programs and certificates which signify competence in this highly specialized area of financial management. The National Corporate Cash Management Association and the South Carolina Cash Management Association are working to develop programs in conjunction with business schools. Georgia Institute of Technology now offers a special graduate program for cash management students. Until recently, courses in cash management were hard to find and college textbooks ignored the subject.

Although several books on cash management have been published, literature geared specifically for the corporate cash manager is sparse. This book describes cash management practices developed by large companies with over $100 million in annual sales. Smaller firms can benefit from the basic mechanics of cash management discussed here. The concepts are the same and just as applicable to their business needs.

The chemistry between banker and corporate customer is essential to good cash management, and it is carefully explored. Bankers can learn more about cash managers and vice-versa.

The first three chapters introduce cash management objectives and vocabulary for the reader unfamiliar with the field. Chapters Four through Ten proceed at a faster clip and consider cash management subsystems in detail. I try to show why carefully planned cash management programs are vital to the financial stability of corporations. I suggest that cash management strategic planning can add to the bottom-line. My intention, however, was not to write the definitive text. My goal was to present cash management, what it is and how it is performed, in a digestable style. I also wanted to discuss nuances of corporate cash management that are often neglected. As such, I have referred to actual corporate situations that reveal how theory applies to practice.

I am indebted to many people who reviewed this book and pointed me in the right direction at critical junctures. I am especially grateful to Craig Sullivan for his tireless help and inspiration. Allen Grieve, John Cardamone, and Bennet Quillan also deserve special thanks. I would also like to acknowledge, and thank, the many people whose speeches, articles, books, comments and other materials are referred to herein. They are: George C. White, John Leahy, Dr. Bernell K. Stone, Dr. Ned C. Hill, Dr. Steven F. Maier, Daniel Ferguson, Robert Losh, Michael Napoli, Steven MacQuarrie, Cindy Yasinski, John Alexander, Raymond Ruzek, William E. Donoghue, and Norman Weinberg. While many people were kind enough to take the time to talk about cash management with me, I am solely responsible for any shortcomings this book may have.

MARY C. DRISCOLL

Boston, Massachusetts
August 1983

Contents

CHAPTER 6 ACCELERATING
CASH RECEIPTS   117

CHAPTER 7 CASH CONCENTRATION
SYSTEMS   151

CHAPTER 8 DISBURSING CASH   163

CHAPTER 9 SHORT-TERM CASH
FORECASTING AND INVESTING   183

Cash
Management

1 Introduction

1 Principles of Cash Management

Walter Hanson, treasurer at American Gadgets, was having a bad day. He'd received a $10,000 bill for tool parts. The invoice terms stated that he could take a two percent discount if he paid in ten days. But Walter was having trouble finding cash to pay the bill. American Gadgets was due to receive a large remittance from a customer at the end of the following week. Walter knew from experience that the customer always paid bills on time, although he waited until the last possible date to mail a check. Furthermore, Walter knew that check arrivals were hard to predict; postal system performance was erratic.

Walter then remembered that Labor Day was five days away. Holidays always disrupted mail service. Frustrated, he realized that he could not depend on the remittance to help win the two percent discount. Even if the customer's check arrived before the holiday, it would take at least three days to clear.

To make matters worse, a memo from the company president landed on Walter's desk. The memo read:

> During a recent golf game, I learned that a company, about the same size as ours, last year added $100,000 to pretax income by using cash management. As you know, I try to stay out of your way when it comes to financial operations. Results are my pet peeve. At your earliest convenience, I would like a complete rundown on American Gadgets' cash management efforts. I am interested in potential earnings from these activities.

Poor Walter was in a terrible state. He had all he could do to keep track of receivables and juggle budgets when the manufacturing division went on a spending spree. The last time he had even heard of cash management was when a college professor breezed through a few short passages on the subject. At the end of his rope, Walter reached for the phone and dialed his account officer at the bank.

CASH—A HIDDEN RESOURCE

American Gadgets, with $50 million in annual sales, is not unlike many other relatively small firms in desperate need of tactics that the Fortune 500 and their banks developed years ago. Large firms sought to manage cash flows and augment earnings by investing temporarily idle balances. While Walter Hanson waits for receipts at the mercy of the postal system, his counterparts at huge American firms debate the fine points of lockbox studies and clearing system slippage. When the prime rate rises, uninitiated treasurers cannot afford to ignore techniques that exploit the earnings potential of cash. Walter Hanson may be shocked to discover what it costs him to let his funds flounder in the mail or at the bank. But Walter will learn quickly, as soon as he figures out the right questions to ask.

This book will help people like Walter by exploring cash management practices refined by large companies who have come to value short-term cash as much as any other corporate asset. We will discuss how firms, large or small, can employ aggressive treasury policies in order to survive in a volatile interest rate environment. We will examine the need for an offensive strategy at a time when corporate America faces a ubiquitous liquidity crisis. In short, we will discover a hidden arsenal, corporate cash management.

This book will offer a perspective on formal systems and techniques, developed by major corporations, for managing cash flows when efficiency and profit are the goals. We will see that when the treasury function is treated as an action—rather than a reaction—center, a firm has a chance of enduring exorbitantly high costs of funds and business uncertainty. Many analysts predict that during the 1980s volatile interest rates will prevail. This environment injects uncertainty into the task of financial management. Astute cash management may be some firms' only life raft.

We will find out how it works and how to implement the necessary systems, and we will discuss ways to capture the productivity of cash.

Cash management can do a lot more for your firm than merely contribute to earnings or help reduce short-term borrowing requirements. A well-oiled cash management program can strengthen your relationships with customers, vendors, and banks; make your firm a better credit risk; and prepare you for growth. Once your cash management program is in place, you will be able to provide top management with helpful cash flow projections that serve as your early warning system for cash flow crises.

Shareholders will also benefit from your efforts. They will feel more secure knowing that you are braced for economic upheavals: a cash management awareness gives you a margin of financial flexibility. At the very least, studying cash management concepts will keep you one step ahead of the boss. With luck, you may someday be able to point to substantial profits that you have added to your company's earnings. The cash manager at one of the largest American oil companies reports proudly that his program added $10 million during one year to the corporate bottom-line.[1] You too can be a corporate hero or heroine.

WHAT IS CASH MANAGEMENT?

Corporate cash management is one aspect of the treasury function. Generally, cash management activities aid the efficient and profitable employment of certain short-term financial assets, cash and marketable securities. Cash management is also concerned with meeting current obligations (vendor payments, bank compensation, debt expenses, taxes, wages, and other financial liabilities). Cash management has traditionally focused on cash gathering and disbursing, called "money mobilization." This is the lifeblood of daily financial existence. The job entails the operational guidance of cash inflows and outflows necessary for a firm to conduct business.

The cash manager measures and guards the certainty, safety, and earning power of cash and near-cash resources. Checks, negotiable money orders, money, and bank balances (after deduction of outstanding checks) are all considered cash.[2] Cash is listed as a current asset on corporate balance sheets. The term "near-cash resources" refers to marketable securities that are often included as current assets on the balance sheet. Marketable securities are highly liquid: usually, they can be converted to cash within one to four days. Most marketable securities are simply IOUs from the government (treasury bills), banks (certificates of deposit or bankers' acceptances), or major corporations (commercial paper). A market exists for these securities because so many companies and financial institutions regularly buy and sell them. Therefore, because such a large market exists, any company holding these securities can quickly convert them to cash. For this reason, they are called marketable securities.[3]

Cash managers are also responsible for amounts represented by outstanding checks. From the moment a customer mails or otherwise transfers payment, until the moment when his payments clear, the cash manager is responsible for those funds' whereabouts. Where funds reside at any given time is of extreme importance to the cash manager.

To understand cash management, it is helpful to recall the textbook axiom about the time value of money. If we have money in a savings account that earns interest, our funds will grow over time. The amount of interest we earn is added to the amount of our principal investment. Since one responsibility of the cash manager is cash balances, he attempts to maintain his balances at levels sufficient to cover his checks presented for payment, compensate banks, and keep certain reserves on hand. When he discovers on any given day that he has more cash than he immediately needs, he transfers the excess to highly liquid interest-bearing mediums that pay the best rate available, given risk parameters defined in corporate investment guidelines. If it makes economic sense for the cash manager to use excess funds to pay down short-term debt, he may do so. Conversely, if he needs to shore up balance levels, he may liquidate a marketable security.

Unlike consumers, corporations are, as of this writing, prevented by law from earning explicit interest on checking account deposits. Additionally, corporations can only have up to $150,000 in savings accounts. This is not an advantageous investment. Therefore, the cash manager must avoid the opportunity cost of allowing funds to remain idle. He must also combat the effects of inflation. The cash manager is driven by the time value of money. Even if regulators ever legalize explicit interest on corporate checking accounts (something now being considered) corporations will depend on cash management expertise for maximizing the value of company cash flows and the information that supports them.

Survival Tactics

As businesses have grown more complex so has the province of the cash manager. Today, the cash manager does more than supervise transactions. Aided by computing power, he orchestrates the timely receipt of information vital to the control of daily cash positions. He directs automated corporate payment systems, moving money to where it best contributes to company goals.

Shrewd cash managers can make a lot of money for their firms. By directing mail to more efficient post offices, a cash manager can increase the speed at which money travels to him. The faster he gets paid, the sooner he can pay off expensive debts or invest. One cash manager added $600,000 to annual profits by changing the address on remittance return envelopes.[4] By manipulating these and other operating procedures, the cash management function can become a corporate profit center. A profit center is responsible for revenues and costs. This is an appropriate cash management goal. Some analysts, however, argue, correctly, that cash management departments should not be viewed primarily as investment centers, where increasing the investment base is an objective on par with fiduciary responsibility.

Cash management strategies never stop with a single coup. The cash manager is involved in an ongoing process of measuring the effects of, and refining, procedures that support the firm's financial health. While many industries do not view themselves as primarily in the money business, cash management is a welcome innovation. As a discipline in its own right, cash management has grown only in recent years when the opportunity cost of idle balances became a paramount corporate concern. Cash management as a profit-making enterprise was a reaction to soaring interest rates and an uncertain economic environment. Nonetheless, it now seems that cash management has become a regular fixture of corporate financial planning. Futurists say that businesses will remain complex and that information—processed by computers—will become a valued commodity. Cash management can help companies of all sizes keep pace with the value of well-managed data, as well as add to the bottom line.

WHERE DOES THE CASH MANAGER FIT IN?

The degree to which the cash manager functions as policy-maker depends on how much autonomy is delegated to his boss, the treasurer. It is awkward to generalize about the treasurer's role in corporate finance since it varies across industries, companies, and even within companies. Often, company size and decision-making traditions define the purview of the treasurer and his staff. Among the largest companies, particularly multinationals, the treasurer (or treasurers) report regularly to a financial vice president, chief financial officer, or chairman of the finance committee. Here, the treasurer is not the chief financial executive. The cash manager may have to contend with strict guidelines on how to execute policies decided at the senior management level.

It is fair to say that the smaller the firm, the more authority accrues to the treasurer and his subordinates. The treasurer of a firm with $200 million in annual sales is usually the resident financial czar. A firm of this size may have two persons responsible for daily cash management activities, while the boss concerns himself with capital formation matters and long-term corporate profitability. The cash manager in a relatively small firm may have a large measure of input on short-term financial management strategies.

A large multinational may have a 20-person cash management department in which, for example, one staffer may oversee collections. A smaller firm, one with annual sales under $100 million (known as a "middle market" firm), may hire an assistant treasurer whose job is to design and implement a cash management system from scratch. Interestingly, middle market firms now practice successful cash management techniques developed in the 1970s by the largest firms and their banks. The smaller corporations have the benefit of learning tested methods for controlling company cash flows and generating extra earnings.

A Sign of the Times

If we think of cash management as creative resource deployment, we see that its recent popularity is actually part of a national trend: obsession with productivity. American businesses are now searching for new success formulas in light of fierce global competition. Cash management is a way of making financial assets very productive, a lesson quickly learned by large American companies in recent years. By 1980, consumers too had caught on to personal cash management. Interest rates crept up and people realized that passbook savings accounts, paying five and one-half percent, could not keep up with inflation. Consumers began to shift their savings into money market funds. In response, bankers lobbied heavily and, in December 1982, won the authority to offer competitive interest rates on certain classes of consumer deposits. Cash management had entered mainstream thinking.

A Typical Tale?

Often, financial newspapers describe corporate cash management with sensational tales of wizardry and intrigue. A favorite story is this: a New York company received a large check on a Friday before a long weekend. The check was drawn on a California bank. The New Yorkers sensed that their customer wanted to have use of the funds over the weekend and still meet a payment deadline. Unawed, the New York firm flew an employee carrying the check to California. He arrived in time to cash the check and invest in the West Coast money markets before they closed. The time difference, and the fact that the New York firm had an account at the California bank, made the plan work. The company earned so much interest over the long weekend that the airfare was inconsequential. Presumably, the staffer enjoyed an unplanned California holiday.[5]

Corporate cash management stories are often exciting because they reveal a unique professional challenge: one individual is capable of contributing inordinate amounts of profit to his company. Unfortunately, cash managers traditionally have been underpaid. Nonetheless, the profession attracts a certain kind of person, someone fascinated by detail but, by the same token, a person who measures an aggregate landscape for perfection. Day-to-day cash management involves grueling attention to minutiae as well as large-scale planning. While suspenseful tales do exist, the perfection of cash and data flows is the cash managers' daily diet. The episode described above represents an occasional taste of caviar. But speeding collections and slowing payments—increasing the cash reservoir—is the meat and potatoes of cash management, a recipe for rewarding corporate financial management.

CASH MANAGEMENT PERFORMED

Efficient corporate treasurers view cash as an asset and a scarce resource that must be conserved and made to earn a reasonable rate of return. Cash management is the treasurer's method of sustaining the proper balance position with which a firm meets its current obligations.[6] Cash management helps the treasurer maintain minimum levels of operating funds. Excess balances that temporarily appear are put to work where they can best contribute to corporate profitability goals.

Primarily, the cash manager has two objectives: efficiency and profit. To meet these, he strives to control the flow of funds and optimize their earnings potential. Sometimes, one cash management activity accomplishes both objectives. For instance, streamlined cash collection procedures may reduce internal operating costs while simultaneously generating extra earnings. Other cash management activities may alone reduce system redundancy or create interest income. But a cash manager primarily attempts to achieve efficiency and profits by increasing and controlling existing cash resources.

Cash Management Activities

Cash management is performed by:
Accelerating cash receipts and concentrating funds in a central cash reservoir.
Planning and slowing disbursements.
Forecasting receipts and disbursements.
Investing excess balances.
Monitoring system performance.

Accelerating and Concentrating Cash Receipts

The object of this activity is to gather and control funds with greater dispatch. This effort can reduce costs and generate profits. A variety of gathering methods—which we will examine in later chapters—are used to shorten the time it takes the cash manager to convert receivables into usable funds. Acceleration involves manipulating the flow of remittances, whether deposited, mailed, or electronically transferred, to corporate coffers. The cash manager then concentrates his funds where they can be easily controlled for paying bills, reducing short-term debt, or investing. This activity, combined with securing short-term loans when needed, is aggregate cash position management. It allows cash managers with widely dispersed accounts to control the network as a coordinated unit.

Using collection and concentration techniques, the cash manager, in effect, reduces what is called "collection float." Collection float is the aggregate cost of delays between the time when a customer writes a check and when that check, having moved through the postal, corporate, and banking systems, becomes available funds to the receiving corporation. Collection float incorporates mail float, processing float, and clearing float, each belonging to operations of the postal service, corporations, and the banking system, respectively. Collection float may be the cash manager's worst enemy because it is expensive to wait for outstanding receipts in transit. Acceleration strategies aim at reducing this burden. We will explore float issues, in depth, in later chapters when we analyze the components of a cash management system. We will learn why float is a cost (when you are managing cash inflows) and why float is a benefit (when you are managing cash outflows).

Part of the cash acceleration process involves monitoring the availability of cash balances. When a check (or other form of credit) is assigned to a depositor's account, he can draw on those funds only when availability has been granted by the bank of deposit. "Availability time" refers to this delay. The time it takes for a bank to move checks through payment systems back to the check writer's bank for collection is called "clearing time." Availability and clearing times are measured in days. Sometimes the availability that a bank grants equals actual clearing time; sometimes it does not.

Cash managers depend on information systems to track the location and accessibility of cash collections. Large corporations do this with the help of computerized deposit and balance reporting systems. In addition, these sophisticated reporting systems provide current data that other departments can use. For example, shipments which may be held back pending payment can be released as soon as collection information pops up on a computer screen. Conversely, shipments may be easily prevented if a down-payment check bounces. Also, automated cash management data can be integrated into other corporate data bases, for example, the accounting general ledger system. This allows for enhanced accounts receivables updating and faster, more accurate profit and loss reporting capabilities.

Planning and Slowing Cash Disbursements

To the cash manager, planning and slowing cash outflows is another way to generate cost reductions and profits. This can be accomplished by centralizing the accounts payable function when information on subsidiary payables is easily accessed. This procedure allows a corporation to exercise control over payment scheduling and method. The cash manager can take advantage of discounts, when appropriate, or, at least, assure that bills are paid only when due. When bills are paid from central bank accounts, the cash manager can better monitor his cash position and allocate daily cash balances. He can also benefit from the increased disbursement float (checks outstanding) produced by planned and slowed clearings.[7] As mentioned earlier, when managing disbursements, float becomes the cash manager's best friend. Astute disbursement strategies can be effective even when payment authority is decentralized, but balance information management responsibility rests with the corporate cash manager.

If a cash manager can hold on to his funds longer, he has the opportunity to keep that money working for him until the moment when it is needed to pay bills. Later, we will discuss techniques that cash managers use to manage disbursements and generate additional funds by investing previously committed cash. Using such strategies, the cash manager can profit and still be assured of having adequate funds to pay outstanding checks when they are presented.

Disbursement programs, tied to balance reporting systems, produce vital data the cash manager needs to better gauge balance levels required for bank compensation, whether for credit or noncredit services. A cash manager aims to minimize idle balances; cash disbursement and information systems support this goal.

Planned cash allocation contributes to financial flexibility as well. It injects added degrees of certainty into funds flow management. It helps a cash manager know where his money is when he needs it. Funds transfer technology is an important part of this process and lets the cash manager react efficiently to unexpected emergencies. Planned allocation strategies can enhance a corporation's creditworthiness and its vendor relationships. Controlling an organized disbursement program helps avoid overdrafts and assures timely trade payments.

Forecasting Receipts and Disbursements

The basic purpose of forecasting is to provide the best approximations of future events. Central to the use of daily cash forecasting is recognizing that it supplies information upon which to base reasonable decisions.[8] Forecasting cash inflows and outflows helps the cash manager create a cash plan. He can then make daily allocations and be prepared for future cash uses and sources. The bases for forecasts are historical requirements and future activity projections.

Cash managers usually forecast cash sources and needs that will occur days and weeks hence. The extent of this forecast is primarily an immediate period—at most, 12 weeks ahead. An operational forecast breaks down the first few weeks of a three-month forecast into an estimate of daily receipts and disbursements and, thus, daily cash positions. Because there is a one-day, bank time-lag in reporting total corporate account activity, the cash manager constructs his own version of how much cash is in an account on a given day. Large banks are now working with computers to provide customers with real-time balance reporting for special disbursing accounts. Monthly forecasts are useful for identifying significant divergencies from quarterly accounting projections. Treasurers can thus be warned of unexpected funding needs.[9]

With careful scheduling of incoming and outgoing funds, the cash manager can match current assets and current liabilities, an essential requirement for financial survival. The cash manager needs to know the cash position for each account that he controls early enough in the day so as to take action before investment opportunities are lost—by 11 A.M. New York time. This is when East Coast money market trading begins to peak. Cash forecasting methods are crucial to the cash manager's goals: efficiency and profit.

Investing Excess Cash

The payoff in cash management comes from mobilizing funds and putting them to work where the firm most needs them. If a cash manager is efficient, he will be able to generate excess balances which he can then invest. The cash manager's playing field is short-term investments, and they catapult him into the world of Wall Street and regional money markets.

With short-term investments that range anywhere from overnight to 360 days, the cash manager can earn the best available rates on temporarily idle funds. Most cash management investments, however, are made for 90 days or less. Those investments that a corporation approves for its short-term investment portfolio represent a firm's sensitivity to considerations of security, marketability, and yield factors. A cash manager usually works with investment guidelines that spell out how senior management wants excess cash used.

Investing in short-term money instruments is only one possible use for unobligated short-term funds. A cash manager may pay down short-term borrowings, thus reducing interest expenses. The expense of short-term debt outpaces probable short-term investment yields. The manner in which a company structures its debts often dictates how a cash manager invests excess cash. A firm typically aggressive in its expansionary policies may want to place working profits back into business development, rather than pay off its outstanding loans. We will see in Chapter 9 how corporations invest. We will discover the significant contributions cash management can make to the bottom-line.

Monitoring System Performance

Once corporate cash management programs are up and running, the cash manager turns his energies to refining system performance. He examines, through formal and informal studies, how well his program achieves its goals. Banks and other service providers can help measure the efficacy of each aspect of the cash management system. Results can be quantified with reasonable accuracy and made into reports for senior management.

The cash manager may also monitor how his department's work affects other areas of the corporation. For instance, he may discuss with the credit manager how well information is being shared. The two may then discuss ways to coordinate, say, discount policies. A fine-tuned cash management system can close existing credibility gaps between the cash management department and other corporate domains. Data from cash management endeavors can prove what works and what does not.

The monitoring function can also help a cash manager negotiate with customers and vendors. Equipped with data, the cash manager can make funds transfer suggestions which may benefit his company and its customers. Conversely, the cash manager may be able to negotiate with vendors over payment terms. When a cash manager knows the extent of his disbursement float, he may then have a valuable bargaining chip when the time comes to plan large trade payables. A vendor may agree to more favorable terms if the cash manager is willing to forego a fraction of his disbursement float.

THE CASH MANAGEMENT TOOLBOX

In order to introduce you to the tools cash managers use on the job, we are going to solve Walter Hanson's problems. Remember Walter? He's the poor guy who can't get his hands on a customer payment needed to take advantage of a large discount. When we left Walter, he was calling his banker for advice. After several long and sober meetings with the banker, Walter had a grip on things. We'll see what he learned in each area.

Accelerating and Concentrating Cash Receipts

Bill Faster.   Walter needs to keep his trade credit terms competitive, so he should not reduce the time that customers are allowed to remit. Invoices specify that they are due thirty days from the billing date. In order to get money in sooner, Walter will change the way he sends out invoices. Rather than mailing statements for all customers at a certain time each month, he may include invoices with shipped goods. This requires coordination among sales, shipping, and treasury staff. They will all work to reduce internal processing lapses. In effect, the billing date is moved up. Additionally, Walter eliminates the time and expense needed for separate bills to travel through the mail to customers. Other firms may be unable to include invoices with shipped goods. Alternative billing strategies will prove useful nonetheless.

Bill Accurately.   Walter will also review invoice legibility; maybe current invoices are hard to understand, and designed so that errors are inherent.

Customers often resist paying bills that are complicated and full of mistakes. He'll create invoice forms that are clear and concise.

Offer Discounts.   He will review whether it is economical to offer discounts for early payments. Discounts may be the incentive for some firms to remit in ten days rather than the standard 30-day credit period. The accelerated cashflow may more than offset, for Walter, the discounting of invoice face value.

Decentralize Receipts.   Walter's firm receives all payments at corporate headquarters. But many customers are on the other side of the country. How about instructing them to send payments to the regional office, where the manager can cut short the checks' long journey and deposit them quickly into a local bank account for collection? Walter's objective will be to accelerate remittance flows and have sooner access to cleared balances. Several funds transfer techniques, which we will study later, are used to move money from field banks to the lead or concentration bank. The point is that Walter just cannot afford to have single checks for $150,000 meandering in the mail for five days. Having that money delayed is a calamity akin to having an investment's earning power shut off for a week. This example is used to illustrate the concept of decentralized collection systems. In practice, however, large companies with national customer bases rely on lockboxes to intercept large, mailed trade payables from credit sales. Lockboxes are described below and explored in-depth in Chapter 6. Methods for efficiently gathering funds taken in by branch offices or field units, typically noncredit sales, are described below and analyzed in Chapter 7.

Collecting and Concentrating Receipts.   Often, regional branches of major corporations are sales outlets, and receive payments over-the-counter, mostly from noncredit sales. Cash management strategies for accelerating cash inflows from numerous branches nationwide are used by large companies to gather funds in a central cash pool for aggregate cash position management. How might such a system operate? If Walter worked for, say, a hotel chain, he could have local managers deposit daily receipts, (cash, checks, and charge card receipts) in a specially selected local bank account. The field unit managers, after making the daily deposits, then phone headquarters and report the deposit information. The funds, including checks that have been cleared through the banking system, are transferred to the concentration bank where Walter can best manage the aggregate cash pool. The deposit reports, among other things, help him plan for cash inflows to the concentration account.

If the transfers are effected at the local level, by the branch managers or their banks, the system is referred to as "field-based initiation." Either wire transfers or depository transfer checks may be used. Depository transfer checks are unsigned checks for moving money between a corporation's accounts. In field-based initiation, the depository transfer checks are mailed either to headquarters or to the concentration bank; they are then entered into the banking system for clearing back to the local bank. This is the most simple form of acceleration and concentration; however, as a cash management technique, it is now, for the most part, obsolete.

Firms with hundreds of branches making deposits often use automated deposit reporting systems operated by banks or third-party vendors. Basically, the local managers phone in the daily deposit reports to a computer center where systemwide data is consolidated and transformed into information necessary to prompt the next step: funds transfer. In this case, funds transfers are initiated by either the corporate cash management staff or by the concentration bank. This is called "central initiation," and there are various applications of the basic concept now in use. We will consider these in Chapter 7. Depository transfer checks, wire transfers (called "draw downs" when initiated by the concentration bank) and electronic versions of depository transfer checks are the ways money is moved out of local banks in a central initiation concentration system.

With a well-run collection and concentration program, Walter will be able to transfer funds quickly to his lead bank, from which he disburses, reduces debt, or invests. However his system is configured (company size determines which methods are best), he can count on reducing significant levels of costly collection float. We have just described methods for accelerating receipts from noncredit sales. We will now look at the most well-known device for quickly gathering funds from credit sales: lockboxes.

Lockboxes. If Walter usually receives many deposits, large or small, in distant regions, he may want to set up lockboxes in cooperation with local banks. Most companies use lockboxes because the regional sales staffs are not geared to augment cash management efforts. Lockboxes are also appropriate in locations where no regional corporate offices exist. The decision to set up lockboxes depends on the size of remittance volume. A cost/benefit analysis will determine whether it is economical to install lockboxes in given regions: the value of reduced collection float has to off-set the expense of this specialized bank service.

Lockboxes are post office boxes rented by a corporation. Customers are instructed to send payments to that special box. The local bank is authorized to open the box—in reality, a canvas bag of envelopes containing checks earmarked for the bank. The bank picks up incoming mail, often many times a day, sorts checks and deposits them into the company's account. Payment data can be tallied for the company. Once the checks are collected locally, funds are transferred to a concentration or lead bank for deployment. The lockbox location should receive prompt local mail service; the bank should have good wire transfer, computer, and ACH (Automated Clearing House— an electronic funds transfer network for sending and receiving debits and credits) capabilities, and be close to a Federal Reserve District Bank or branch. A good lockbox bank must also have an efficient "direct send" program, whereby the bank transports volumes of checks to other banks or Fed facilities for fast presentation. If Walter sets up a lockbox, he can speed collections and reduce internal processing of receipts.

Many large American firms employ computer modeling methods for determining optimum cash transfer schedules. But Walter may not require this level of sophistication. It is appropriate for companies with hundreds of retail outlets making daily deposits, or for firms with numerous lockboxes. However, he will learn to transfer local deposits when it is economical and when it enhances balance control.

Preauthorized Checks. Walter could also speed collections and better predict inflows by arranging with customers to use preauthorized payment plans. In essence, a preauthorized payment plan would allow Walter to issue a check drawn on his customer's account, upon the standing authority of the customer. Usually, such a device is appropriate for regular payments, like mortgages or insurance premiums. Corporate customers may be reluctant to agree to preauthorized plans for many purposes; after all, one person's collection float is another person's disbursement float. However, if Walter can institute uses for preauthorized checks, he can further accelerate certain types of payments. Lease payments are a potential application.

ACH Debits.   An electronic form of preauthorized payment transfer, ACH debits occur when a company accesses customer funds through the ACH network. Preauthorized debits are useful for quickly and inexpensively collecting fixed as well as variable payments from consumer or corporate customers. If Walter's company experienced a high volume of customer remittances, this method could be used to efficiently reduce check charges and check clearing float.[10] Corporations can pay other corporations through the ACH, but the payor is usually unwilling to sacrifice disbursement float enjoyed with the paper-based system. ACH debits give the transaction beneficiary usable funds the day after initiation—unlike checks that experience delays in the mail, in company and bank processing systems, and in Federal Reserve or private sector clearing mechanisms.

GIRO Payments.   Often referred to as customer initiated entries, GIRO payments are credit transfers through the ACH. A customer instructs a bank to debit his account for money which is then moved through the ACH network to the account of the firm receiving payment. GIRO payments, discussed here for corporate collection use, are electronic. Since ACH credits, as well as debits, represent usable funds the day after transaction initiation, payors are reluctant to sacrifice disbursement float, a concept understood by any American who has a checking account: you can pay your rent with a check on Wednesday but cover it on Friday, payday. Electronic GIRO payments are widespread in Europe, not because that continent embraced the computer revolution before America. Paper GIRO systems have been around since the 1600s. When the electronic version came to the fore, Europeans adapted easily. American consumers, ironically, have been resisting electronic banking ever since the first automated teller machine was installed in 1964.

By 1982, automated teller machines were the subject of slick television ad campaigns, and America's love affair with electronic money had blossomed. Although widespread corporate use of this collection tool has not yet materialized, electronic GIRO payments will someday play a significant role in corporate cash management. Corporations with large retail customer bases will, sooner or later, find it cost-efficient to convert accounts receivables and collections systems to this electronic wonder. Corporate-to-corporate trade payments will remain check-based as long as paying cash managers can profit by investing previously committed funds—outstanding checks. We will see later how some innovative firms have already begun the march to electronic consumer initiated entries.

Plan and Slow Payments

Centralized Payment Control.   At Walter's firm, all large trade payables
are made by him at headquarters. This way, he alone is authorized to
disburse hefty trade payments to suppliers. From his chief bank account,
he also meets all the firm's current obligations such as payroll, taxes, and
operating expenses. Branch office expenses, over a certain amount, are
paid when invoices arrive on Walter's desk. Local bank accounts are
maintained by the branch business manager, who may need to pay for
small expenses with a local check. Walter is fortunate that his disbursements are mostly centralized; he already has control mechanisms in place.
Although Walter's disbursement system is simplistic compared to those
at very large corporations, he can adapt some of the basic payment tools
and techniques used by the giant firms. We will describe here the common
strategies and later analyze their applications in Chapter 8.

Plan Payments.   Once Walter's plan to accelerate and concentrate receipts is implemented, he will be able to better allocate payments. For
one thing, he will benefit from speeded cash inflows, which, at opportune
times, will allow him to capture lucrative discounts on bills he pays. He'll
begin to match large receipts and large disbursements, in effect, adding
control to daily operations. If warranted by company size, he will also
develop a plan for funding necessary branch accounts at appointed intervals, thereby reducing the need for local idle balances. In effect, his
disbursement system will be designed to reflect the time value of money.

Take Discounts.   Since Walter always pays his bills on time, taking discounts regularly will soon become a profitable exercise. He must review
state laws; in some states, checks mailed on the day a discount expires
still qualify for the discount. Moreover, Walter will learn how to judge
when it makes economic sense for him to take a discount or to keep funds
invested elsewhere.

Slow Payments.   Primarily, he will begin to schedule payments. He will
no longer automatically pay an invoice the day it arrives. He will learn
to calculate how much it costs him to pay a bill before it is due. For
instance, Walter now sacrifices $138.89 when he pays out $100,000 five
days before the invoice due date. (This assumes Walter could have kept
the money invested at 10% for the five days.)

Remote Disbursing.   Although discouraged by the Fed, remote disbursement is one way cash managers slow down payments. Walter could enhance his disbursement float by paying vendors with checks drawn on a bank situated in a remote corner of the country. The Fed cannot usually clear such checks efficiently; poor winter weather conditions and equipment failure sometimes prevent the Fed from reaching remote destinations for days.

Remote disbursement has come under fire from all sectors in recent years, and rightly so. It is a scheme that takes advantages of inefficiencies in the Fed check collection system, and contributes to unacceptable levels of burdensome Fed float carried at the taxpayer's expense. Remote disbursement can jeopardize relationships with vendors whose funds are subsequently delayed. (Objections aside, cash managers in recent years have used this technique to extend their disbursement float by ten or more days. We will see in later chapters that cash managers use computers to select optimal disbursement sites.) Until the Fed modifies its practice of granting availability on uncollected funds, or begins to charge for float (both now under consideration), Walter may want to strive for added disbursement float with this plan.

Criss-cross Disbursements.   While not truly remote, criss-cross disbursing attempts to add to the amount of time it takes for checks to travel through the payments systems and clear. Companies pay East Coast vendors with checks drawn on West Coast banks. West Coast vendors are paid with East Coast bank checks. If Walter were to use this technique, he'd need to have a reliable way of measuring check collection performance of large banks and the Fed. Many big banks regularly have direct send programs that thwart such schemes. Direct sends are used when a bank finds it worthwhile to physically transport high value checks to the banks on which they were drawn for collection on the same day they are received. Criss-cross disbursing, while widespread, can be tricky. Often, New York checks clear faster to Los Angeles than they do to Detroit when a collecting bank is especially aggressive with direct sends.

Zero-Balance Accounts.   If Walter's company needed to maintain regional disbursements accounts—local suppliers want to be paid with local checks—he could convert branch disbursement accounts to zero-balance accounts. These are special checking accounts that contain no cash balance, or a very small balance requirement. Zero-balance accounts, usually held at branches or affiliates of a lead bank, become overdrawn when checks are presented for collection. The lead bank funds the zero-balance accounts through a master account on the day of presentment, not when checks are written. Sometimes, this technique adds disbursement float, but it is primarily used for keeping some disbursing authority and accounting integrity at the regional level. Of course, Walter may want to use zero-balance accounts for special classes of payments: taxes, payroll, and so on. The device automatically separates cash outflows and provides the cash manager with an easy way to monitor certain account balances while reducing the need for idle balances.

Many large banks that specialize in cash management provide cash managers with the ability to monitor zero-balance account activity with computers. Funding from the lead bank, typically the chief concentration bank, can be automatically triggered when checks presented for collection overdraw the accounts. (We will see later the role of funds transfer mechanisms in these systems.) With this disbursement method, Walter's task will be easier, and he will have better control of account activity. He may reduce the number of independent accounts that his firm uses and thus eliminate redundant banking expenses.

Controlled Disbursement Accounts.   Walter may set up special accounts for controlled disbursing of substantial cashflows. Also organized in a tier system, controlled disbursement accounts maintain zero balances and are funded through a master account after the bank informs the cash manager early each day which checks have been presented for collection. Money may be kept earning interest in another medium until it is needed to cover checks. Controlled disbursement accounts are usually maintained at branches or affiliates of large banks. These branches or affiliates are not in major cities and, therefore, receive early, final check presentments from the Fed each day. They also have certain daily cutoff times after which checks presented by other private banks for collection become the next day's work.

The cut-off times are early enough in the morning to allow banks the time to sort and identify checks, then notify cash managers of their daily funding requirements. Money is transferred into the controlled disbursing accounts before the end of the day, generally by wire transfers. Other transfer mechanisms, such as depository transfer checks, can be used; however, as we shall discuss, banks may require back-up balances. The key reason for using controlled disbursement accounts is that cash managers have a way of knowing how much excess daily cash exists for investing in the money market on a timely basis. Since optimal investment decisions must be made before 11:30 A.M. New York Time—before the daily market for certain investments winds down—these disbursing plans give the cash manager a valuable hedge: he is assured that no other major funding requirements will arise after the last batch of checks has been presented against his controlled disbursing account.

Controlled disbursing plans are also valuable because they enhance the cash manager's balance control: idle funds are minimized and payment information is organized, often by special computer programs. Walter can review with his lead bank the need for this cash management technique. His bank will be eager to keep his business and may be willing to design a controlled disbursement plan for him. However, like remote disbursement accounts, controlled disbursement accounts have been criticized by regulators who view the device as another disbursement float extension gimmick. We shall see, in later chapters, new Fed operating procedures—called noon presentment plans—that are causing cash managers to reformulate their controlled disbursement strategies.

Payable-Through-Drafts (PTDs).   Unlike checks that are drawn on a bank, PTDs are drawn on the corporation. The bank acts merely as a collecting agent and assumes no liability for the instrument. PTDs flow through the Fed as checks and are presented to the bank that delivers them to the firm. Although PTDs require special bank handling and, sometimes, minimum bank deposits, Walter could use them to monitor certain disbursements that require the issuer's examination prior to their being paid. One proper use for PTDs is an insurance claim settlement in which the payee's endorsement constitutes a release of the issuing company from further liability.[11] He could use PTDs for branch expenses when no local bank account exists. PTDs afford a critical, centralized control ability: the cash manager reviews payments and is able to ward off potential embezzlement or unauthorized liabilities.

When banks experience operational snags and cannot deliver PTDs for same-day corporate payment authorization, the device extends disbursement float by at least one day. Cash managers have traditionally used them for this reason. However, potential float benefits with PTDs may now be drying up. Many large banks have adopted automated ledger systems that help measure float and charge back to the customer any float earned at the banks' expense.

Money Fund Disbursements. Walter may use a money market mutual fund much like he would use a bank checking account, especially when he does not need to maintain average levels of collected balances to compensate banks for either credit or noncredit services. The benefit of paying bills from a money fund account is that balances continue to earn competitive interest rates until checks clear the fund's custodian bank. One disadvantage, though, is that checks written on money funds are often for a minimum of at least $500. Furthermore, funds that are primarily oriented to a retail customer base do not encourage corporations to move large amounts continuously in and out of their accounts. Such wide swings can adversely affect daily dividend payouts to other fund shareholders. This is due to the fact that money funds calculate the net asset value of their portfolios, hence shareholder gains, daily.

Walter can use a money fund to pay certain bills, such as taxes, which sometimes experience lengthy government processing delays. This way, he'll be sure to keep idle funds working judiciously for him. The key feature of disbursing from a money fund is that competitive interest rates are paid on balances. As long as banks are prohibited from paying explicit interest on corporate checking accounts, money funds provide cash managers a way to earn money market yields on temporarily idle cash. As of this writing, there is a proposal before regulators to allow banks this privilege. We will analyze relevant issues in Chapter 9. For now, it is fair to say that the cash manager who is understaffed, or who has little portfolio management expertise, can benefit by drawing on the professional investment skills found among money fund portfolio managers. And there is another boon: money funds do not charge investors for purchasing or redeeming shares; management fees are built into the daily net asset valuation calculation.

EFT Trade Payments. Walter may be able to obtain consideration for paying bills via the ACH, an electronic funds transfer system that provides transaction beneficiaries with funds the day after a transfer is initiated. If so, he will engage in what we call negotiated settlement. The benefit to the vendor is that he enjoys payment certainty; he does not have to wait for checks in the mail or for those held up in processing. He can better predict the cash inflows. Another benefit to both parties arises when funds are value dated; that is, initiated at a time convenient for the payer but guaranteed to be available to the payee on a certain date.

Generally, Walter will give up disbursement float with electronic trade payments, but he'll negotiate for discounts in return from his suppliers. Traditionally, corporations have been reluctant to sacrifice float benefits: the profit that cash managers can make by investing previously committed funds has been the driving force behind many cash management programs. However, there are times when electronic trade payments make economic sense. For example, using the ACH may allow a paying company to reduce processing and check charges to an extent that justifies the loss of float. We will consider later how corporations are now using the ACH for both debit and credit transactions. Although Walter may not be ready to use the ACH for trade payments, he will want assurances that his lead bank can easily accommodate this kind of operation.

Forecasting Receipts and Disbursements

Daily Cash Forecasting.   Walter will learn to predict cash inflows and out-flows and develop a daily cash plan. While accounting departments prepare forecasts that reflect expected changes in levels of working capital for an accounting period, the cash manager needs to predict very short-term changes to levels of bank balances. Accounting forecasts may predict that, during a given month, receipts will exceed disbursements. But any cash manager knows that during the month there will be days when there is not enough cash available to meet current obligations. Furthermore, because company books often reflect disbursements when checks are written, rather than when they are presented to the bank for payment, the cash manager needs his own system for estimating patterns of check clearings. He also needs to chart when field unit sales forecasts, accounts receivables, and daily check deposits will become usable funds at the bank. He needs to estimate for certain days, how much excess cash is available for investment or debt reduction or, conversely, how much he will need to borrow short-term to cover deficits.

The daily cash forecast, which typically looks ahead two weeks, is updated every day as actual cashflows affect the level of bank balances. Usually, the cash manager forecasts ahead as much as three months, broken down into weeks, but the current two-week estimate of daily cash flows is his vital concern. This activity provides him with crucial cash planning ability. For instance, if he knows he will have an extra two million dollars for five days, he can prepare an investment plan and attempt to secure the best possible yield on approved instruments. If he knows that in one week, he will have a deficit cash position, he can plan to sell securities or arrange for credit. We will see in Chapter 9 that the cash management control afforded by an accurate cash forecasting program translates into cost-savings or profits for corporations. For Walter, developing a reliable daily cash forecasting program is essential to his management role. Otherwise, he is merely a fireman, extinguishing cash crises that have been smoldering without his knowledge. There are very sophisticated computer modeling techniques that large corporations use to forecast daily cashflows. Although they may not be appropriate for Walter's firm, the concept of developing a cash plan is still essential.

Investing Excess Balances

Short-Term Investments.   Once Walter is in a position to invest temporarily excess balances, he will be able to choose among a range of money market instruments. We will look at each of these in Chapter 9. Walter and the company president will discuss the need for, and develop, investment guidelines that will establish the firm's investment philosophy and risk parameters. Then he will know that his decisions represent proper use of company funds. He and the company president will decide whether to manage short-term investments internally or let a professional manager oversee all or part of this function. He will establish a method for monitoring the performance of his short-term investment portfolio. He may use a benchmark yield, like the 91-day Treasury bill rate, to measure how well his investments fare. He will also review annually whether approved investments bring desired returns without jeopardizing corporate financial assets.

Walter will also review short-term borrowing expenses. He will identify short-term debt parameters which indicate when to pay down lines of credit or repay other loans. He will be able to track how well his policies utilize the earning power of excess cash.

Monitoring System Performance

Monitoring Float.   Walter will carefully scrutinize current operations and determine where he suffers from high levels of collection float, and misses opportunities to maximize disbursement float. He will perform cost-benefit analyses to determine when it makes economic sense to install or change systems for dealing with both kinds of float. For instance, before he opts for a lockbox system, Walter will determine the proper trade-off between collection float reduction and the expense of lockbox service. He may discover that the annual cost of maintaining a lockbox, including charges for bank fees, concentration costs, and internal management costs are too high, given the expected float reduction. He will quantify the trade-off by finding the opportunity cost of the collection float. That is, he will calculate, at a rate which may be a potential investment yield or an internal rate of return on funds, how much earning power he sacrifices by not using a lockbox and allowing receipts to flow in at their normal, slow pace.

Once he begins to use cash management techniques, Walter will monitor how well they address float concerns. For instance, he will periodically review whether his disbursement sites were proper choices; that is, is he receiving expected float extension benefits at a certain disbursing account location? As we will see, cash managers regularly monitor float and its components, sometimes by asking bank cash management consultants to study their programs.

Monitoring System Expense and Efficiency. Throughout this book, we look at how cash managers review how well their systems are working at justifiable costs. We see, for example, that cash managers can use wire transfers to easily concentrate funds from field banks but that excessive use of this tool for certain applications can drive system costs sky high. To address this problem, cash managers decide when and how to gather funds at the concentration level. A field bank that receives small daily deposits may be a candidate for wires only twice per week. Maybe other transfer devices would then be appropriate, such as depository transfer checks or ACH concentration debits—the electronic version of the depository transfer check. Walter will learn to monitor system expense and efficiency by assuring that his cash management programs achieve desired results at reasonable cost. He will look at each component of his system, then consider how each interacts with the system as a whole. He will constantly fine-tune the different working parts of his cash management program. Once things are running smoothly, he can try to quantify the results of his program either in terms of cost-savings or investment earnings.

Probably one of the most critical monitoring functions a cash manager faces is regularly inspecting the monthly account analyses he receives

from his banks. These are reports on how many cash management services
were used each month, and what each cost the bank to provide. The account analysis also indicates the month's average levels of collected and
uncollected balances. From these figures, a bank determines how well it
is being compensated by the corporation for services provided. A corporation may pay for bank services in fees, balances, or a combination
of the two. The account analysis review process, which we cover in-depth
in Chapter 5, allows the cash manager to study whether he is over- or
undercompensating his banks. Walter will learn to review account analyses
as if they were monthly invoices from his banks. Then, he will be able
to get a handle on how much he spends annually for banking services.
He may even be able to prepare yearly banking expense budgets and,
thus, create a valuable management report for use by senior management.

Computer-Assisted System Monitoring.   Desktop computing is fast becoming
a regular feature in cash management departments. Microcomputers are
now the rage; they are stand-alone machines that do not rely on mainframes
for calculating and storage power. As the lever assists the arm the computer
aids the brain, and cash managers are turning to microcomputers in order
to easily perform the many mundane tasks generic to their profession. A
microcomputer can automatically retrieve daily balance reports from a
network of bank accounts. This replaces having to phone banks every
morning to learn the current opening cash balances. Since banks do not
finish posting the total day's debits and credits until the early hours of
the following morning, the cash manager needs updated information on
yesterday's closing balances before he plan's daily investments. With automated balance reporting, the cash manager's computer can be on the
phone to bank computers, gathering the crucial data, long before the cash
manager is out of bed.

Microcomputers can keep track of investment portfolios and even suggest optimum investment strategies given parameters supplied by the cash
manager. They are used for forecasting daily cashflows; computers can
perform in moments calculations that would take a human hours. Treasury
terminals, either as stand-alone computers or tied to timeshare systems,
can access external data bases, providing up-to-the-minute reports on
money market rates. Remote access terminals provided by banks can help
the cash manager track balances as each day unfolds. He can even initiate
funds transfers through terminals tied to his banks' systems. A desktop
computer can track debits and credits posted to individual bank accounts,

in effect, replacing the need for manual bookkeeping while, at the same time, recording current data useful to the accounting function. Cash managers at large firms are now trying to integrate their computer output with the mammoth corporate data processing systems. The idea is to trade valuable information with other departments automatically, reducing task redundancy and the burden of manual data translation and storage. Walter's firm may not be ready for the savvy techniques used by large corporations for managing information. But there is nothing stopping him from getting a small micro—maybe he can borrow one from his children. He will be amazed at how much time and energy he can save with such inventions as the electronic spreadsheet.

SUMMARY

We have quickly described popular cash management tools that Walter can employ to greatly improve the performance of his firm's treasury department. The purpose of this section has been to present these basic concepts so that the reader new to the field can sense how various collection, concentration, disbursing, forecasting, investing, and systems monitoring tasks fit together and form a cash management strategy. We have seen that although the cash manager strives for profit, his primary role is to operate efficient systems that safeguard the earning power of short-term financial assets. We will examine all tools and techniques in great detail later and see how they are commonly used by American businesses. We will see that optimum performance may be achieved when savvy techniques are combined with well-developed strategies.

2 A Strategic Approach to Cash Management

A classical definition of management is: accomplishing objectives through directing others.[12] We can think about the cash manager's job as one that directs his firm's most liquid assets, cash and marketable securities. Then, the cash manager becomes a task master of some very valuable resources. His job changes from supervising repetitive transactions to nurturing the productivity of cashflows and the information systems that move them. To do this, the cash manager plans and oversees systems that render his resources profitable. In effect, he uses strategies that deal effectively with uncertainty. The proactive cash manager may be likened to an airline chief executive. His resources are the aircraft; his systems are the schedules and routes that put his planes to work. He plans, organizes, and directs the people who operate the resources and systems which return a profit.

A PROACTIVE VIEW OF THE CASH MANAGER'S ROLE

Quickly we sense that strategic cash management requires an ability to diagnose and solve daily problems as well as constantly monitor the efficiency of the function as a whole. He may, for example, set up a lockbox to speed receivables in one area. But he will also review, at appropriate intervals, optimum schedules for transferring funds to concentration banks. He may discover that daily funds transfers are unnecessary; receipt volumes at certain locations only warrant transfers two days per week. But, he will not ignore funding needs; if they are constantly severe, he may decide to incur the expense of daily transfers. He will consider how each element of the cash management system interacts.

The strategic cash manager sets objectives which all the moving parts of his system strive to meet, individually and as a working machine. But for objectives to be meaningful, they must be attainable and measurable. Furthermore, objectives should be sanctioned by top management; this way, cash management efforts are in line with corporate philosophies for growth and return on investment.

For objectives to be attainable and measurable, policy and procedures must be developed in concert by applying logic, judgment, and information analysis. The person setting up a cash management program must decide:

What is to be implemented and the results required.

What decisions have to be made.

When to achieve the required results.

Who is responsible and accountable for decisions.

How such decisions should be made.[13]

The cash manager then approaches each of his subsystems in the same way. He defines policies and procedures for cash acceleration, concentration, disbursement, forecasting, investing, and monitoring. Each has its own set of objectives which, combined, produce the best cash management results for the company.

We have seen in Chapter 1 that the cash manager's system objectives are efficiency and profitability. We have considered the need to view a system as a whole, made up of operations that are, individually and collectively, efficient and profitable. One way the cash manager accomplishes this is to maintain both short- and long-term goals. When developing strategies, he must consider how well they can adapt to organizational, regulatory, economic, and technological changes, as well as solve daily problems.

If his company is new and its prospects for growth are good, the proactive cash manager builds a system that he can upgrade as his firm expands. When he chooses a cash management bank, he studies how well that bank is prepared to meet his needs as they grow more complex. He compares prices for bank services, but these alone do not motivate his decision. Aware of the importance of bank expertise, the proactive cash manager includes a quality factor in his eventual choice. We will now look at some additional strides the cash manager can make.

The cash manager will not attempt money mobilization improvements (speeding receivables and slowing disbursements) without an idea of what he will do with the extra funds once he has them. He should have prepared an acceptable investment plan for temporarily idle balances. He must research the best direction for investments: is it more efficient to reduce short-term borrowings, fund subsidiaries, or earn interest income in the money markets? How can he apportion uses of excess cash? He should rely on analytical skills like computing required rates of return on liquid assets versus borrowing costs, capital expenditures, and money market yields possible with investments approved by senior management. This way, he can produce immediate results that fit into a long-term plan.

He should also employ conceptual skills that help him decide how to best adhere to overall corporate philosophy. Will he be an aggressive or conservative cash manager? Does he forsee future need for bank loans for expansion, or will his company's credit requirements remain stable? If he shops for cash management bank services too aggressively, he may find that when his firm needs bank credit, relationships have been unduly strained. He must review how his plans affect subsidiaries or branch office functions. He will realize that he cannot afford to be myopic; strategies that benefit him may aid or burden other departments.

He will make decisions in light of the regulatory climate. For example, when choosing a controlled disbursement site, he will consider Fed threats to change presentment and availability schedules (timed allotments of credit for deposited checks), actions that could wreak havoc on his disbursement system. A proactive cash manager will have another controlled disbursement account reserved for system back-up or be prepared to alter cash balance forecasting methods.

It is important to keep abreast of economic developments. He can predict fairly well approaching business downturns or upturns when he is aware of business conditions nationwide and within his own industry. He can then sense whether or not it is appropriate to negotiate with customers for certain, albeit discounted, payments. Conversely, he will know when his vendors are likely to offer favorable discounts in return for sooner and/or certain payment.

Armed with data on bank availability schedules and fund transfer techniques, the proactive cash manager may be able to stave off a rash of bounced checks when the economy goes sour. Although in many companies the cash manager alone does not set credit policies, his operational savvy can help other departments confront business upheavals.

The proactive cash manager will know what are realistic office automation needs. Does he need a computer terminal to minimize manual processing of commercial paper issues? Does he need it today or ever? How cost-efficient are computer models that recommend optimal balance allocation? How much time and money can be saved with computerized balance and deposit reporting systems? Can the accounting department use computer-transmitted lockbox remittance data?

To answer questions like these, the cash manager needs perspective. This he gets, in part, when he undertakes independent research. How can perspective help? Using the issue of technology, we see that perspective aids decision-making. A cash manager planning a major enhancement may research how similar companies are using available technology. What methods and suppliers are satisfactory? What are the pitfalls of customization?

There are other useful benefits to having a perspective on technology. Since the cash manager reigns over bank balances, he is, in effect, the director of his corporation's payment systems. He is qualified to assist top management with decisions about all banking services. If the head of personnel decides that employees should have the option of direct deposit of their payroll checks, the cash manager can then advise on which banks are most capable of performing this function. The current payroll bank may have a long and valued relationship with the company, but if it can't do a good job that is no reason to let it foul up such a sensitive operation. All banks are not alike; the cash manager with perspective will be the first person to know this.

Good cash management foresight will coordinate various activities so that they reinforce each other's efficiency and profitability. We have seen that an effective money mobilization plan is worthless without an established investment function. Moreover, an ability to allocate excess balances is useless without a way to monitor short-term investment or debt portfolio performance. The cash manager must use performance benchmarks so that he can tell if all the effort is paying off. He may compare the results of his short-term investments with the average yields of selected money market funds investing in similar instruments.[14]

A proactive cash manager will predict and prevent undesired results.

He may have to avoid showing a negative cash balance at audit time, but if he is very good at his job, the cash manager will often have negative book balances because he invests previously committed funds, playing the float. Ironically, some stockholder groups, unaware of what cash management can do for a company, may interpret the lack of cash as troublesome. The cash manager may be in the unenviable position of having to break an investment or increase bank credit at audit time just to show that the company has surplus cash. This is called "window dressing." One alternative is to explain the negative cash balance in the footnotes to financial statements.[15] Whatever recourse he takes, the smart cash manager will solve such a potential mess before damage is done.

A cash manager who takes a large view of his operation will understand, and appreciate, the sensitive politics of bank balances. Bankers have traditionally priced services and earned profits according to their ability to hold on to deposits. With the current pressure on banks to compete with nonbank providers of financial services, losing balances to cash management strategies is just another blow to the banking industry. Mindful of the banker's dilemma, the cash manager can approach the bargaining table confident that balances he leaves on deposit are worth something in return. He may negotiate for special services at little or no cost. Cash managers must recognize, however, that there is a limit to how far banks can be pushed. The careful cash manager will not unnecessarily jeopardize the banking relationship—his hedge in time of need, his partner in innovation.

We have just explored a few examples of how the proactive cash manager thinks. He looks at his own operation and the environment around it. He considers short- and long-term needs and developments. In effect, he examines the causes and effects of scenarios, an activity that can mean the difference between reaching objectives and failing miserably.

CASH MANAGEMENT BY OBJECTIVE

So far, we have described cash management tools and techniques, how they are used, and potential corporate benefits. We have suggested an approach to cash management that stresses setting goals for efficiency and profit. When we look at each cash management activity and tool in subsequent chapters, a clear picture of generic industry practices will emerge. The reader may then apply policies and procedures suitable to his or her company. Let's now examine how a cash management program supports a key treasury objective: maintaining a proper capital structure. One element of capital structure is net working capital, defined as current assets less current liabilities. A firm's investment in its working capital is represented at different times during a firm's natural business cycle by the sum of components of that cycle. A company's business cycle, or cash cycle, begins when cash is invested in raw materials, merchandise, supplies, or services. As the inventory of finished goods is sold, accounts receivable are produced. The cycle is completed when customers pay for goods or services, and accounts receivable become cash. (See Exhibit 2.1.)

One of the treasurer's tasks is to make sure that the right level of working capital is maintained. He has to assure that it is high enough to support business activity, such as extending sufficient credit to customers in order to stay competitive. But investment in working capital must not be excessive. Let's see where the cash manager fits in. Before accounting for current liabilities such as obligations to suppliers, working capital is made up of cash, marketable securities, accounts receivable, and inventory. These are short-term assets. A short-term asset is one that can usually be converted to cash within one year. The treasurer's job is to keep funds, represented by investments in working capital, fully and profitably employed. One way that the treasurer measures his own efficiency is to evaluate how many times in one year the initial cash outlay goes through a complete cycle. This will vary according to company, industry, and economic climate, but the idea is to keep investment in working capital at an efficient minimum. Part of this task is delegated to the cash manager who is given the responsibility for, among other things, keeping cash and marketable securities productive and profitable.

Because the firm must forgo opportunities to invest or repay debt in order to maintain a cash balance, a cash management imperative is to keep only the minimum levels of cash balances necessary to pay bills, handle emergencies, and compensate banks.[16] While he may work closely with the treasurer when decisions about accounts receivable and inventory levels are made (depending on company size and structure), the cash manager's domain is cash and marketable securities. (Checks, we remember, are a form of cash.) He helps the treasurer manage working capital by maximizing the use of cash and marketable securities: generating additional cash, controlling operating expenses, and monitoring the performance of programs that he implements to carry out his job.

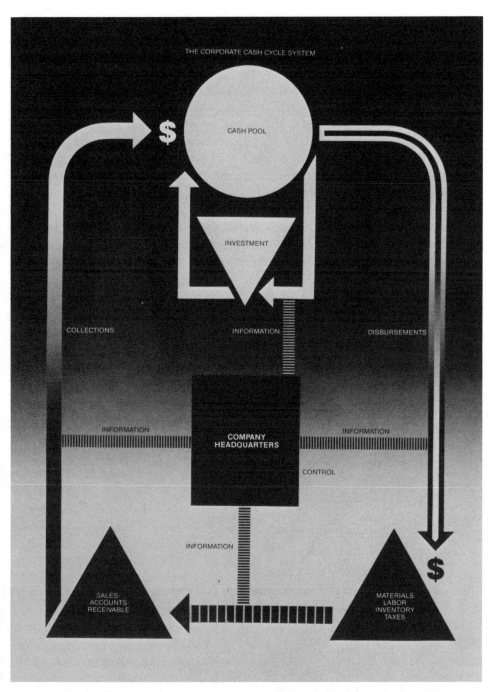

Exhibit 2.1. The cycle of cash that supports business activity. *(Reprinted from "Cash Management Brochure," The First National Bank of Chicago.)*

A cash manager's program has to be efficient and profitable for him to support the treasurer's goal of controlling levels of working capital. We saw in Chapter 1 that the cash manager accomplishes this by staging five activities: (1) accelerating and concentrating cash receipts; (2) planning and slowing disbursements; (3) forecasting receipts and disbursements; (4) investing excess balances; and (5) monitoring system performance. He has to be able to plan and direct each component of his cash management program and report the results of his efforts to the treasurer. Effective reporting is vital; in short, he has to turn raw data into information that the treasurer and senior management can use to manage the financial health of the company. Obtaining meaningful management information is best achieved by planning ahead. When designing cash management systems, it is important to build into them the objective of producing understandable and usable reports.

STRATEGY, WHERE TO BEGIN?

You start by evaluating your current business practices. You may discover that your operation suffers from some of the symptoms of weak cashflow control listed below. These common symptoms are encountered by companies in need of better cash management. The point is to diagnose problems before you plan your strategies. In so doing, you'll learn where you are now and where you have to go.

Some key symptoms of a weak cash management program are:

High short-term borrowings.

High deposit float time.

Consistent bank overdrafts.

Failure to consolidate cash balances.

Decentralized responsibility for cash management.

Holding accounts payable checks.

High volume of intracompany checks.

A limited ability to obtain short-term credit.

Lack of disbursement planning.

Mail transfer of cash.

Absence of cash flow projections.

Poor collection performance.

Large cash balances in demand deposit accounts.

Lack of current analysis of bank performance.

Lack of formal investment program.[17]

Bankers who cannot explain how the ACH works.

Weekly payroll when biweekly payroll would suffice.

No methodology for regularly reviewing bank account analyses.

Unnecessary wire transfers.

No sense of competitive bank service charges.

Infrequent and unreadable account analyses.

Poorly trained staff.

A redundancy of paper and phone transfer advices.

Obsolete investment guidelines.

Little understanding of the Postal Service, commercial banking networks, and the Fed.

Poor communication with top management.

These are examples of dilemmas companies face when cash management is practiced intermittently or not at all. We sense quickly that a firm suffering from some of these problems cannot use stopgap measures to chart a course for efficiency and profit. Successful cash management programs begin with an approach that stresses planning, organization, direction, and control. This is strategic management. It provides performance objectives and measures how well these are met. Techniques are regularly fine-tuned; momentum is preserved.

THE BANKING RELATIONSHIP

Probably the most crucial strategy that a cash manager can implement is to develop a mature relationship with his banks. The word "mature" is used here to denote an interaction in which two parties appreciate its inherent value. When a treasurer and his banker set out to design a cash management system, each will try to reap the most rewards for his organization. Business is business, and getting the most for your dollar is the name of the game. However, the banking relationship is not so cut and dried. A truly profitable banking relationship is one that fosters creativity and fairness. When the cash manager and the banker treat each other fairly, they learn to trust. When this happens, both parties win.

There are now over 250 major banks in the United States that are actively involved in cash management. Given that there are close to 14,000 commercial banks in the country, the cash management cadre seems small. The statistic reveals that cash management operations are highly specialized. (Don't be surprised if your small-town banker knows little about it.) Because cash management requires so much special expertise by bankers, the issue of a trusting relationship is compounded: decisions take on expensive implications for both banker and treasurer.

Often, a treasurer just getting into cash management will turn to his bank for help. Most likely, that bank will be the one with whom he has had a primary credit relationship. Cash management techniques drain the bank of its beloved cash balances and can reduce a company's need for short-term credit. So, many banks have seized a hidden opportunity. A smart banker will realize that although he may lose balances, he will gain an opportunity to offer the corporation a whole range of new services.

Many banks develop cash management services at the request of their customers. Aware that the treasurer may go elsewhere, the banker is eager to hold on to the relationship. Many banks have innovated for this reason alone. Most of the products we will discuss in this book grew out of joint efforts by banks and their customers. But services constantly evolve; the need for creativity is persistent.

It is imperative that cash managers approach negotiations with their bankers with a sense of fairness for an ideal relationship. The cash manager who is too aggressive, shopping far and wide to squeeze the extra cent out of bank service charges, may find that the relationship is strained at a time when he needs a special favor. A cash manager who always wants too much for too little may remember the value of a good relationship only during times of credit emergencies. Having your banker on your side is also critical on days when you receive money late in the afternoon and need to quickly find an overnight investment. While searching for the best services that your money can buy is implicit in your job description, you should not neglect the importance of equitable dealings. The former assistant treasurer at Pickwick International puts it this way: "I know what

I need to spend to get quality service, and I know enough not to jeopardize my operation simply to save a few pennies." Quality service is more often present in banking relationships when both parties treat each other fairly.

However, cash managers, especially new ones, will find that not all bankers are fair. There are those institutions that take advantage of new-comers to cash management; invariably, those banks pay a heavy price. One bank was found to be charging a small company three times the average price for lockbox services. This news emerged at an industry conference with over 300 cash managers in attendance. It is unlikely that the mischievous bank won many new accounts that day. An important part of a cash management strategy is regular bank service evaluation. We will look at this more closely in Chapter 5 and learn how to judge banking relationships. We will see that companies who spend hundreds of thousands of dollars annually for bank services must constantly appraise performance and price. We will also see how they do it from a position of strength and equity.

There is a natural stress to any relationship in which one party pays the other to perform a service. This applies to the arena of cash management. Cash managers, as a group, often exhibit adversarial attitudes toward their bankers. It is easy to understand that a cash manager wants his peers to sense his professional authority, but it would be superficial to say that antagonism describes the extent of a good banking relationship. Many cash management innovations were conceived by corporate and banking professionals working together to solve problems. Teamwork has produced rewards; the smart cash manager never for a moment forgets this.

Attitudes within banks toward cash management have been relatively slow to evolve. Traditionally, bankers have been trained to think in terms of credit services and the deposit base. Cash management service groups within banks were organized as early as the 1950s. But these functions were never considered the glory assignments, and many young banking executives waited out their "operations" stints, eager for promotion to the credit side of the bank.

This has changed considerably since cash management blossomed as a discipline in its own right during the 1970s. Additionally, banks have had to face major repricing issues since the Fed, in 1981, began charging for services. (We will look at this in detail later.) These events have forced bankers to view cash management in a different light. Unfortunately, some bankers still hold on to the notion that cash management is mundane. They make the mistake of imparting this attitude to their customers when making calls. They fail to note what a poor impression this attitude gives the corporate financial executive. It shows that the banker is trying to sell something he barely understands, and it warns the cash manager that service may lack commitment. According to corporate banking surveys done by Greenwich Research Associates, Inc., it is not uncommon for cash managers at large companies to be called on by at least ten bankers with whom they do not do current business.[18] With competition this fierce, bankers cannot afford to offend their customer with ignorance.

The corporate treasurer looks to his banker for ideas and news of products evolving in the marketplace. Even if his cash management program has been long established, the treasurer or cash manager wants to feel that his banker is always interested in his operation. Marketing cash management services does not end when the company signs up for a product. A smart banker knows the value of sticking with the cash manager as his program moves through different stages of growth.

It is often difficult for cash managers in large corporations to switch service banks. A large corporation has multilayered banking relationships which help it finance expansion and arrange mergers, among other things. Boards of directors have been known to terminate a proven relationship simply because a bank is also the lead bank of the perpetrator of a hostile takeover. But the cash manager in a large company cannot fire his bank willy-nilly. What does he do when, for example, he feels ignored by his bank or is unsatisfied with a service? He may threaten to let another of his major banks provide a new service. Indeed, politics play a large role in banking relationships for companies of all sizes. For example, the small business treasurer may be bound to a relationship because his president and the bank president are golf partners or sit on each other's boards. The treasurer will do his best to accommodate both his boss's and his department's needs.

Banking relationships involve people, and, hence, egos, politics, attitudes, and a wide assortment of skills and knowledge. The most profitable relationships are those that foster creativity and trust. Cash management functions and products will continue to evolve in the 1980s, and fair and trusting relationships among cash managers and bankers are the key to success.

3 The History of Cash Management

WHEN THE PRIME WAS ONE PERCENT

Prior to the 1950s, the banking industry did not have to contend with corporate treasurers demanding many services and draining the banker's profit base: deposit balances. Bankers did not have to compete for corporate accounts. Through the 1940s and into the early 1950s, the banking system was awash with money. Bankers clearly had the upper hand and granted loans on a highly selective basis. Treasurers who wanted to protect their credit sources made sure that ample funds were always on deposit. With balance levels high, banks made large profits from loans, built huge government securities portfolios, and kept their costs low. During this period, few bankers worried about costs for corporate services; many companies assumed their services were free.

THE LOCKBOX: RCA's GAMBLE

With the prime rate stable at near one percent for years, corporate treasurers worried little about the time value of excess cash. Radio Corporation of America (RCA) in 1947 made a big gamble when it established the first lockbox network in New York and Chicago. RCA hoped to reduce its loans when it asked The First National Bank of Chicago and Bankers Trust to collect certain mailed remittances directly and deposit the funds in RCA's respective accounts. Little did they know what a Pandora's box they had opened. The banks were less than excited about performing the menial tasks, even for a giant like RCA. Nonetheless, it was a landmark event in cash management and had a profound effect on New York and Chicago banks.

Regulations on the Move

Just a few years later, the wheels of cash management began to grind when the Accord of March 4, 1951, between the Federal Reserve System and the U.S. Treasury, gave the Fed complete freedom in its open market operations. The Fed was no longer obligated to buy all government securities offered to it at minimum established prices, a practice that had kept prices from falling and yields from rising.[19] The Accord helped to trigger a rise in short-term interest rates, an environment which spawned corporate interest in the money market. Another catalyst to the rate movement was the restoration of convertibility to Western European currencies during the mid-1950s. International investors were then allowed to move money from low-yielding U.S. investments into more lucrative European issues.

The Accord reintroduced market risk for government securities. This risk factor accounts for the threat of lost principal that occurs when a fixed return security must be sold before maturity and the market value of that security fluctuates in the opposite direction of interest rates offered on new instruments entering the market. To compensate for this risk, the market demanded higher yields and rates were bid up. The European convertibility opportunity heightened the new competition for funds. A period of tight money and resultant strain on corporate liquidity during the mid-1950s fueled the fires. Corporate treasurers became active investors in Treasury Bills and other short-term securities. The cost of money soared; cash management became rooted in corporate finance.

Meanwhile, the lockbox idea had caught on with corporate treasurers who began to ask their banks to provide them with this service. By 1954, regional banks got into the act. The Boatmen's National Bank of St. Louis began to receive and deposit remittances for the Purex Corporation of Lakewood, California. In 1956, treasurers experienced their first credit crunch since World War II and began to seek ways to better control balances, turnover of receivables, and payables. As a cash management awareness grew among corporations, balances began to dwindle to working minimums.

The tables had turned; funds were scarce and the prime rate did not dip below two percent in 1960. Bankers had to scramble to design services to hold onto corporate money. The competition for funds encouraged the development of new short-term investment vehicles. In 1961, the Fed authorized negotiable certificates of deposit, and The First National City Bank of New York (now Citibank) was the first to offer them. Banks were also authorized to trade repurchase agreements and Federal Funds. Some banks sensed that depositors had legitimate concerns about profit improvement opportunities and started to assist corporate investment through bank money market centers.[20]

MOBILIZATION COMES OF AGE

During the 1960s, treasurers formalized their approaches to cash management, and segregated functions emerged: mobilization, forecasting, investing, and bank relations. Banks first emphasized their roles in money mobilization because it was the one function that entirely depended on bank involvement in the payment system. Cash management services, especially collection programs, further evolved because there grew an awareness of the impact of payment system timing on collections. Lee Hecht, from the University of Chicago, conducted the first mail-time study in 1968. Western Union mailed 109 envelopes to 47 lockbox locations.[21] This analysis led to the formation of Phoenix-Hecht, Inc., which has since studied mail times regularly in an attempt to quantify mail time and assist in selecting lockbox locations across the country. As this activity grew, banks competed for collection business by joining the mail-time study.[22]

Cash gathering programs—part of money mobilization—focused on overcoming the weaknesses of the paper-based payment system. We call these weaknesses, collectively, "float," the dollar value associated with the delays occurring between the issuance and payment of a check.[23] Cash management sought at this time to speed the flow of remittances and concentrate deposits where they could be optimized. Corporations also began to look at ways to coordinate the handling of paper checks. Companies asked banks to perform more of the processing functions involved with managing the flow of remittances and customer account information. Cost avoidance became paramount as bank services matured.

EFTs EMERGE

Another movement took root durng the late 1960s: electronic funds transfers (EFTs). The banking industry was alarmed over an explosion in the use of checks that occurred as Americans of all income levels embraced the household checking account. Gone forever were the days when Americans stuffed cash into mattresses. Banks had won back the confidence of many consumers stunned by the Depression. Moreover, the babyboom generation unleashed a wave of young families eager to join the consumer ranks. Check volumes skyrocketed and bankers questioned their ability to process all that paper. But, by 1968, the computer age had dawned. Bankers turned to dazzling technology that promised inexpensive and efficient methods for processing payment data electronically.

Electronic funds transfer systems can be defined as any system that replaces the paper-based payment processes with electronic impulses.[24] Today, we recognize a variety of EFT networks that are used to move paperless money and/or related data transactions around the country and around the globe.

These systems include:

Automated clearing houses (ACH).

Fed wire.

Bank wire.

Bank wire II.

The Society for Worldwide Interbank Financial Telecommunication (SWIFT).

Clearing House Interbank Payments System (CHIPS).

GIRO systems.

Data processing vendor services.

Bank-owned systems.

Corporate information systems.

A major component of EFTs in the United States is the ACH network, which got its start in 1968 when people began to explore alternatives to paper-based payments. Four groups contributed to the development of ACH technology and the services ultimately offered by that network. The first was the Special Committee on Paperless Entries (SCOPE), formed in April 1968 under the auspices of the San Francisco and Los Angeles Clearing House Associations. (Clearing house associations have long been the bulwark of banks in all regions of the U.S. They provide the coordination that banks need in order to meet daily to exchange checks for payment. This is an alternative to sending local or regional checks through the Fed for collection.) The purpose of the SCOPE study was to recommend procedures and standards for:

Interbank exchange of preauthorized debit transactions.

Preauthorized debits using magnetic tapes or punch cards.

Magnetic tapes accompanying clearing checks.

The focus of the study was the timely clearing of debit transactions.[25] Four years later, in 1972, the first operational automated clearing house system was established in California.

On another front, the Monetary and Payments System (MAPS) Planning Committee, sponsored by the American Bankers Association, researched the need for change in the paper-based payments system. Their conclusion was:

> To remain static with the present payments system and rely too heavily on the check processing method of funds transfer would be a costly mistake for the banking industry. Rising labor expenses will continually expand the relative costs of bank operations. These additional costs will either reduce profitability, which is already a concern, or increase the expense to our customers. Neither outlook is attractive.[26]

MAPS recommended the establishment of automated clearing houses at local and regional levels, in essence, an electronic version of the traditional clearing house concept. MAPS recommended standardized transaction formats so that all banks could send and receive electronic messages with ease. The banking industry wanted to avoid the chaos experienced by industries such as the audio and recording industry. When cassette recording became a rage, many manufacturers inundated the market with a wide variety of odd-sized cassettes; standards were lacking.

The third organization to contribute to the development of the ACH was the Federal Reserve. In 1971, the Board of Governors set forth a policy that defined ACH objectives:

To decrease the number of paper items handled.

Increase payment settlement speed with minimal handling.

Reduce float.

The fourth group involved with ACH development was the Atlanta Payments Project, working under the auspices of the Federal Reserve Bank of Atlanta and the Georgia Institute of Technology. That effort then expanded to include representatives from the five largest commercial banks in Atlanta. The result was the establishment of the Georgia Automated Clearing House, which became operational in May 1973.[27]

The number of automated clearing houses continued to expand. In 1974, the American Bankers Association ACH Task Force prompted the establishment of the National Automated Clearing House Association (NACHA). NACHA was conceived to oversee the development of standards and rules for inter-ACH activity. By February 1982, there were 40 regional ACH facilities (computer centers) and 32 ACH associations (rule-making bodies in various regions owned by private banks). All but one of the facilities are operated by the Federal Reserve. The New York ACH is owned and operated by the New York Clearing House Association.

MODELING

The late 1960s also witnessed the introduction of computer modeling techniques for cash management. Among other researchers, Robert Calman at MIT's Sloan School of Management developed a linear program model that helped corporations with numerous bank accounts decide how to best allocate balances. Calman's work was published in book form in 1968,

Linear Programming and Cash Management/Cash Alpha.[28] Linear program models have built into them—in the form of mathematical equations—all of a company's activities, including agreements with banks, bank prices, and relevant internal policy guidelines. The company feeds into the computer data from monthly account analyses and cash-flow forecasts. The computer suggests optimum configurations for bank balances that conserve cash and support its earning power. Since corporate cash management is in part a distribution problem, the linear program models, used successfully for production planning and scheduling, were welcomed as appropriate treasury tools. The largest firms found modeling helpful because it solved complex problems that eluded conventional analytical techniques.[29] Phoenix-Hecht also employed modeling programs for its lockbox location studies by 1970, and banks flocked to subscribe to the service. Models were later developed for cash transfer scheduling, forecasting, and disbursement planning.

TECHNOLOGICAL REVOLUTION

Successful computer applications for cash management continued to blossom during the 1970s as computer timesharing allowed corporations, banks, and data processing service providers to work cooperatively with affordable technology. Someone once described computer timesharing as "one computer using 200 people." In effect, this innovation opened up a whole new world for cash managers. Timesharing prompted cash managers to develop refined techniques for cash concentration.

National Data Corporation (NDC) was an early pioneer in this area. NDC provided a way for post offices around the country to efficiently report daily, by phone, deposits into local bank accounts for next day transfer to the appropriate concentration bank. NDC at the time was processing inbound WATS line calls for Master Charge franchises, reporting negative credit verification.[30] NDC was familiar with needed technology. The postal system designed the first concentration system which used information compiled by NDC's computers and inaugurated the concept of the automated depository transfer check. The automation label refers to the practice by which a concentration bank receives data transmissions containing field deposit information and then prepares the depository transfer checks, placing them into the collection system on behalf of the corporation. This is sometimes called "central initiation," because it differs from the procedure whereby field locations prepare their own DTCs and then mail them to the concentration bank. (See Exhibit 3.1.)

The new procedure for speeding the concentration of local deposits revolutionized cash management. By the early 1970s, many companies were using this tool to significantly reduce collection float. The automated DTCs also reduced costs: many companies were able to replace expensive wire transfers with this innovation. By the late 1970s, very few companies were still using the old mail DTC procedure. Rapidata and General Electric Information Services further refined the procedure during the 1970s when they developed touchtone and synthesized voice input enhancements.[31]

Meanwhile, the Fed and the banking industry were racing onto the new technological playing field. During the 1960s, MICR encoding—computerized numbering of checks—allowed the Fed and banks to implement streamlined check processing procedures. By the late 1960s, bankers were convinced that they would soon be drowning in a sea of paper as check volumes continued to explode. The cashless society was heralded, and the large computer manufacturers had a heyday supplying banks and the Fed with mammoth reader/sorter equipment that revamped check processing. Ironically, the cashless society failed to materialize; the new technology was so efficient that by the late 1970s, banks found that they had more than enough processing capacity. They soon began to take on workloads for smaller banks who could not afford the expensive computers. The fruits of technology trickled down, and computerized banking became commonplace by the end of the decade.

1970 also witnessed the implementation of the Fed's Culpeper Switch, a computer facility in Culpeper, Virginia. The Culpeper Switch brought Fed wire transfer procedures into the new technological era, reducing significantly the amount of time required to process money movements. The Culpeper Switch also provided computer-to-computer transmission capabilities necessary for Fed member banks to adequately respond to customer demands for faster money transfers. Funds transfer technology bloomed throughout the 1970s as CHIPS, Bank Wire II, and SWIFT became operational.

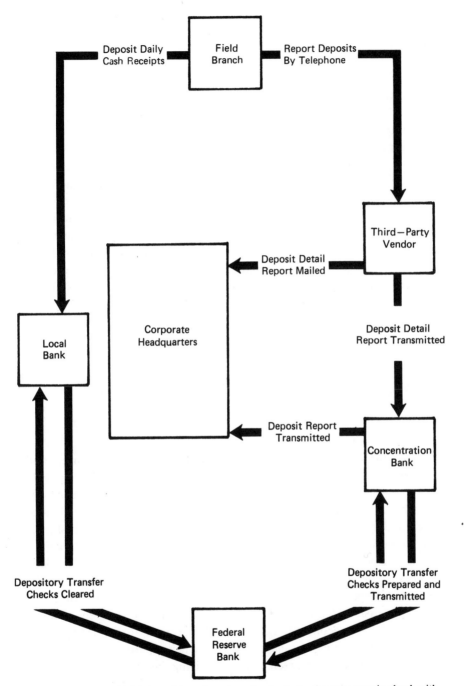

Exhibit 3.1. Central initiation of depository transfer checks by the concentration bank with a third-party vendor collecting and automatically transmitting deposit data.

FLOAT MANAGEMENT CATCHES ON

During the early 1970s, cash managers focused on the disbursement side of their functions. The innovations seen in the 1960s on the cash gathering side emphasized information management. With this perspective, cash managers began to search for ways to lengthen disbursement float and control payment timing and expense. Remote disbursing made headlines by 1975, and many corporations rushed to cash-in on the benefits of "playing the float." Enhanced methods for tracking account activity came to the fore, and banks raced to provide customers with computerized balance reporting programs. Automatic account reconciliation was introduced. Cash managers began to boast of huge gains made by manipulating payments and investing funds tied up in the payments system. Zero-balance accounts were inaugurated, and the notion of controlled disbursing became popular.

CASH MANAGEMENT MATURES WITH HIGH INTEREST RATES

The decade of the 1970s saw unprecedented interest-rate spirals and swings. From 1967 to 1981, the nation's money supply grew at relatively high but variable rates. This growth, which seemed out-of-control, was primarily responsible for longer-term rise and increased volatility in interest rates. Exhibit 3.2 shows representative short- and long-term interest rates for the period of 1954 to the second quarter of 1981.[32] We see that the rate movements created a terrible state of uncertainty and highly priced funds for corporations. In 1974, the prime hit 12% and short-term rates soared. Companies became extremely cash conscious at this time and turned to cash management techniques to help them effectively confront an unpredictable economy. Yet when rates seemed to stabilize for short periods, interest in cash management still remained strong.[33] Corporations had discovered a hidden arsenal for maximizing the earning power of temporarily idle funds.

Chart 1

Representative Short-Term and Long-Term Interest Rates

Yield on long-term government securities

3-month Treasury bill rate

Latest data plotted: 2nd quarter

Exhibit 3.2. Interest rate behavior that accompanied the emergence of cash management as a discipline in its own right. *(Reprinted from the Federal Reserve Bank of St. Louis Economic Review.)*

Cash managers in the late 1970s sought to enhance their investing abilities. For example, they formalized programs for buying short-term securities. Aggressive investors turned to the Eurodollar market which offered attractive yields and slightly higher risk. Money market mutual funds, which arrived on the scene in 1972, caught the attention of corporate cash managers who experimented with money fund disbursing after The Fidelity Group in Boston introduced check redemptions in 1974.

The scramble for cash productivity in the face of volatile interest rates also justified the purchase of new management tools. By 1982, cash managers were using mini- and microcomputers to interface with securities dealers and financial institutions for enhanced money market investing. They were also beginning to look for ways to link with internal accounting systems and trade precious data. Terminals that allowed access to market data bases also became popular with companies that regularly issued commercial paper. Mini- and microcomputers were used to evaluate debt and investment portfolio performance. These savvy machines allowed cash managers to greatly enhance the accuracy of daily cashflow forecasts; furthermore, calculations that took hours by hand were available at the push of a button. Desktop treasury computing had arrived and cash managers began to use mini- and microcomputers to gain valuable commodities: calculating and information management power. With these resources, cash managers battled volatile interest rates and liquidity crises.

High interest rates sparked corporate attention to the need to watch treasury expenses; they turned to the big ticket item: bank service costs. By the late 1970s, cash managers were implementing bank service budgets and carefully monitoring the costs of numerous bank accounts. Advanced information management techniques allowed corporations to reduce the number of banks they needed in order to conduct daily transactions. One large retailer reduced its banking relationships from over 1000 to 300 in 1981. Cash managers focused on account analyses and began demanding accurate and understandable documents from their banks. The former assistant treasurer at J. C. Penney, Andrea Bierce, reported in 1981 that a year-long review of account analyses from 650 different banks revealed over $1 million in mistakes made by the banks. Large firms found it worthwhile to assign a staffer to regularly pour over account analyses and search for errors.

FED PRICING

The Depository Institutions Deregulation and Monetary Control Act of 1980 instituted charges for Fed services. Prior to this event, Fed member banks received check collection, money transfer, and other Fed services for free. In return, member banks left reserves on account with the Fed. The new legislation allowed the Fed to provide all banks (not only Fed members—and including thrifts) with services, priced so that the Fed would recover its costs. Fed prices were adjusted for taxes and other costs incurred by private sector service providers, to keep Fed charges in line with the realities of market competition. As a partial offset to price initiation, reserve requirements for members were slated for gradual reduction; reserve requirements for nonmembers were scheduled to be gradually phased in. The Act intensified the need for banks to scrutinize charges for cash management services. Many banks had traditionally offered these services at little or no cost as an inducement to continued strong credit relationships with corporate borrowers. When assertive cash management strategies drained large, idle balances from corporate accounts, and when Fed pricing raised banks' costs of doing business, banks began to restructure costs for cash management services.

The Act also forced bankers, already facing profit pressures, to pass the increased operating expense along to their customers. Additionally, as banks reviewed the profitability of cash management services, they began to realize that they could no longer afford "loss leaders." By 1981, banks were identifying which services made sense in their respective market segments. Morgan Guaranty eliminated its New York wholesale lockbox program in 1982 because it could not justify the expense of the program considering the geographic location and poor mail service associated with New York City.

By 1982, cash managers and their bankers had experienced consistently volatile interest rates and the introduction of Fed pricing. Cash management for large corporations entered a mature phase in which systems in place would be maintained and refined. Bank cost accounting procedures were enhanced; banks began to have a better idea of what they were earning and losing with cash management services. Corporations also began to take a closer look at cash management costs and how to make their programs as efficient as possible.

DISBURSEMENTS UNDER FIRE

In the spring of 1979, the Board of Governors at the Fed declared war on remote disbursement. The Fed was concerned that corporations who disbursed large payments from small, remote banks were jeopardizing the solvency of those banks. The Fed had a point: some companies that were making payments in this manner could have placed the small banks in technical bankruptcy. If a small bank received for collection large checks that the company had failed to cover with a wire, the bank would have been technically bankrupt if the checks represented amounts larger than the bank's capital assets. The issue of unsound banking practice was also a concern; if the remote bank had to loan money to the corporation to cover checks, the bank may have had to go beyond its legal lending limit. The bank may have had to make an unsecured loan while it facilitated corporate exploitation of funding delays.

The Fed blamed remote disbursing for high levels of Federal Reserve float. The Fed had been under pressure from Congress to reduce its float which resulted from Fed System inefficiencies. The Fed undertook a campaign of intimidation, many in the banking industry felt, when it began calling on banks around the country and warning them not to allow remote disbursing. Corporations argued that they were really interested in controlled disbursing from branches of large money center banks. Cash managers sought the benefits of information flows available from these controlled accounts. They were able to know early in the day the amount of checks presented for collection and, hence, the amount of excess cash they had to invest. The corporations tried to point out that remote disbursing, while popular for a while, had come to be considered child's play by the savvy cash managers who could earn interest income in more respectable ways. By 1982, the controversy was still raging. Fed officials believed that the difference between remote and controlled disbursing was academic; they were not concerned with cashflow control in a private enterprise.

The Monetary Control Act urged the Fed to eradicate or charge for float. Since the Act was passed in 1980, the Fed began work on various proposals aimed at reducing Fed float caused, Fed officials said, by large corporate payments. (Industry analysts contradict Fed assertions that large portions of Fed float stem from corporate payment practices.) Schemes for electronic check collection were discussed in 1981 and shelved in 1982. In July, 1982, the Fed met with bankers to discuss its plan to change presentment schedules at banks located in Federal Reserve cities. In short, this change would significantly alter controlled disbursing in these locales. We will see later how cash managers and their controlled disbursing bankers are trying to deal with this.

The Fed had its way with remote disbursement. While it still is practiced today, bankers and corporations do not like to discuss it publicly. But controlled disbursement can be a life-saver for the corporate cash manager. To date, the Fed has yet to find virtue in the practice, but cash managers hope to educate Fed officials. The National Corporate Cash Management Association (NCCMA), founded in 1979, has established a liaison committee which will work with the Fed on issues of concern to corporate cash managers. No doubt, a formal channel for dialogue between regulators and cash managers will serve to shed light on misconstrued issues which, in the past, have plagued the industry.

CASH MANAGEMENT TODAY

For many large corporations, applying cash management strategies to global operations is gaining popularity. With advances in technology, cash managers at multinational corporations are designing computer-assisted programs for reducing cross-border payments and subsequent foreign exchange expense. Cash management concepts are also filtering down to the foreign subsidiary level where investment management is badly needed. Bilateral and multilateral netting schemes offer corporations mechanisms for reducing the costs of international funds flows. Cash management operations, whether directed domestically or overseas, are now viewed as vital profit centers.

Many corporate treasurers at the largest firms today believe that the existing generation of cash management products, such as automated balance reporting, have reached a mature stage. These treasurers are now concerned with linking their systems with other corporate data bases, in effect, integrating financial management.[34] Cash managers in the 1980s will seek ways to totally automate routine tasks. They will increasingly use microcomputers—smart technology—to analyze information and plan cashflows. Generally, cash managers today want to learn how to best employ the fancy products they bought and installed in the late 1970s. More and more time will be spent on refining procedures for managing company cash and maintaining the systems they use on the job. As cash managers become better at getting the most out of their systems and procedures, they can function more and more in true managerial roles. This will coincide with heightened interest at top management levels for cashflow data.

Analysts maintain that the next generation of electronic banking services will prompt cash managers to view themselves less as float managers and more as information managers. Already, a few companies are researching paying dividends electronically. This means that, for some firms, the cost-efficiency of ACH credits outweighs the value of disbursement float on dividend checks. Since dividend checks are typically written for small amounts, the cost of all the paper handling and mailing expense may be relatively excessive. Therefore, this is one application for electronic payments that we are likely to witness in the 1980s.

Electronics spell the eventual demise of float. There is no value in delaying a blip. Cash managers at the largest firms are already planning for the new floatless era of cash management. The really smart companies are looking at how they can get customers to pay them electronically. The Fed is mandated to eliminate or charge for float sooner or later, but that in no way means the end of cash management. Corporations have discovered that information, and the people and systems to manage it, are the keys to efficiency.

Bankers are facing severe competition in the cash management marketplace. There are now over 250 banks that stress cash management products. Regional banks are entrenched in their marketplaces. The large money center giants find that they now have to go further and to smaller companies in order to sign up new cash management customers. This is indeed the hot new market for banks, the firms with under $100 million in annual sales. To reach new markets, some of the large city banks are teaming up with regional banks. Large banks like Chemical of New York are franchising their sophisticated systems and bringing advanced technology to the hinterlands. Some regional banks are buying data processing capabilities from third-party service vendors like NDC.

Banks are taking a new tack with product planning. Gone are the days when bankers simply developed something new and then searched for users. Because banks are competing to keep their deposit bases stable, both retail and corporate, they can no longer afford the loss leaders. Product plans at some banks now undergo heavy scrutiny before much investment is made. Product lifecycles and potential markets are pegged. Generally, banks are focusing on profitable services, letting the losers die a slow death.

Much of the action in cash management today is found in small and middle market companies. Consultants, banks, vendors, planners, are all queuing up to sell their wares to the small firms that have recently been introduced to cash management. Banks are strengthening their training programs for the officers who call on this special middle market, generally defined as firms with annual sales between $1 million and $100 million. In many ways, the small company can adapt basic cash management concepts, but bankers are learning quickly that the small firm has very special needs. While product standardization is a worthy trend now among banks, the small company will often require customized programs. Banks are learning to juggle these conflicting demands.

The cash management movement is officially recognized under the auspices of The National Corporate Cash Management Association (NCCMA). Established in 1979, the NCCMA brought together under a national logo many local cash management organizations that formed after 1975. The NCCMA is headquartered in Newtown, Connecticut, and publishes *The Journal of Cash Management* through the Georgia Institute of Technology in Atlanta. The NCCMA has several working committees that are engaged in research and advocacy efforts. One committee now is developing guidelines for a cash management certification program. The association sponsors regional seminars and an annual national conference. The area of cash management education is a ripe one for the NCCMA.

The NCCMA is also attempting to give a voice to cash managers. Because corporate finance is a sensitive topic at many companies, for years it was difficult for cash managers to reach public consensus. The NCCMA Federal Reserve liaison committee hopes to close the gap between regulators and cash managers.

2 Components of a Cash Management System

4 Corporations, Payment Systems, and Float

Bankers and corporate cash managers have a curious habit of referring to any type of time delay as float. We hear of invoicing float, processing float, mail float, clearing float, disbursement float, and so on. One cash manager even reported experiencing ACH float, a concept that seems out of place since the ACH involves EFT which is supposedly float-free. Basically, all these terms refer to transaction delays that are quantified because someone either gains or loses.

THE MANY FACES OF FLOAT

We are now going to look at different kinds of float and how they occur. In effect, we will look at the nation's payment systems, another favorite industry phrase that describes the machinery that moves money around the country. Cash managers need to know how the external environment works if they are going to meet their goals of efficiency and profitability because implicit planning involves understanding alternatives. So, when we examine float, we will see different ways that money moves: through the Fed, through commercial banks, through local clearing houses, and through the ACH network.

THE FED AND ITS FLOAT

Federal Reserve float is a very notorious form of float because it is ultimately an expense to taxpayers. Fed float occurs when a Federal Reserve Bank credits the account of a depositing bank before it collects the funds from the paying bank. The Fed does this often because of certain policy issues which we will discuss below. This action increases the overall level of bank reserves. Fed float is a cost to taxpayers because it prematurely increases member bank reserves at the expense of Fed interest income. This increase in reserves must be offset by Federal Reserve Board sales of securities, assuming that the Board is attempting to manage the money supply by keeping member bank reserves within certain predetermined ranges. (By selling securities, the Board reduces reserves, the money supply, and its interest income.)[35] Fed float costs the Fed the forgone earnings on the securities it had to sell. Since earnings from such securities would ultimately be passed back to the U.S. Treasury, taxpayers, in essence, pay for float by forgone revenue that must be made up either by taxes or borrowing. While the Fed does not offset every float variation, it does accommodate the average float prevailing over a period of time.[36]

The Fed's Float Dilemma

Intolerable levels of Fed float caught the attention of the Congress in recent years and became a major controversy in Washington. Fed float hit a record daily average of $12 billion during the Blizzard of 1979—when airports close down, the Fed cannot present checks for collection. But the Fed experienced problems in its air transport network during the late 1970s that could not be blamed on the weather. (See Exhibit 4.1.) Fed check clearing volume increased by 20% from 1976 to 1980, but a cost reduction program was in force and staff levels remained virtually constant during this period.[37] Congress finally clamped down on the Fed for high float levels in 1980 and passed the Monetary Control Act which urged, among other things, that the Fed eradicate or charge for float. We will see later how the Fed plans to charge back to banks the cost of float.

Fed float is an interest-free loan to banks who receive credit for checks before they are collected. (Fed float is associated only with checks that flow through the Fed's check collection service.) This happens when the

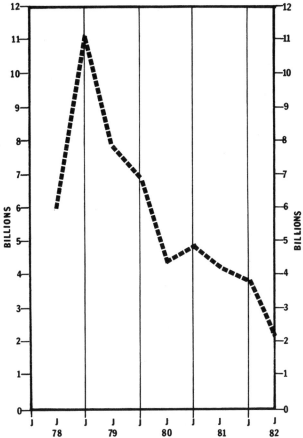

Exhibit 4.1. Beginning with June 1978 and depicting subsequent January and June increments, various levels of Federal Reserve System float.

Fed cannot transport paper checks from one of its facilities to another within published availability schedules. These schedules give commercial banks, hence corporate customers, actual or deferred credit on checks deposited with the Fed for collection. As of this writing, the longest that credit can be deferred according to the Fed schedule is two days. Fed float arises when actual collection time exceeds stated availability. Now we see why the Fed deplores remote disbursement: it takes advantage of Fed collection problems. The Fed has difficulty reaching remote locations, especially during bad weather.

In addition to superficially inflating bank reserves, Fed float provides cash managers with interest income when they can keep previously committed funds working until the last possible moment. So, why in the world would the Fed allow this to happen? The answer lies in the Fed's role. The Fed is charged with, among other things, maintaining adequate levels of service to all of the nation's banks. The large commercial banks that have their own programs for transporting checks to other large banks do not bother to go to many small, remote banks. The Fed has to guarantee service to places like Helena, Montana in the dead of winter when weather often makes check deliveries erratic. The Fed has to provide emergency check clearings when disasters —hurricanes, floods, and so on—wipe out commercial bank deliveries.

So why doesn't the Fed simply lengthen its availability schedules? The Fed argues that lengthening the schedules would unduly burden small banks who have no alternative means of collecting interterritory checks. A lengthened Fed availability schedule would ostensibly punish those smaller banks: their means of providing competitive collection times would be hampered. Industry analysts, however, contend that the Fed refuses to lengthen the schedules because it would drive away Fed check processing volume. Private commercial banks can always devise ways to collect checks faster than the Fed. If the Fed were to defer credit on a certain check for three days, the depositing bank, if it had the option, might clear that check through a large private bank that offered a more attractive collection schedule. Because the Fed now charges for its services, much of its competition with private sector check collectors is based on performance. Issues concerning the Fed's proper role in the payments system are complicated and require discussions of free enterprise that are inappropriate here.

Let's look at how the Fed system works. The Fed operates 48 processing centers referred to as regional check processing centers (RCPCs), one at each of the 12 district banks, one at each of 25 branch banks, and 11 in cities where no bank or branch is located. Each center is linked by air courier and wire services. Each processing center serves a given geographical area, known as a zone. Except by permission, banks using Fed services must deposit checks for collection with the processing centers in their respective zones. (See Exhibit 4.2.)

The majority of checks processed by a center are for collection within the center's territory. Although the processing centers work around the clock, the busiest time is after midnight when RCPC checks are sorted according to paying banks and prepared for dispatch early the same day.

.

GROUPING OF FEDERAL RESERVE DISTRICTS

GROUP 2
Cleveland.   Minneapolis
Chicago   Kansas City
St. Louis

GROUP 1
Boston
New York
Philadelphia

GROUP 3
Richmond   Dallas
Atlanta   San Francisco

Exhibit 4.2.   The twelve Federal Reserve Districts, divided into three regional groups.

The Federal Reserve estimated in 1979 that it cleared 45% of the nation's transit items, checks drawn on banks other than the bank of first deposit. The Atlanta Fed Check Study estimated in 1979 that 32 billion checks were written that year. To sort all this paper, the Fed uses fast, computerized machines that read the magnetic encodings on checks that indicate amount, Fed zone of paying bank, and the specific paying bank on which the check is drawn.

The Fed uses published availability schedules that state how soon a check presented for collection will be given credit. (Remember, cash managers try to increase the availability of remittance checks and decrease the availability of payments they make.) The Fed gives depositing banks immediate credit for city and regional items—these are within the RCPC zone—provided that they reach the Reserve Bank prior to a designated time cutoff. Country checks are collected outside the RCPC zone but are still within the center's processing territory. These country checks are assigned a one banking-day deferred availability. Checks to be collected in the territory of another processing center are called "other Fed" checks and qualify for one or two banking-day availability, depending on collection time required. There are exceptions to these groupings which allow banks to gain better availability.

Settlement occurs through banks' reserve accounts held at the Federal Reserve District Bank or branch within their zones. The Monetary Control Act of 1980 opened the door to all banks, including thrifts, that agreed to maintain reserve accounts and thus have access to Fed services. Prior to that event, a bank had to be a member of the Federal Reserve System to use its services. The Fed District Banks post credits, deferred credits, and debits to the accounts of appropriate banks. At the end of each day, each bank receives a status report of the net settlement results. The report includes adjustments for returned items, mistakes, and disputes. In the same manner, Fed District Banks and branches settle among themselves. On a daily basis, net amounts are transferred among Fed banks using the Fed wire system, but the Fed's Interdistrict Transportation System (ITS) moves the actual paper. This way, money is shuffled around the country with the Fed District Banks swapping debits and credits on behalf of banks within their zones. The Federal Reserve Wire network and the Federal Reserve Interdistrict Transportation System are the cornerstones of this activity.

The Fed Wire system is often the vehicle that corporations choose to make large money transfers. Fed wire is the safest way to move cash; these transfers represent good funds the moment the wire is executed. Payments are credited the same day of transfer: debits and credits are posted to the Fed accounts of sending and receiving banks. (Cash managers find, though, that the Fed Wire can be expensive. Prices range between $6.00 and $11.00 for each transfer, depending on the charges levied by sending and receiving banks. As a result, they often perform cost/benefit analyses to find the lowest, economical transfer amount appropriate for their operations.)

The Fed Wire currently handles over 200,000 transfers per day. In 1981, this system moved over 50 million transactions worth approximately $100 trillion. In 1975, The Fed began work on FRCS-80 (Federal Reserve Communication System for the 1980s), an enhancement to the current wire network. This new system, which will be fully operational by 1985, will employ packet-switching technology to easily handle burgeoning wire transfer volume.

ALTERNATIVES TO THE FED

Correspondent Banking

Another way that banks collect checks is through direct send programs which are run by large commercial banks that have many correspondent relationships with other banks around the country. A correspondent bank accepts deposits in the form of a cash letter and collects items for its bank depositor. A cash letter is a deposit ticket, listing checks drawn on one or more banks in another city, which is sent to the correspondent who immediately credits the account of the sending bank. Direct sends present checks to the paying bank, its Fed District Bank, or a clearing house in its area.

At both ends of this process, the large banks perform collection chores for smaller banks, called "respondents." This network allows smaller banks to circumvent the Fed. Settlement occurs at all levels by debit and credit entries made on the accounts of the appropriate banks kept by the correspondent. Often, checks sent directly to correspondents for collection receive same-day credit. It is this feature which prompts all the frenzy. Time is money, and direct sends are often the quickest way to get paid on a check. Obviously, banks are willing to go out of their way to collect checks for very large sums. Although it is expensive to do so, banks would rather clear a $10 million check through a direct send than to risk its becoming an item returned for insufficient funds. Banks compete for corporate business based on how quickly they can get credit for the depositing corporation. This activity helps corporations reduce clearing float. Small checks sometimes "ride free"; when there's room on a plane for bundles of small checks, a bank may include these along with the high-value items.

Bank Wire

Fund movements by correspondent banks are also facilitated using the Bank Wire system, a communication utility owned by over 180 of the nation's leading banks. Bank Wires provide a media for information exchange essentially through administrative messages. Transactions are settled through correspondent banks' balances. (The Cash Wire system, an enhancement, settles differently. We will consider this below.) In the traditional use of Bank Wire, when daily trading of funds transfer messages concludes, net debit balance positions—how much who owes whom—are covered with Fed Wire transfers from one bank to another or through bookkeeping entries to correspondent accounts. Bank Wires are extremely useful to cash managers who receive same-day use of Bank Wire credits, but a slight degree of risk is involved. Although transferred payments may be immediately available, the credits are not considered finally collected (irreversible) until all bank balance positions are covered at the end of the banking day. Theoretically, problems could arise in the event of a sudden bank failure. A cash manager may invest the proceeds of a Bank Wire payment only to discover later that the credit did not represent good funds. In practice, many cash managers ignore this potential scenario; the chances of sudden bank failure are considered by many people to be extremely remote, and the intimate nature of correspondent banking relationships precludes unforeseen credit risks.

This is how Bank Wire works from a corporate perspective: Bank A notifies Bank B to transfer Bank A funds from its account for credit to a receiving corporate account in Bank B.[38] Bank A covers the transaction with funds from the originating company's account. Presumably, Bank A determines that its customer has the money available for transfer before the process begins. As of October 1981, Bank Wire handled approximately 20,000 communications daily. Bank Wire II is the name for the current computerized system that effects all data transmissions.

Part of Bank Wire II is the Cash Wire. The Cash Wire system is an enhancement of this network, and, as of October 1982, system administrators finished years of negotiations with the Fed which authorized actual net settlement on the books of the Fed. Cash Wire determines a single net balance for each participating bank at the end of each day. The Fed adjusts its books, and banks with net debit positions have to cover those positions right away. Banks (and corporations) with net credit positions are free to use those funds for investments or any other purpose.[39] Funds are available for use on the same day of initiation, but final settlement occurs on the morning of the next business day. Cash Wire transforms Bank Wire from a mere communications network, that prompted bookkeeping adjustments among correspondent accounts, to a true funds transfer system, settling through the books of the Fed. Cash Wire now takes its place along with the Fed Wire as a national, domestic settlement device. The large banks that own Cash Wire hope to compete vigorously with the Fed for wire transfer business. Indeed, they hope to have an edge with prices that are significantly less costly than Fed Wires.

SWIFT (The Society For Worldwide Interbank Financial Telecommunication) is a communications network that carries funds transfer instructions among over 800 international correspondent banks around the globe. CHIPS (Clearing House Interbank Payment System) is an actual funds transfer system used by over 100 international banks in New York to settle dollar transactions. CHIPS now handles over 90% of all foreign exchange trades. We will discuss these two networks in Chapter 10.

Local Clearing Houses

In each major metropolitan area, bank clearing houses service local members. One banker suggests that to depict the activities of local clearing houses, all one has to do is imagine a large room, filled with people holding boxes of checks. At the appointed hour, the people, each representing a bank, begin to slide the boxes across the floor until all the checks have been presented to the proper paying bank. A net settlement tally is given to each person, and the proper amounts are transferred to satisfy transaction adjustments. While this may be a simplistic version of an honorable banking tradition, the image helps the uninitiated understand what check exchange is about. Banks developed clearing houses to gain better availability on certain classes of items: a one banking-day processing time is, in many cases, a better availability time than the Fed can provide. Thus, clearing float is minimized in this manner.

Automated Clearing Houses

The Automated Clearing House network (ACH) replaces the manual check clearing processes described above. Instead of banks exchanging checks and settling accounts, magnetic tape files are processed on a central computer, and all entries for a particular receiving bank are recorded on one file that is delivered to that bank for automated processing. No physical checks are required to effect payment.[40] Banks sending or receiving ACH items depend on the physical transportation of magnetic tapes to or from the ACH computer center. To get around this, a few banks have installed direct computer links with the ACH; tape data is transmitted over high-speed lines. In either case, funds are available for use the day after an ACH transaction is initiated.

There are 32 ACH associations located across the nation. ACH associations are comprised of private member banks who formulate local policies. The National Automated Clearing House Association (NACHA) is the national umbrella authority for the 32 associations. Although ACH transaction volume is relatively small—about 1.5% of all checks written in the U.S. yearly—analysts expect the network to play a major role in EFT proliferation. To date, the federal government is the largest user, applying electronics to benefit payments, such as Social Security, and government payroll items. We will discuss in-depth the various corporate ACH uses in Chapters 6, 7, and 8. The Fed operates 39 of the 40 ACH facilities in existence (as of May, 1982); the New York Clearing House Association owns and operates the New York ACH.

ACHs simply provide an electronic means of sending data similar to that on checks from an account at one financial institution to a checking or savings account at any of the over 14,000 participating banks, savings and loans, and credit unions. The standardized "bank address" and account number, printed on the lower left corner of a check in magnetic ink, was developed to facilitate paper processing but is also used to route ACH transactions to their proper locations. ACH volume, although presently small, is growing as more corporations, banks, and consumers realize the advantages of payments made on an exact settlement date at low cost. The greatest success of ACH technology is the direct deposit of ten million monthly Social Security payments.[41]

CORPORATIONS AND THE ACH

While initial applications of the ACH network primarily involved electronic credits to individual accounts, such as direct deposits of payroll for government employees, corporations have found the ACH valuable for concentration of funds from field bank accounts to regional concentration or lead bank accounts. This involves electronic debits. Until recently, the principal vehicles for moving these balances were either Fed Wire, Bank Wire or depository transfer checks. During the late 1970s, another method of concentrating balances, using the ACH network, was initiated. Instead of issuing depository transfer checks, concentration banks began to originate electronic depository transfers (EDTs) through their local ACHs. Cash managers found that by concentrating through the ACH, they had a method of gaining uniform, next-day availability at a low cost. Mellon Bank was one pioneer in the use of the ACH for cash concentration. Its first EDT customer was the U.S. Postal Service in 1978. Mellon estimated later that processing costs for ACH cash concentrations were 10% to 20% lower than the traditional DTC method. DTCs, remember, are less expensive than wires. Banks across the country have since developed this service for their corporate customers who were eager to take advantage of its many benefits.

An unexpected benefit to corporations using EDTs is the current inability of many banks to properly debit the corporation's account on the day that the funds are to be transferred. Many banks, particularly those with unsophisticated check availability systems, depend on techniques that may leave funds available to the corporation in the field bank or second tier concentration bank for an extra day. These funds are not from the bank's Federal Reserve account. That Fed account has been properly charged; the internal bank system has failed to charge the customer on a timely basis.[42]

Another ACH application, debiting a customer's account, speeds the collection of funds and provides certainty that money will arrive in a bank account on a specific day. This is a preauthorized payment plan. Of course, most consumers and corporations have no desire to pay bills sooner than necessary. However, with the rising cost of funds and check payments— paper, postage, and reconcilement—more and more companies are beginning to negotiate with customers, offering discounts when ACH debits are allowed to pay for goods or services. This is called negotiated settlement. Bergin Brunswig, the Los Angeles based drug supply distributor, recently began a pilot program for debiting the accounts of customers who receive weekly shipments. Reducing costs is important to all companies, but for those in a low-margin area such as distributing, the cost-savings realized by using creative EFT methods can be significant. One large insurer uses the ACH to receive premium payments, credit transfers initiated by consumers using pay-by-phone technology. The insurer also uses ACH credit transfers to electronically pay out benefits. The rewards are great: among them, predictable cashflows and streamlined accounts processing.[43]

Payroll systems can be greatly enhanced using direct depositing through the ACH. Although some disbursement float may be sacrificed—funds are paid out on the pay date rather than when employees actually cash their checks—many corporations have discovered that they save costs for late or lost checks, local bank accounts, and lost productivity when employees have to leave to cash checks. Retirement benefits are another illustration of the productive use of the ACH for corporate payments. Companies are often obligated to pay such benefits on a certain date each month. But to meet this obligation using the traditional mailed check, many firms experience "negative float." This happens because checks sometimes arrive and are cashed sooner than intended. Using the ACH, and even arranging with banks to warehouse ACH payments, and value-date transactions, innovative firms assure that retirement benefits are available in the retiree's account no sooner than the contracted date. Dividend and interest payments are also particularly suited to firms that can offset the loss of disbursement float by enormous reductions of processing costs. Consolidated Edison, which handles its own stock transfer system for its 220,000 stockholders, in 1981 began paying a pilot group this way. Firms like Con Ed find that making traditionally small payments such as dividends with paper checks is simply not cost-effective.

Payments to financial institutions by low-cost ACH batch payments is another innovative application of this EFT network. The Associates Corporation of North America in Dallas (part of Gulf and Western) now makes quarterly repayments of multimillion dollar revolving credit agreements to 500 financial institutions using a timesharing service through a Chicago bank. These repayments replace expensive single message money transfers.

Pay-By-Phone

Very few corporations have yet to establish ways to receive telephone bill payments to their accounts as happens in the European GIRO system. Exceptions are companies such as Exxon USA and Equitable Life Assurance Society which are able to receive ACH payments this way. However, less than 10% of the banks in America now offering pay-by-phone banking can link this service with the ACH.

More innovation with the ACH is bound to occur in the 1980s because of the Fed intention to charge for its float. When this happens, cash managers will have less incentive to continue paper-based payments. As well, the costs of the paper-based system will continue to rise; sooner or later, corporations will have to look to EFT alternatives.

(The author is indebted to George C. White for the discussion of the ACH given above.)

CORPORATIONS AND FLOAT

We have seen why Fed float exists: the Fed grants availability on checks before it can collect them according to its published schedules. We have seen how correspondent banking networks clear checks and effect funds transfers on behalf of corporations who seek to have available funds as quickly as possible. We have explored uses of the ACH that decrease collection float and disbursement float. Now, let's look at float—time delays—often caused by corporate inefficiencies:

Invoicing Float. The time it takes the accounting department to create invoices and mail them.

Payables Processing Float. The time it takes a company to process an invoice and mail a payment.

Accounts Receivable Float. The time it takes a company to open envelopes, record customer remittance data, and prepare a bank deposit (assuming no lockbox tools are used).

In Chapter 1, we discussed mail float and clearing float, each belonging to the Postal Service and banking system, respectively. Together with internal time delays experienced in a company's collection system, these time lags constitute collection float. We saw in the *Toolbox* Section of Chapter 1 how cash managers attempt to reduce collection float by using lockboxes, depository transfer checks, concentration banking networks, ACH cash concentration, and other techniques for accelerating cash inflows. The point to remember is that collection float costs a company time, and because of the time value of money, collection float represents lost revenue. That is, when a company has to wait to use its funds, it forgoes the chance to reduce short-term debt or invest that money and earn interest. The cash manager's objective, then, is to develop efficient strategies for reducing the collection float that occurs because of internal and external delays inherent in business transactions.

Disbursement float is the other side of the coin. Cash managers attempt to increase disbursement float and keep money invested until the moment that it is needed to cover outstanding checks. Managing disbursement float is an important part of cash management because the amounts of money involved are often substantial. A company may make a $250,000 payment that takes over a week to travel from the accounts payable clerk, through the mail, into the vendor's accounts receivable department, to the vendor's bank, through the banking system, until it finally arrives as a debit to the payor's account. A cash manager would be negligent if he merely forgot about the $250,000 the day that the payment was mailed and entered into his books. His job is to keep that money efficiently employed until it is needed at the bank.

MANAGING FLOAT

Managing disbursement float—the sum of outstanding checks at any moment in time—involves monitoring bank account balances. The corporate books will show a payment entered on the day a check is written. However, the collected balance shown by the bank will not be reduced until checks are presented for payment. A collected balance—money cleared for use—at the bank is the ledger balance less collection float. Again, we see why the cash manager attempts to reduce collection float and increase disbursement float: the goal is to swell the amount of usable funds at any given time. He may use remote disbursement techniques to slow payments and/or controlled or zero-balance accounts to monitor bank account activity and enhance the certainty of when cash outflows will occur. In Chapter 9, we will see why this is so important.

A portion of the collected balance may be used for bank compensation, unless the company pays for all bank services in fees. However, many companies use strictly average monthly collected balances to compensate for credit and cash management (noncredit) services. Using one predetermined, fixed balance to compensate the bank for credit as well as cash management services is called "double counting." Although banks prefer not to double count, some corporations are able to negotiate this arrangement. Double counting, though, has become less widespread in recent years as banks have undertaken restructuring of their cost accounting methodologies. Of course, clout comes into play in negotiations of this kind. In Chapter 5, we will examine bank account analysis and how banks calculate check availability, hence, clearing float deducted from the ledger balance. We will see how cash managers determine the cost of float, and see that monitoring the availability that a bank assigns to check collections is crucial. Different banks use different methods, some better than others, in order to determine availability factors; cash managers must regularly review whether or not their banks are accurately reflecting the true availability of checks deposited in their accounts.

SUMMARY

The trick to "playing the float," a common nomenclature for disbursement float control, is predicting actual funds flow through major disbursement accounts after those funds no longer show on the company's books. This practice will normally result in company books showing red or negative balances.[44] Many housewives are experts at this practice; they cash checks at the grocery store on weekends but only cover those checks with cash deposits on Monday. Needless to say, cash management involves strategies that coordinate cash inflows and outflows and adequately compensate banks. The cash manager determines approximately the levels of disbursement float residing in the system at any given time. He monitors the availability assigned to deposited checks. In sum, he selects disbursement, funds transfer, check collection, and concentration alternatives that will increase this usable cash reservoir. Thus armed, investment of temporarily idle funds is possible. Interest income is one brass ring the cash manager tries to grab. Reduced levels of short-term debt is another. Surely, he attempts to reach his goals in the most efficient manner possible.

5 Corporate Banking

Selecting a cash management bank is no easy task these days. There are now over 250 banks active in the cash management market. Operational capabilities vary, and product quality runs the gamut from top shelf to lackluster. Sifting out the winners from the losers is an arduous chore for the corporate cash manager who must thoroughly evaluate current and prospective bank partners. Services range from basic lockbox networks to sophisticated balance and information reporting packages tied to automated funds transfer. The cash manager in a typical, large corporation now uses over 14 cash management banks to perform an average of 15 specific services. In addition, this cash manager has an average of ten banks calling on him to sell cash management products.[45]

BANKING IN A STATE OF FLUX

Trends now affecting the banking industry make the cash manager's job even tougher. Competition is heavy as banks scramble to position themselves in a fast-paced market. Regional banks are battling the encroachment of the large money center giants. Some small banks, simply outclassed in their ability to innovate, watch corporate customers migrate to more savvy competitors. Furthermore, the technology that banks use to

79

provide corporate services is evolving so quickly that some bankers have to struggle to keep pace with new concepts and terminology.

The banking industry is contending with the upheavals of deregulation as well. Banks' costs of retail deposits are rising at the same time that more and more companies are practicing cash management, thereby draining idle funds from demand deposit accounts. Additionally, the Monetary Control Act of 1980 has forced the Fed to charge for its services, including check collection, wire transfers, ACH transactions, and others. Banks' costs of providing cash management services are rising accordingly, and these increased costs are being passed on to corporations.

In response, bankers are now reconsidering the traditional view that deposits are a bank's primary profit source. Cost accounting systems are being restructured so that banks can unbundle product packages and assign realistic prices for individual services. The days of giveaway cash management services are over. Price predictions and comparisons among banks are therefore difficult as the industry revamps its own business plans. How well a bank carves out its niche and concentrates on profitable products in the next few years will affect how it delivers dependable cash management services.

Also, there are new providers of cash management programs emerging, further intensifying the competition for corporate business. For instance, a mutual fund family, Boston's Fidelity Group, recently unveiled an integrated line of cash management services at an industry conference. Other mutual fund organizations have developed sweep arrangements with banks, whereby daily idle corporate cash is automatically invested in a money market fund. The entrance of mutual fund groups into such areas as cash concentration will no doubt complicate the service selection process for the corporate treasurer looking for better ways to mobilize and employ his funds.

This all amounts to a very unsettled market for corporate cash management services, with banks leapfrogging each other in price and product innovation. A bank seeking market share with a certain new product may try to attract customers with a relatively low price. Cash managers may then be frustrated when prices double or triple a few years later as the bank tries to recoup costs. Because it is burdensome to dismantle a working cash management system, corporate treasurers often have to accept price increases as a way of life. We quickly sense the importance of developing a meaningful strategy for evaluating cash management banks. It is obvious that selecting the low-cost provider, with price the only performance criterion, can prove to be shortsighted.

Competition among cash management bankers sometimes prompts other unpopular scenarios. Occasionally, cash managers are sold a service before the bugs have been worked out. Bank sales staff have been known to misrepresent operational capability, using the phrase "totally automated" when a service is not. One corporate treasurer reports having been sold a state-of-the-art lockbox program that promised to greatly reduce the time required to deposit receipts and transmit data. When he attempted to quantify the promised savings by reviewing the availability given on deposited items, he noticed skewed results. He called his bank for an explanation and was informed that there had been an unfortunate system malfunction. When the situation prevailed over the course of several months, the treasurer knew he had been had. He confronted his banker who finally admitted that the service still required much human intervention and simply could not deliver what was sold. The treasurer negotiated with the bank for a better availability than he would have received had the service operated properly. Until the bank can deliver what it promised, this treasurer receives special treatment.

A BANK EVALUATION STRATEGY

The preceding episode underscores what many experienced cash managers profess; the burden is on the cash manager to:

Know why you need a new service or bank.

Determine exactly what programs and operational capability you require.

Use available networks to prescreen bank and nonbank service candidates.

Know how much and how you are willing to pay for products.

Negotiate prices.

Follow-through with performance evaluation and skillful communication.

Treasurers and cash managers who have been successful with initial and ongoing bank evaluations often take strategic approaches to keeping banking expenses under control and relationships stable. Whether it is reviewing account analyses from over 50 regional depository banks, budgeting for banking expenses, or staging surprise tours of lockbox facilities armed with intelligent questions, rewards exist for the cash manager who plans how to get the best services his money can buy.

For instance, one large hotel chain now saves thousands of dollars annually, compensates for an understaffed cash management department, and keeps bankers and timesharing firms honest with the help of an automated account analyses program designed by the assistant treasurer. He realized that he could not manually review over 100 different account analyses arriving in a variety of formats at haphazard intervals. Efforts to standardize account analyses are now underway in the cash management industry, but this assistant treasurer could not wait. He studied his operation with a view toward internal resources that could help him evaluate the efficiency of his deposit reporting network and the availability that banks were granting for deposited items. He found that by working closely with the data processing manager he could create his own system for standardizing and reviewing account analyses.[46] One of the most interesting aspects of this tale is that the assistant treasurer took the initiative to work with the data processing manager. He did something that many corporate managers cannot: break traditions of rivalry and share ideas with another planner.

This shows that cash managers who plan, organize, direct, and control their company's strategy for bank evaluations—whether on a basis of price, performance, or creativity—can be powerful and reasonable bank customers. These are proactive cash managers who can be tough negotiators but who are also pleased to fairly compensate banks for quality service.

Why a New Bank or Service?

It may be helpful to ask yourself why you are looking for a new cash management service or bank. Are you unhappy with your present bank? If so, you may want to take the time to list some of the causes of your discomfort. This exercise can help sharpen your awareness of the kind of bank customer you are and what you expect from a bank. Are you seeking better prices, more sophisticated operating capability, knowledgeable account officers and consultants, or a sense of being an appreciated account at the bank?

A banking relationship succeeds when both parties, customer and banker, have a clear view of their expectations. A cash manager can become a strong and mature negotiator by first asking himself, "what am I like to deal with?" The ideal answer to this question is, "I know I am sometimes a thorn in my banker's side, but I am fair and straightforward about my needs." Because corporate banking in many ways depends on solid communication skills between human beings, a first step in developing a strategy for evaluating banks is to understand your business needs and how successful you are at expressing them to your banks.

Some soul-searching may be in order for the cash manager who is about to undertake an evaluation of banks. He may ask, to wit, "is it fair that I've already picked my next operating bank, although I am asking ten other banks to answer lengthy service questionnaires so that I can show price comparisons to my boss?" On another score, cash managers can improve the evaluation process by reviewing the effectiveness of service questionnaires. Bankers have complained that cash managers too often send out questionnaires that contain irrelevant requests, a clue that the cash manager is either incompetent or, more likely, too busy to design a useful document. Work is underway on several industry fronts to standardize service questionnaires. This sorely needed effort will surely make for better communications between cash manager and banker.

Headway has been made on one front: a model lockbox questionnaire provided by the Bank Administration Institute's Center For Cash Management Studies. (See Appendix A.) Its purpose is to enable lockbox banks to establish a comprehensive set of answers to lockbox questionnaires sent by corporations, and it provides cash managers with a model from which to select appropriate questions and a way to make meaningful comparisons among bank respondents.

Needs Assessment

Focusing on why you need a new bank or service can determine how you will go about evaluating candidates. Do you need to start operating relationships with banks in areas you are unfamiliar with? For example, if you are opening a new branch, the business reasons for needing a new field bank are straightforward. You may then turn your attention to the task of prescreening banks. You can use your local cash management association as an avenue for researching the operating reputations of different banks. You can streamline the selection process by narrowing your choices down to those banks which have performed well for colleagues using the types of services you seek.

Do you need a bank that can better handle the growth of your company? If so, you may want to assess where your firm will be in five years. Are you looking for a long-term relationship and access to credit? Then, you may consider not only how creditworthy your firm is and how that is perceived by banks, but also a bank's capacity to write new loans during tight money periods. You may want to investigate a bank's ratio of net loans to its deposit base. You can discover if a bank routinely spreads itself too thin, which could pose a problem for you if your firm does not have enormous clout. You could find yourself competing for credit when you need it most.

Bank credit analysis is an art. Many corporate treasurers turn to specialists who help them evaluate bank capital adequacy, liquidity, asset quality, profitability, interest coverage, and market versus book value of bank stock. Firms such as Keefe, Bruyette & Woods, A. G. Becker, and Cates Consulting Analysts, Inc. specialize in both domestic and international bank credit analysis. Cash managers who need this kind of assistance, and who are willing to pay the hefty charges, can receive segregated financial data of individual banks, analytically measured and formatted to highlight existing or potential problem areas. This way, cash managers and treasurers can obtain meaningful credit examinations of depository, credit-line, disbursing, and investment bank partners.

Why you need a bank or service illustrates what programs or combinations of programs you will settle on. Can you estimate future credit as well as cash management needs? Which will be more important to the success of your firm? Is your company selling word processing equipment or typewriter parts? Credit versus cash management priorities, now and in the future, weigh heavily in today's selection of a banking partner. Will you need merger and acquisitions help? Will you require special lines of bank operating expertise because your company is planning to expand into new markets? Will you need a bank that is aware of your industry's nuances?

What about international cash management consulting and operations? Are you looking for a bank that can help you consolidate overseas cash management functions? Do you need bilateral or multilateral netting programs, a reinvoicing center, or other assistance in reducing the costs of cross-border payments? You will want to determine a candidate's commitment to international financial management products, its level of staff expertise, and its global clout.

How quickly is your firm embracing computer technology; are five-year plans incorporating computerized business tools? If so, you will need a banking partner who has a good track record of providing corporations with innovative solutions to technological quandaries. Is your accounting department planning to automate or upgrade its systems? Will you want to link external cash management data sources, such as automated balance and transaction reports, with the main corporate computer system? What can a bank tell you about this rocky road?

With questions like these, the strategy-minded cash manager can intelligently select a banking relationship he, or someone, will have to live with for years. The bank you choose today may have to guide you as your company expands or falters. Thinking about why you are seeking a new bank or service can help you pinpoint concerns crucial to your bank evaluation strategy.

Such planning also helps you to realize when service selection involves factors beyond your control. The word service is used here intentionally to suggest that operational requirements are often generic until corporate/bank politics add dimension to the evaluation task. Your objective need may be a lockbox location close to corporate headquarters, and you may want weekend lockbox processing. Politics may play a role when your company president sits on the board of the local bank, which does not happen to do weekend lockbox work. So you may or may not wind up with your ideal service. Many cash managers are well aware of unspoken rules regarding bank selection and traditional loyalties that sometimes dictate who their banking partners will be. Other cash managers report no interference with purchasing services, even though relationships exist with certain banks at the board level.

Make Service Make Sense

When selecting or evaluating service banks, the cash manager performs the role of a systems engineer. He first reviews existing operations, noting strengths and weaknesses. He then compares strengths and weaknesses with the objectives he has in mind for the improved system. He looks at components of the existing cash management function and decides which areas need enhancement and which areas need to be scrapped and replaced with a new approach. In short, he looks at where he is now and where he wants to go and how he'll get there.

This sounds like a tidy prescription. In many ways, it is because planning merely implies a rational approach to achieving goals. Upon closer inspection, however, we find that the words "rational" and "goals" mean somebody has to do some serious legwork. The cash manager who studies what he wants a new system or service to achieve in terms of efficiency and profitability will have a better way to gauge which service provider can best match his expectations. The burden, then, is on the corporate person charged with cash management to become familiar with service options and to keep in touch with cash management industry news. Walter Hanson, who we met in Chapter 1, was in the unfortunate position of having to call his banker and ask, "what is cash management?" By the same token, you do not want to be in the position of calling your banker to ask "what is a payable-through-draft?" (Banks despise them.)

Should a new disbursement account be located at an affiliate of a sophisticated West Coast bank in Grand Junction, Colorado? What about using a money market fund as a disbursing account? How stable are these options given the regulatory climate? Do improved float, control, or investment scenarios outweigh the risk that such a disbursement site may be short-lived because of regulatory or market events?

The proactive cash manager attempts to make decisions armed with an acute sense of service costs, options, provider reputations, technological trends, industry events, regulatory environment, and, most important, his own cash management needs.

How to justify service expense? Consider a treasurer setting up a lockbox network for the first time. He will need to analyze his existing collection system and perform a breakeven study to determine that a lockbox would be economically beneficial. First, he will have to determine his average daily collection float by multiplying annual sales by the average daily collection time (in days) and dividing by 365. This produces a dollar amount that represents average daily collection float. To determine the negative effect of float—its cost—the cash manager multiplies the average daily collection float by an interest rate that reflects the value of funds to the company. This rate may equal the potential average yield on a money market investment or some internal indicator of required return on capital. He then divides the result by 365 to quantify the cost of average daily collection float.

With this approach, he discovers how much of an opportunity cost—the return on investment that could be made if funds were available for corporate use—he incurs because he has not yet speeded the flow of receipts. Float calculations can also be designed to reflect seasonal sales fluctuations, changing collection times, and investment rates. This process focuses on the true value of corporate funds.

Banks can help in this area, especially if they are eager to perform a service for the treasurer. The First National Bank of Chicago's marketing literature actually shows treasurers how to conduct a breakeven analysis. It states:

> To calculate a breakeven point, the incremental benefits of a service are set to equal the incremental costs and the equation is solved for the unknown. For example, you might want to determine the necessary reduction in collection time to justify an $.08 incremental differential between your present check processing cost and a contemplated service such as a lockbox. Assuming an average check size of $750 and a 12% annual cost of capital for purposes of illustration, the equation is solved as follows:
>
> Incremental Costs = Incremental Benefits
> Incremental Cost/Unit = Days Saved (DS) × Average Check
> Size × Daily Cost of Capital
> $.08 = DS × $750 × 12%/365
> DS = 0.324
>
> The lockbox in this example must accelerate collections by about ⅓ of a day to be economically justified. If it accelerates collections by less than ⅓ of a day, the benefit would not justify the cost. The same equation can be used to determine breakeven check size if the number of days saved is known, or breakeven incremental cost if the other variables are known.[47] (This example is reprinted courtesy of The First National Bank of Chicago.)

This method of determining whether or not a new service makes sense for your company can be applied to other cash management subsystems as well. For instance, you may decide to concentrate with ACH debits rather than paper depository transfer checks. But the decision to make such a radical change involves a lot more than just cost considerations. You may need expert advice. Banks can help in this regard—they will be particularly eager to help you solve problems if they want to sign you on as a credit customer. They will study your current operation and suggest how to best proceed. But how do you know which banks are skilled at handling ACH concentrations? Generally, the reputable cash management banks understand the value of providing treasurers with unbiased recommendations. But the burden is on the treasurer or cash manager to undertake a rational approach to purchasing cash management products. Let's now look at other bank and service evaluation criteria.

SERVICE INTEGRATION

No component of a cash management system operates in a vacuum. For example, a good lockbox bank not only efficiently processes and deposits receipts but is also able to assign actual, rather than Fed, availabilities on your deposited items. This assures you that you are receiving proper credit for checks cleared through direct-send programs—Fed availability schedules do not reflect the fast collection times associated with private bank direct sends. A good lockbox bank also makes its deposit and balance reporting function a priority, with adequate staff and planning committed to the task of providing you with the timely information.

An optimum concentration bank links your various cash management functions. As such, it must efficiently handle deposit and balance reporting, telecommunications (data transmissions between a computing system and remotely located devices), automated processing of paper and ACH debits, ACH transaction value-dating, funds transfers of all varieties, controlled disbursing operations, funding of zero-balance accounts, and account analysis. The concentration bank also has to have knowledgeable personnel to assist you in investing and borrowing. (We will consider how the concentration account operates in Chapter 7.)

It is crucial that the cash manager see how his system, using different banks and service providers for different purposes, operates as a whole and how well funds and data are captured and used by each system participant. In so doing, the cash manager matches a new service provider to his needs. He assures that the new provider is able to plug into his banking network insofar as the new service role requires it to keep pace with the level of technological sophistication established systemwide. A cash manager does not always need a field depository bank capable of satellite data transmission, but he does need a field bank that gets transit items to the Fed or to the local clearing house for collection as quickly as possible.

Analyzing the existing cash management system not only segregates individual weak spots and service enhancement needs but can also prompt the cash manager to investigate how this cash-flow information can be integrated with other corporate data bases. A treasurer may decide that his field deposit operation has grown to the point that an automated deposit reporting feature is warranted. He may then realize that the accounting or sales departments could benefit by receiving data captured by his system. For example, the cash manager of a restaurant chain could build his deposit reporting system so that when each restaurant reports daily deposit figures to a concentration bank or third-party vendor, it also reports sales data, such as the number of hamburgers sold. Some very large companies are able to automatically update the general ledger and accounting forecasts with deposit and sales data, respectively, captured by the cash management system.

The concept of integrated information flows that feed central corporate data bases is important to cash managers today as new technologies are becoming affordable and usable. Microcomputers, used to retrieve information from varied external sources as well as from corporate mainframes, promise to become an exciting cash management tool in the next few years. The important point to remember is that purchasing cash management services today requires a perspective on how information is best routed through a company.

CASH MANAGEMENT BANK CRITERIA

Several key factors affect how well money-mobilization banks perform: bank location, size, staff expertise, and operations capability. It is important to keep these factors in mind when evaluating potential cash management banks.

Bank Location

Four common location criteria for corporate selection of cash gathering banks are:

Access (for lockbox banks) to an efficient Post Office where around 90% of lockbox mail is received within one day of intracity mailing.

Lockbox and, where possible, field banks must be close enough to the Fed Bank in their areas to take optimum advantage of check presentation deadlines.

Proximity to the local clearing house where average availability granted is one and one-half days.

Access for lockbox banks with direct send programs to busy and well-run airports that have generally good weather.[48]

Disbursement bank location is critical to the cash manager operating remote or controlled disbursement programs. Obviously, for remote disbursing, the ideal bank is one that is located in a place hard to reach for physical check presentation. Controlled disbursing, typically, is accomplished using branches of large banks situated so that only a few Fed check presentments are made daily. This allows cash managers to know early in the day the amount of cash disbursements they have to cover. (We will analyze this in Chapter 8.)

Bank Size

It is reasonable to assume that size affects a bank's processing capability. A small bank (under $50 million in assets) probably cannot generate enough check processing volume to warrant its investment in techniques for providing cash management services. Cash management industry analysts generally agree that for a bank to be large enough to provide cash management services it must have no less than $100 million in assets. There are, however, examples of very imaginative country banks who, working with city correspondents, offer cash management products. Conversely, bank size does not guarantee adequate cash management expertise. One only has to hear cash managers swap stories of big bank fiascoes to realize that, sometimes, the bigger they are, . . . Where size really matters is investment in equipment and technology needed to provide sophisticated cash management products. Consider that, in some regions, banks have to spend $25,000 to become ACH members. The latest developments in lockbox processing—video and digital imaging—require cash commitments that can run into millions of dollars. Only the large banks intent on leading with technology can afford to develop computerized cash management.

Staff Expertise

A bank truly interested in providing quality cash management services will pay close attention to the kinds of expertise represented among its staff. Persons charged with product development, planning, cost accounting, marketing, operations, consulting, and systems design must be well-trained in their respective areas and committed to their roles within their organizational structures. The need for competent and committed personnel is probably more important than ever to the bank cash management department, since the field is evolving with the technology that accompanies it.

Successful banks are those that create an environment in which staff expertise is shared and customers are able to take advantage of a consortium of knowledgeable people. Bank generalists need to have a working knowledge of operations and finance, as well as enough sense to bring in a specialist to assist a corporation with sticky cash management problems. Often, a bank's organizational structure determines how well this kind of interaction at the bank occurs.

Account Officer Training

A bank is often judged by the competence of its account officers. Therefore, account officer training is crucial to the sustained success of corporate-bank relationships. Properly trained account officers can reveal the level of a bank's commitment to cash management. The bank account officer functions in a key role, not only representing the bank and booking loans but also relaying a company's needs to senior bank management. However, not all banks assure that account officers are well-trained or are adequately briefed about a customer's business nuances. Cash managers resent having to re-educate account officers who have not familiarized themselves with company background or, for that matter, cash management operations.

Too often, new account officers show up at the cash manager's office and merely say, "Hi! How *are* you? Now, what can I *do* for you?" These kinds of visits have been dubbed "Howdy Doody Calls." Cash managers generally agree that this kind of call is a waste of time and reflects poorly on the bank. One corporate treasurer even gives his secretary an approved list of people he will see in his office in an effort to weed out unprepared account officers.

Cash managers count on account officers to bring them news of product innovations, regulatory changes, and industry events. They also prefer that account officers come armed with probing questions that make the visit a useful fact-finding mission. It helps if the account officer receives and reads company financial statements regularly. Account officers function best when they are more than superficial marketeers of products developed elsewhere in the bank. They earn ultimate respect from cash managers when they can help solve problems or suggest where a solution might be found if it is unavailable at the bank.

The point to remember here is that the caliber of bank calling officers can be a useful criterion upon which to judge a bank's commitment to its customers and their sensitivities. An account officer who understands your cash management as well as credit requirements can be an invaluable partner.

Bank Consultants

The quality of a bank's consulting staff is another area you can investigate when evaluating a cash management bank. At least 50 of the top cash management banks now have formally organized consulting units. Some of these units are run as profit centers and are therefore organizationally independent from the cash management sales and product management functions. This aspect of independence is meant to support the consultant's ability to deliver objective analyses of corporate cash management systems, including: billing, receivables collection, deposit procedures, concentration, payables management, check reconciliation, cashflow budgeting, information management, short-term investments and, so on.

You are more likely to get better quality work from bank consultants who are independent of the sales function. But, because these independent units charge for their services—the work is not a "gift" tied to other cash management products—you must be willing to pay premium prices for objective and professional counsel. A typical lockbox analysis, which recommends lockbox locations by studying company remittance patterns, mail time, and bank availability criteria with computer models, may cost $5000. Some large company studies run as high as $100,000. You can pay for this work in fees or balances, depending on your existing, if any, relationship with a given bank. By contracting with a bank consulting unit that is run as a profit center, you can often assure that the advice you receive will be objective and professional. If a consulting study is free, most likely it is a disguised marketing proposal, recommending that you buy other bank products.

It is important when selecting bank consultants, whether from credit or noncredit banks, to realize that the kind of study you need will dictate a corresponding level of consultant skill. Cash managers selecting bank consultants do not hesitate to check references. They know that a study's quality depends on the consultant's expertise, not the bank's name. A consultant with a proven track record working for companies with similar cash management requirements can work best for you. Furthermore, studies differ in size and scope. Some prove successful using a standard approach; others demand special skills and a customized design. A relatively standard model-based lockbox system analysis can be performed by a competent consultant who need not be the head of the unit. However, if your needs are complex—say, a look at multidivisional collection, concentration, and disbursement—you may insist that the senior consultant be involved. Part of the evaluation task, then, is to investigate just who will be supervising your study. The senior consultant may be present when you close the deal; make sure he or she remains an active participant.

When contracting for a study, you can also evaluate how willing a bank is to schedule follow-up reviews of your system. The analysis need not be recalculated, but it is helpful to have the consultant visit with you on a yearly basis to discuss how well the recommendations are working. You may be able to negotiate for these check-ups when contracting for the initial work.

We will look quickly at some components of cash management consulting in order to help you formulate questions useful in the evaluation task. In general, a bank consulting engagement should consist of three elements: (1) the proposal, (2) an interim analysis, and (3) a final report.

    1 The proposal should state study objectives and scope, an outline for an approach (on-site interviews or surveys, data gathering, and analysis techniques), estimated consulting hours, estimated costs and cost ceilings, expense reimbursement agreements, payment terms, payment options (balances or fees), billing method (invoice on completion or progress billing), and, most important, the project timetable.

2   The interim analysis may be verbal or written, but it should provide initial results upon which you base subsequent decisions. Depending on the kind of study, the interim analysis delivers a progress report in quantifiable terms. It gives the cash manager and consultant an opportunity to fine-tune directions and resolve any problems with the study.

3   The final report should identify major problems, present key findings and study conclusions, show cost/benefit analyses, and recommend solutions accompanied by an appropriate implementation sequence. You should also receive appendices to the final report which include charts, statistics, and methodologies used and an evaluation of current industry events which may affect your operation.

A successful study is practical yet innovative. Its recommendations should be appropriate for your corporation's current and projected levels of technological savvy. A good study is also proactive: it considers your company's growth and attempts to anticipate your cash management needs a few years hence. The best studies, however, grow out of a working rapport between corporation and bank. When evaluating consulting candidates, be sure to weigh how well you think you can communicate with the consultant. Investigate how willing the consultant is to deal with you directly, rather than through your account officer.

Finally, be fair when you request proposals. Banks invest time, energy, and money when they bid on a consulting contract. In one instance, a bank spent $20,000 on the proposal alone. If you have your heart set on having your lead credit bank do your consulting work, do not ask five other banks for proposals only so you can go to the bargaining table with price comparisons.

For a variety of reasons, you may want to have an independent consultant or one of the Big Eight accounting firms perform cash management studies. As the practice of cash management has gained much attention during the past ten years, the large accounting firms have begun to build staffs of treasury management specialists. Respected cash management thinkers like Paul Beehler and Andrea Bierce, left the banking and corporate worlds, respectively, to become Big Eight consultants. Other cash management pioneers, like Allen Cohen and George C. White, left banking to consult in the electronic funds transfer areas. If your bank cannot provide you with specialized consulting, it may be willing to recommend firms that can. Or, if you require a nonbank perspective on your cash management system, you may investigate alternative consulting sources.

Operations Expertise

A cash management bank can do more for you than reduce collection float or add control to your disbursement function. If a bank has solid operations capability, you can then delegate certain processing tasks to it, thereby reducing your corporate overhead. For instance, you can have a bank automatically perform reconciliations and eliminate several clerical positions from your budget. A bank's ability to run a smooth "back office," as operation departments are called, is important. Yet true operating skill may stem from a bank's approach to technology. A bank that is willing to invest substantially in cash management product development proves its commitment to the needs of the corporate treasury function, and a bank that sets up training programs for cash management product managers clearly wants to be known in the marketplace as consistently innovative. Furthermore, a financial institution that is willing to try out new applications of computer technology with pilot programs demonstrates that it takes its role as a market leader very seriously.

Industry analysts concede that many cash management operations, like lockbox processing, are mature products. This means that they are developed to a relatively sophisticated degree and are common from bank to bank. Banks who were pioneers in the 1970s with the cash management services we use today are now involved with research on, and development of, new cash management tools. No doubt, these efforts are concentrated on ways to best interface with corporate data processing systems, using a new generation of technological skill. On the other hand, many banks simply follow the leader and devise product imitations simply to hang onto corporate business. Therefore, wisely evaluating a bank's operational capability includes investigating that bank's attitude toward innovation.

Looking at a concentration bank, the crucial turnstile for cash inflows and outflows, you may ask: does it provide reliable money transfer, communications, and balance reporting services? Can it automatically prepare depository transfer checks, wire transfers, and ACH transactions? Does it automatically interface with third-party data-gathering services? Can it accept company tapes or teleprocessing as part of its data and funds management responsibility? Who maintains the necessary software; is internal systems support adequate? How fast can it move your funds? If your concentration bank is also a disbursing bank, can you arrange for controlled disbursements? How well can the bank perform the kinds of information reporting tasks needed to support the service? How detailed and understandable are account reports? With questions like these, you can gauge a bank's preparation for a continuing role in the cash management business.

Is the bank that you are evaluating a market leader or follower? If the bank is a leader, then, it takes its role seriously, developing profitable products in areas where it has proven expertise. Commitment to creative product management and problem-solving is obvious among a stable staff. Product line profitability is targeted and periodically reviewed, while product eliminations are less likely to occur. The cash manager can strategically plan his objectives in tune with this bank's commitment to program support.

A market follower, on the other hand, may not be an organization that is prepared to offer consistent service quality. Staff turnover may be high, and senior management support may be lacking. Such a bank may have no true sense of its profitable and nonprofitable accounts. Sometimes, this kind of bank focuses too heavily on high-pitch sales campaigns and ignores the importance of careful product planning. It rushes into the marketplace simply because its competitors are there. While these comments are general, they are meant to suggest important criteria for evaluating a bank: long-standing dedication to cash management services, indicated by innovation and support of services that have proved profitable to the bank.

When we discussed bank size, we noted that size alone does not guarantee quality bank service. In the same way, it is fair to say that slick ads and marketing proposals also do not guarantee that you will get the operational expertise you need. Cash managers have a favorite saying that sums up the dilemma. It goes: "A bank is only as good as its back office." This relates to what goes on behind the scenes. Take, for example, the wire transfer desk, where banks have been known to subjectively define "automated wire transfer services." A cash manager may believe that he is executing a wire instruction from his terminal to the bank, whose own computerized system, in turn, reliably moves the money. The cash manager may not know that a clerk tears off a printout, spindles it along with 50 other wire instructions, and eventually sits down at a machine to manually rekey the messages. While many banks have dedicated staff and capable managers handling your company's money in the back office, it is important to remember that most cash management services are labor-intensive and involve mountains of paper. How well the back office functions, not how flashy the ads, determines how reliable bank services are.

So, how can you get a glimpse at the back office? Go and look. Your local cash management bank should be happy to give you a tour of its lockbox facility, proof department, check processing function, investment desk, and money transfer operation. In fact, the bank will be proud to have you meet its respective department heads who can explain the various systems. If possible, schedule your tour, preferably a night visit, with as little notice as possible. Then you are apt to get a true picture of workflows. For if left to the discretion of the bank, your tour might be slated for an afternoon during a week when work volumes are not typically hectic. Also, take advantage of business travel and tour current and potential regional banks. When touring a lockbox location, ask for sample customer operating instructions. Ask not only how many mail pick-ups are made daily, but also how often accounts are processed. See how custom work is performed. Note employee attitudes and their work surroundings. Question key personnel about equipment and its use. In short, look before you leap.

BANK COMPENSATION

Part of the bank selection process requires a comparison of bank service charges. This task, however, is not as simple as it sounds. The cash manager first has to find common price denominators among bank candidates before a meaningful analysis can be made. But many factors complicate this process. Banks figure their costs and, hence, service charges using various methodologies. Local market competition can pressurize prices and render national bidding illogical. Bank costs can vary because of different asset structure, capitalization, or operating and regulatory requirements. Furthermore, banks have responded incongruously to the environment of deregulation. The large banks, for the most part, have revamped cost accounting strategies to reflect product profitability, while many smaller banks have been slower to unbundle cash management services. Some banks still rely on the *Federal Reserve Functional Cost Analysis*, which uses arbitrary averages to estimate bank costs. This method is considered by many experts to be inaccurate. As a result, many smaller banks have yet to accurately determine individual product costs, a shortcoming which contributes to service charge instability. (We will look at the account analysis later and discuss its components.)

Banks are far from uniform in methods for documenting compensation requirements. Some banks treat local customers with whom they have credit relationships better than they treat regional operating account customers. For similar reasons, the cash manager shopping for a new bank partner must approach price comparisons with caution. He will need to understand well the mechanics of bank compensation and determine whether explicit fee-based or implicit balance-based payment best suits his firm. In short, knowing what you'll pay and how you'll pay for it is critical to your bank evaluation strategy.

Before we discuss the merits of fees versus balances to pay only for cash management activities, we have to consider the importance of the credit relationship. Compensation for cash management (noncredit) services in balances can contribute to a bank's willingness to extend credit. Remember, banks earn most of their profits from commercial loans, and they need deposit money to carry on this business. Corporate checking account balances represent an inexpensive resource to banks. Therefore, banks have traditionally favored corporate customers who have maintained sizeable deposits. If your bank relationship includes both credit and noncredit services, a special perspective on potential borrowing needs must be taken.

COMPENSATING BALANCES FOR CASH MANAGEMENT

In Chapter 1, we saw that banks are prevented by law from paying explicit interest on corporate checking accounts. As a sort of end run around this prohibition, banks use an applied earnings credit rate on collected bank balances in order to return to corporations an implicit value for idle funds left on deposit. This computation generates credits—expressed as an earnings allowance—which offset cash management activity charges. When more credits accrue than are used by the corporation, the excess is absorbed back into the bank. When service charges during a month outpace the earnings allowance, either additional balances or a fee is required. Cash managers often review required compensating balance targets, using a 12-month moving average, and make adjustments on a monthly basis. Banks typically analyze compensating balance requirements monthly and review overall account profitability and prices at least annually.

The earnings credit rate can be based on a moving average of the 91-day U.S. Treasury Bill rate, a combination of U.S. Treasury Bill rates and an internal cost of funds rate, or a combination of U.S. Treasury Bill rates and repurchase agreement or commercial paper rates. Banks have varying policies concerning how often the earnings credit rate is adjusted to reflect market movements.

Cash managers unable to reduce balance levels to zero (and invest liberated money at market rates) find balance-based compensation to be a handy way of paying for such things as check processing and coin and currency exchange. Some cash managers prefer balance compensation because it allows them to hide the extent of bank service costs from senior management. In other instances, for example, at an outlying field bank where accumulated balances are relatively small over time, cash managers cannot justify the effort necessary to manage the account to zero. It is easy to simply let average balances compensate the bank for deposit activity.

As we stated previously, double counting refers to the practice of applying earnings credits to balances kept on deposit for loan compensation and allowing these credits to offset noncredit service charges. Banks have traditionally done this to attract credit customers and, furthermore, because they were not adept at tracking a customer's net monthly balance position. The prevalence of double counting in the past led to the perception that many cash management services were free. Today, however, cash management banks have improved systems for analyzing overall account profitability. Moreover, many banks have formal policies that disallow double counting. It may still be possible, though, to find a bank willing to negotiate on this score.

Sometimes, cash managers compensate for noncredit services by maintaining balances in the form of noninterest-bearing certificates of deposit.[49] This arrangement takes advantage of the low reserve requirements—now at a 3% maximum—on this kind of instrument. Ostensibly, the reserve requirement savings is passed on to the corporation in the form of lower average balance requirements. The certificate of deposit can be double counted and used to offset both credit and noncredit charges. A cash manager who could afford to tie up funds in a time deposit may find this alternative useful.

Most corporations still rely on the balance method of compensating banks, although fee-based payments are becoming increasingly popular. Often, cash managers have "inherited" their bank management responsibilities and discover that instituting wholesale changes too quickly draws fire from senior management. Balance compensation is useful to corporations who are relatively unsophisticated in cash management. It is possible to arrange a compensation plan that combines fees and balances: balances are used to cover activity charges, whereas intermittent balance shortfalls are recouped with explicit fees.

To pay in fees demands accurate systems for tracking banking expenses and monitoring bank statements and account analyses. No doubt, we will see the trend toward fee compensation continue with vigor as cash managers implement treasury applications for microcomputers. It is fair to state, however, that there is more room to negotiate compensation packages when balances are used. Banks fear being accused of uneven dealings if they negotiate structured fees. But banks can, and do, favor special customers in many ways. Goodwill is more easily dispensed when balances are used for compensation.

FEES VERSUS BALANCES

Where no credit relationship exists with a bank, say, at a field depository used to clear local checks, the issue of fees versus balances is pronounced. It has long been a sore spot among cash managers who argue that balance compensation does not deliver full value to the corporation. (Trust services, data processing, and investment advice have traditionally been fee-based.) By nature, banks dislike fee compensation; the practice drains beloved balances from banks. Moreover, bank growth is measured by deposit base. This problem is exacerbated at small banks who have difficulty assigning accurate costs to individual services. Some banks, large or small, add a premium when corporations insist on paying with explicit fees. Such actions, however, are not bound to dissuade cash managers from considering fee-based compensation arrangements.

The central arguments for payment of banking services with fees are:

Banks do not provide earnings credit on the portion of corporate demand deposit balances assigned to Federal Reserve requirements.

When corporations generate more earnings allowance than can be used on a monthly basis and compensation is balance-based, the excess is absorbed by the bank as required by law.

Corporations can typically achieve a higher return on investment by buying short-term instruments (or greater interest savings by reducing loans) than is available from the assigned earnings rate.

Cash management techniques, such as balance reporting and disbursement float control, have given cash managers a better handle on cashflows which can be productively deployed elsewhere at market rates.

Larger firms, especially, are concerned with budgeting for, and managing, banking expenses, an endeavor facilitated by expense itemization.[50]

Some cash managers prefer fee compensation because it delineates tax deductible business expenses. One could argue, though, that there is a corresponding tax liability incurred when liberated balances earn interest income. The tax question is a complicated one, and solutions depend on the particulars of a company's business environment.

As cash managers continue to be concerned with cost containment and control, fee-based compensation arrangements will proliferate because they serve the process of budgeting for banking expenses. Companies will increasingly establish banking expense budgets for all departments and subsidiaries. Then, cash managers can more easily note variances between budgeted and actual expenses and competently perform the ongoing task of bank evaluation. With commercial banks nationwide going through product unbundling, bank service charges will continue to spiral as prices are brought into line with actual costs. Fee compensation will help cash managers make more valid comparisons of bank service prices.

COMPENSATING BALANCES FOR CREDIT LINES

Now, we will take a quick look at using balances to compensate banks for credit lines. A credit line is an agreement by a bank to provide a firm with a specified level of cash on relatively short notice. A credit line is typically negotiated for a one-year term, although revolving credit lines extend longer than one year. Usually, companies pay for usage of credit lines by making monthly interest payments based on a nominal interest rate. The rate is variable and is tied to a base rate such as prime. Usually, an increment is quoted along with the base rate, such as prime plus one percent. Credit-line rates change as the bank's prime rate moves up or down. Beyond the nominal interest rate, additional compensation is required to pay for the line. One or more of the following methods are used:

1 Compensating Balances on the Credit Line. The lender may require the borrower to maintain an average level of demand deposit balances equal to a specified percentage of the line. This average compensating balance must be maintained regardless of how much is actually used.

2 Compensating Balances for the Unused Line. Sometimes a bank requires a compensating balance on the amount of the line unused during any one time period.

3 Compensating Balance on the Amount Borrowed. A compensating balance may be required based on the amount borrowed against the line. This amount is sometimes called the "usage" or "draw."

4 Commitment Fee. A lender may require a fee payment when establishing the line. Generally, this is a percentage of the size of the credit line. Occasionally, there is an additional fee on the unused portion of the line. This is sometimes the case with revolving credit lines.

5 Earnings Credits on Compensating Balances. This is double counting, which we discussed above. It allows corporations to offset charges for tangible services with earnings credits accrued from balances kept for credit compensation.[51]

Negotiating credit-line terms is a common practice among money center and large regional banks. Balance requirements can be traded off with nominal rates and commitment fees. But negotiating for credit lines can involve complex decision-making. It deserves an in-depth discussion of the difference between nominal and effective rates and their relationships to compensating balances. Readers can refer to work done by Ned C. Hill and William L. Sartoris, at Indiana University's Graduate School of Business for a thorough treatment of the effective cost of bank credit-line borrowing.

Regulated Payments

A source of account balances used for compensation, in addition to those which cannot be controlled in a cost-effective manner, are regulated payments. Dividend payments are one example of regulated balances for which receipt of earnings credits can be negotiated. Others are certain federal grant funds to public entities and segregated customer funds in the brokerage industry.[52] Corporations can pay federal taxes by either remitting directly to the U.S. Treasury or paying an authorized bank. Up until recently, banks enjoyed the use of these deposits for a while, since the Treasury did not always immediately draw on tax funds. Cash managers were occasionally successful at pressuring banks to give them earnings credits on tax deposits.

However, new treasury and tax loan regulations now require banks to remit federal tax payments immediately, or pay interest to, the U.S. treasury. Needless to say, smart cash managers do not make tax payments long before they are due. It is important to remember that when you approach the bargaining table with a prospective bank partner, be sure to ascertain the bank's posture on earnings credits for regulated balances. You may be surprised to find that the bank is flexible on this issue.

UNDERSTANDING ACCOUNT ANALYSES

Probably one of the most important documents to cross a cash manager's desk is the account analysis, a monthly report prepared by banks that gives a snapshot view of noncredit service activity and corresponding charges. (See Exhibit 5.1.) It is a document prepared from the bank's

THE FIRST NATIONAL BANK OF BOSTON

Boston, Massachusetts 02110

Analysis of Checking Account Activity

Company Name	Date	April 1982
Statement Address	Group Summary	
	Assigned Officer	

Average Monthly Balance Data		Earnings Allowance	
Ledger balance	1,078,300	Collected balances	10.95%
Less float	707,600	Investable balances	12.75%
Equals collected balances	370,700		
		Next months allowance on collected balances	11.16%

Services Rendered	Volume	Price	Total
Checks paid	795	.10	79.50
Deposits	57	.50	28.50
Transit items deposited	151	.06	9.06
Lock box items deposited	1,211	.06	72.66
Maintenance	8	5.00	40.00
Summarization	206	.02	4.12
Fine sorting	587	Minimum	20.00
Stop payments	1	7.50	7.50
Returned deposited items	3	1.00	3.00
Additional statements	2	1.00	2.00
Lock box processing			618.48
Depository transfer checks			31.09
NEACH deposits			20.41
Account Reconciliation			.05
Bostonlink checking account			337.65
Bostonlink wire transfer			34.00
Balance advice			42.00
Controlled disbursement			667.26
Money transfer/PHN/Repetitive		4.00	4.00
Money transfer/Book/Repetitive		3.00	69.00
Money transfer/Fed/Repetitive		4.00	40.00
Money transfer/Via Fed		5.00	20.00
Money transfer credit		2.00	24.00
Automatic transfer debit		2.00	8.00
Automatic transfer credit		1.00	4.00
Zero balance transfer		1.00	42.00

Total Price of Services Used	2,228.26
Earnings Allowance in Collected Balances	3,364.49

Exhibit 5.1. Sample account analyses statement. (Reprinted courtesy of Steve MacQuarrie, The First National Bank of Boston.)

perspective and depicts whether a company has maintained sufficient average monthly balances to generate an earnings allowance used to compensate the bank for tangible services such as wire transfers. The earnings allowance is computed by applying an earnings credit rate to average monthly balances after Fed reserve requirements, credit-line balances and availability float (uncollected funds) have been deducted. Banks differ, however, on whether earnings credits are allowed before or after credit-line balance deductions.

The account analysis lists which services the corporation has used during the monthly analysis period and the prices assigned to each unit of service. It gives a summary of activity expenses and illustrates the level of required average available balances necessary to produce enough earnings to cover each service unit type. The account analysis shows how much of an earnings allowance was created and whether the bank broke even or whether an excess or deficit of earnings credits exists. It also indicates the excess or deficit balances in the account after all bank-relevant deductions have been made.

In essence, the account analysis is a picture of account profitability. Yet it may not represent the total profitability of the bank-corporate relationship, since it often excludes independent services such as stock transfers. The cash manager uses the account analysis as a banking expense control mechanism. He checks to see that balances are in line with his own records, daily balance reports, and monthly statements. The cash manager can discover that summaries of daily balance reports and the monthly statement reflect different balance levels. According to the daily deposit report from the bank, a branch manager has deposited $1500 on a certain day. But when the statement arrives, it indicates a larger amount. A cash manager may reason that both figures come from the bank and, therefore, he is justified in assuming the higher number in his favor. Or, if the account analysis reports less balances than the cash manager expects to see, the cash manager, no doubt, will immediately phone the bank for an explanation. He will want assurance that his account is appropriately adjusted with credits assigned on proper dates. Reviewing the account analysis allows a cash manager to ascertain that he is receiving expected availability on deposited items and a suitable earnings allowance.

Cash managers differ in their approaches to account analysis review. Some tackle the task with vigor, assigning staffers the primary job of checking over the monthly analyses. J. C. Penney followed this course and discovered over $1 million worth of errors in one year, an event which more than justified staff time. The endeavor also put Penney's vast banking network on notice that expense control was a priority. Craig Sullivan, assistant treasurer at Ramada Inns, Inc., recently designed an automated account analysis review system that has already saved the company thousands of dollars.

But account analysis is a tedious task, one that a busy cash manager can easily put off. A cash manager may receive numerous account analyses, one from each major operating bank, arriving anywhere from five to sixty days after the end of analysis periods. A complaint among cash managers is that banks do not use standardized formats, either in documentation or computation. As a result, the cash manager has to review each analysis in light of varied methodologies. For example, different banks set their analyses programs to run at different times during the month: some run from the first day of the month to the last day of the corresponding fourth week; others run from the first day of the month's second week forward, and so forth. While bankers argue that asking for standardized account analyses is like asking all corporations to use identical cost accounting methods, a fledgling industry effort to reconcile some inconsistencies is now underway. The fact remains that tangible and intangible rewards exist for cash managers who can get a handle on account analysis review, manually or, more likely, with computers. There are now software packages available for cash managers who want to use sophisticated computing techniques for analyzing account analyses. This software can run on mini- or microcomputers stationed in the treasury area, or it can be accessed through timesharing. But until cash managers become comfortable with these approaches, the review process will remain a laborious one.

Obviously, the biggest rewards for cash managers are to be gained from reviewing account analyses from major banks. Many cash managers concede that it is unjustifiable to try to track every field account, where daily deposits are miniscule and, when cleared, are quickly moved to a concentration bank. To the associate treasurer of one of the largest insurance companies in the world, it makes little difference if he is receiving 1 or 1.3 days availability on local checks deposited at a small and remote bank. Sometimes, however, cash managers have to use small banks for relatively large operations. One cash manager for a Las Vegas casino had no choice but to rely on a local bank to clear checks written on banks nationwide. He ran into problems when he tried to use computer systems to help assure that proper availability was being assigned to his deposits—the bank did not know how to compute its own availability schedule. The cash manager actually constructed a make-shift availability schedule for the bank, working with airline departure times and Federal Reserve Bank deposit deadlines in San Francisco and Chicago. The cash manager wound up with an availability schedule he could use to negotiate for more favorable availability on checks deposited with the bank.

How Account Analyses Differ

Account analyses are not always useful when comparing banks. This is due to the fact that banks differ in how they manipulate components of the account analysis to compute charges and earnings allowances. For example, a bank may assign a high per item lockbox charge, but grant the corporation an earnings allowance based on a generous earnings credit rate, for example, the previous month's average 91-day Treasury Bill rate. Another bank may assign a low per item lockbox charge, but use a comparatively low earnings credit rate to compute the earnings allowance. For this reason, cash managers comparing banks have to ascertain how each bank pegs the earnings credit rate, whether or not a rate is based on a discount factor, how often adjustments are made to reflect market movements, and how the earnings credit rate behaves during different economic climates. For example, an earnings credit rate may be based on the previous month's average 91-day Treasury Bill rate. In a rising interest rate environment, the earnings credit rate will follow, on a one-month lag basis, market values for funds. Conversely, a bank may peg the earnings credit rate on a previous three-month average of 91-day Treasury Bill rates. If money market rates are rising, the rate applied to corporate balances will not as quickly catch up with market realities. If rates are dropping in the money markets, however, the value of compensating balances in the first example will be devalued more quickly than the value of balances in the latter example. It is important to ask questions about rates and how they affect the implicit value that the earnings allowance scheme grants to corporate funds, and it is crucial to ask whether a bank adjusts earnings credit rates when money market rates are gyrating or adjusts rates only at set intervals. Generally, cash managers prefer that adjustments be made consistently and frequently, since few expect rates to plummet to a perpetual low. Volatility has been and will continue to be a market watchword.

One comparison exercise that cash managers perform when evaluating banks is to ask why two banks using the same basis to peg earnings credit rates come up with a large basis-point disparity between earnings allowances.[53] One hundred basis points equal one percent. While this may put account officers on the spot, it gives the cash manager insight into how well a banker knows his business. Another comparison that cash managers make concerns reserve requirements. Reserve requirements are those portions of collected balances that banks have to set aside in order to satisfy a legal requirement imposed by the Federal Reserve Board. Reserve requirements are exclusive of vault cash and bank deposits held by correspondents. While cash managers argue that reserves represent a bank operating expense, it is traditional that this expense is built into a bank's pricing structure.[54] Bankers contend that they do not get to invest that portion of demand deposits that are held on reserve with the Fed.

Astute cash managers review account analyses for equitable treatment of reserve requirement deductions from collected balances. Where appropriate, they check whether banks judiciously pass on reductions in reserve requirements that are now accompanying banking industry deregulation and change. The Monetary Control Act of 1980 called for a gradual reduction of reserve requirements for banks who are members of the Federal Reserve System. Nonmember banks face a mandatory, gradual phase-in of reserve requirements. Reserve requirements for large member banks averaged 16% in 1980; they are currently at 14%, and will drop to 12% by 1984. The Fed views lowered member reserve requirements as helping to offset the whopping rise in bank business expense that began when the Fed started charging for its services in 1981.

The checking account balance before any deductions are made is described on the account analysis as the average daily ledger balance. The average daily collected balance is the average daily ledger balance minus a dollar amount which represents checks which have been assigned deferred availability by the bank. This deferred availability accounts for float that occurs when a check takes one or two days to clear. We will see below that banks use different methods for determining how much float to assign to corporate deposits. It is important to note that a bank's method for calculating availability on checks can give it a competitive edge with cash managers. Furthermore, banks sometimes assign availability that is more advantageous to a corporation than actual experience merits in an effort to secure market penetration. Cash managers sometimes study the mix of checks that flow through an account. They compare expected, assigned, and actual availability factors; they complain only when results indicate that the bank is assigning an unfavorable availability factor.

Let's look at some ways banks calculate the basic components of an account analysis. The monthly average daily ledger balance can be determined by simply summing each day's ledger balance and dividing that amount by the number of days in the month. Another way to do this is by summing the ledger balances on, say, the first, fifth, tenth, fifteenth, and twenty-fifth day of the month, then dividing this amount by the number of days selected. One treasurer suggests that a variation of the latter method can be beneficial to a clever cash manager: if the bank computes average ledger balances by selecting only one or two days on which to judge a monthly average, the cash manager can keep balance levels very low most of the month, but fund the account with a large credit the days before each balance test is made. This recommendation may apply only to those cash managers with spare time for such sport. Nonetheless, cash managers should be aware of how their banks compute the average daily ledger balance and, depending on corporate deposit nuances, which methods work best in their favor.

Banks also differ in methods for calculating how much float and, hence, deferred availability, should be assigned to a corporate account. The dynamic float capture method determines funds availability by automatically examining each check deposited. The location of the bank on which the check was written is identified and matched against a collection table. This table may be based on the Fed's stated availability schedule. More sophisticated cash management banks have devised collection tables that reflect bank collection experiences that often outpace the Fed. This is because private banks use direct send programs to speed check collections; the Fed schedule does not indicate improved collection performance demonstrated by the large cash management banks. (See Chapter 4, "Alternatives To The Fed.") In general, cash managers can expect to find dynamic float capture methods employed by the leading cash management banks, since a heavy investment in computer technology is required to automatically determine appropriate availability on individual items.

Other, less efficient ways that banks calculate float and subsequent funds availability is to depend on the average bankwide collection experience or on the average number of days required to collect checks for a specific account. Again, a bank may rely on Fed schedules which may not predict optimum check availability. Cash managers have to be careful when a bank uses one or the other average float methods. The bankwide experience may not fairly represent the actual availability of a company's checks. Conversely, the bankwide collection experience may grant a corporation better funds availability than is warranted. If float is calculated according to company deposit mix, the cash manager has to assure that availability factors are adjusted when that mix of checks changes. For example, a new product line could suddenly inject new types of deposits into a bank account and skew availability factors. This could work for or against a corporation, showing up on the account analysis as a smaller or larger amount of uncollected funds.

Banks also differ on whether compensating balances for credit lines are deducted from (1) collected balances before activity charges for noncredit services are assessed, or (2) from balances in excess of what is required to cover noncredit activity charges. *The Leahy Financial Newsletter* provides an interesting look at how treating compensating balances for credit lines as first or last dollars affects how much a corporation pays for services. It states:

> Suppose the treasurer of ABC Company has agreed to maintain 20% compensating balances on his $2.5 million fully utilized credit line that provides for borrowings at prime. He also needs balances to take care of bank account activity charges that amount to, say, $83,250 annually. Prime is 11.5% and the account earnings rate is 10%.

Annual Account Analysis
Credit-Line Balances Deducted:

	First	Last
Collected balances	$1,000,000	$1,000,000
Credit-line balances	500,000	—
	500,000	1,000,000
Reserves (16.25%)	81,250	167,500
Investable balances	418,750	832,500
Earnings at 10%	41,875	83,250
Acct. anal. charge	83,250	83,250
(Loss)	(41,375)	—
Credit-line balances		500,000
Cost of borrowing—120% Prime		69,000
Fee paid by treasurer	$ 41,375	$ 69,000
Ratio	.60	1.38

It does not seem to make a difference whether the bank's account earnings allowance is high or low, or whether collected balances in any one month are high or low. What does matter is whether credit-line balances are considered by the bank to be first dollars or last dollars. When compensating balances for credit lines are deducted as first dollars, any deficit or fee paid by the customer is calculated with money valued at 83.75% of the earnings rate (83.75% − 10% + 8.4%). When such balances are deducted as last dollars, money is valued at the credit line borrowing rate including balances— say, prime plus 20% (or 13.8% at this time). The spread between the 13.8% borrowing rate and the 8.4% earnings rate is 5.4 percentage points, or almost 40% based on the higher number.

Which of the above calculations are correct? Is there an agreement between the treasurer and the banker on which calculation is preferable? One calculation is as defensible as the other; a cash manager should pick the one that benefits him most. Certainly, profitable banks know the difference between the calculations. Other banks that do not know, may be like my college friend who graduated at the bottom of his class. Later, when asked how he became such a successful businessman, he seriously replied: "I simply buy an article for $2, sell it for $7, and am satisfied with a small 5% markup!"[55]

We have looked at how account analyses work, how they can differ, and how some cash managers use them to control banking expenses. We have seen that tangible rewards exist for cash managers who systematically review account analyses. It is important to remember that the account analysis is a useful tool with which you can monitor not only your cash management activities but also the effectiveness of your bank. A proactive cash manager makes account analysis review an integral part of his cash management strategy. This way, he can improve the efficient and productive use of short-term corporate cash.

THE CHANGING CASH MANAGEMENT BANKING ENVIRONMENT

We have mentioned the Monetary Control Act in Chapter 4 and, again, in this chapter in order to give cash managers a sense of the regulatory upheavals now affecting the banking industry. The Act is a sweeping piece of legislation which will undoubtedly force bankers to change the way they cost their services and position themselves in their respective retail and wholesale marketplaces. On the retail side, bank deregulation is causing quite a ruckus: commercial banks and thrifts are meeting money market fund competitors head-on with new consumer investment products.

As of this writing, there is a proposal before the Depository Institutions Deregulation Committee to allow banks to pay explicit, competitive rates on corporate checking accounts. Although this notion has great value, there is some debate whether such an authorization would affect corporate cash management system design. Consensus is that large corporations have investment goals that differ considerably from those of consumers. To wit, cash managers direct their short-term investment in such a way that they are able to capture high yields easily, while speeding the velocity of cash inflows. They have no interest in slowing down their cash gathering functions merely to gain unspectacular rates on small deposits at field banks. Furthermore, while the consumer cares a great deal about Federal Deposit Insurance Corporation (FDIC) insurance for amounts up to $100,000, cash managers at large corporations find in their job descriptions the task of the fiduciary. They are responsible for the safety of corporate funds, given risk parameters outlined in corporate investment policies. Cash managers are accustomed to being responsible for the safety of millions of dollars. They do not feel great urges to entrust this responsibility to banks. Others argue that explicit interest on corporate checking accounts is an inalienable and overdue right. These debaters insist that cash management would not be needed if we simply allowed interest on corporate checking accounts. This may apply to very small businesses. However, we have discussed throughout this book the systems-engineer role that the large corporate cash manager plays. The supervision of cashflows, and the information systems that give them life, will remain a crucial corporate function. Nonetheless, this issue fosters interesting arguments that underscore the important role of the cash manager.

It is appropriate here to note some of the effects of the Act as they relate to corporate banking such as changes in deposit availability and clearing float, which are key components of the account analysis and crucial factors in a bank evaluation.

We recall from Chapter 4 how Federal Reserve check float occurs: a Federal Reserve bank, acting as a provider of check clearing services, grants credit (check availability alloted in immediate, one- or two-day increments) to a depository institution before it can actually present those checks for collection to a payor bank and receive credit for the funds.

For awhile, dual balances exist for both the payee and payor bank. This policy creates Fed float, which currently hovers above $1.8 billion on an average annual basis, and it is an expense borne by taxpayers.

The Monetary Control Act, among other things, urges the Fed to eradicate this float or charge it back to banks priced at the Federal Funds rate. The Fed has reduced its float levels from a 1979 high of over $9 billion through a program of operational improvements designed to help the Fed speed check processing and better meet its stated availability schedules. However, Federal Reserve officials now believe that operational improvements have achieved the most float reduction possible. They are now proposing to change Fed availability rules with a plan that many analysts fear will make it very difficult for corporate cash managers to predict deposit availability. Analysts also suspect that the plan will create fluctuating availability schedules over the course of a year, further contributing to cash management chaos on both the collection and disbursement sides.

The Fed plan hopes to transfer up to 80% of current levels of annual Fed float—$1.8 billion—onto the banking system and, hence, transform this float into a cost borne by bank customers. The proposal consists of four options of which two or more would be made available to banks by each Fed branch. They are:

1 Actual Availability.   Each depositing bank would receive availability equal to the actual clearing time of the check.

2 Stated Availability with as-of Adjustments.   Each depositing bank would receive availability based on stated Fed availability schedules. Any Fed float occurring would be charged against that bank's reserve or clearing account with the Fed approximately two weeks later.

3 Stated Availability with Balances Maintained at the Fed to Offset Any Float Incurred.   On an individual bank basis, the Fed will estimate the amount of balances required to offset float. Periodically, balances will be adjusted upwards if deficits accrue to the bank, while positive balances will create earnings credits to compensate the Fed for check clearing services.

4 Fractional Availability.   Each clearing bank would be graded on each end point (payor bank) on a 90-day average basis, the result of which will determine the availability of individual items. If significant changes occur in the actual clearing times to a certain end point during a 30-day period, fractions will be adjusted to reflect the actual experience.[56]

The Fed has just recently approved another proposal designed to complement its float reduction efforts. This plan will extend until noon each day the Federal Reserve presentment times for city items. By mid-1983, the extension will apply to checks presented to RCPC and country collection points. This means that cash management banks would be hampered in their efforts to offer effective controlled disbursement services because they could not inform cash managers early enough in the morning of all checks being presented that day for collection. Cash managers would have to wait until the afternoon before they knew the amount of the day's excess funds available for investment. Currently, investment activities are well underway by late morning and stragglers pay premiums for short-term investments. (We will further analyze the noon presentment issue in Chapter 8.)

Another Fed plan, electronic check collection (ECC), recently drew serious criticism from the banking industry. ECC would collect large dollar checks electronically using the Fed Wire network in order to transmit check data to payor banks. The actual pieces of paper were to follow days later. Bankers cited enormous legal and operational problems that would result when banks, and customers, were improperly charged with electronic debits. ECC was shelved in June 1982; however, industry analysts expect the idea to reemerge in years to come. On another front, the Fed has begun a pilot program of transmitting cash letter data to banks using magnetic tapes. In effect, this pilot, called the MICR (magnetic ink character recognition) Line Capture Service, allows a bank to receive individual check information one or one and one-half hours before a Fed cash letter arrives. This arrangement, in turn, allows banks to report sooner to cash managers vital daily check presentment data.

It is difficult, and dangerous, to try to predict what the Federal Reserve will do. But we can draw several conclusions about the direction of regulatory edicts. Probably the most important trend for cash managers concerns Fed float reductions. In coming years, cash managers will emphasize the strategic control of corporate funds and corresponding data flows integrated into company data bases. There will be less emphasis on playing the float since, one way or another, it will become a cost borne by banks and their corporate customers. Electronic funds transfer (EFT) and computer technology will increasingly play a significant role in the nation's payment system. Cash managers will be very aware of controlling banking expenses which will continue to spiral as deregulation and Fed pricing (see Chapters 3 and 4) drive up the banks' cost of doing business.

6 Accelerating Cash Receipts

INTERNAL CREDIT AND COLLECTION POLICIES

Before we look at methods for accelerating cash inflows, we will discuss how commercial transactions occur and consider the effects of credit and collection policies on the cash manager's realm. We will see that the traditional separation of credit and cash management functions is no longer appropriate when electronic payment alternatives exist. For years, many corporations have taken a passive stance toward credit policy abuses; for instance, allowing customers to continuously take expired discounts. These suppliers often ignored opportunities to negotiate with customers for credit terms that would benefit both parties. Cash managers who know how to effectively use the tools of their trade can help credit managers reduce abuse and the amount of time that payments remain uncollected. We will see that proactive cash managers are concerned not only with time delays caused by mail, processing, and clearing float but also with cashflow delays caused by outdated credit policies. We will also look at payables policies and discover when disbursement float can be traded off for improved credit terms.

Trade Credit

American business practice has long observed a tradition of granting a period of credit to buyers of goods or services. This credit period may extend from the time a seller ships goods (or renders services or mails invoices) to the time that the buyer is required to make a payment. In effect, the seller loans the buyer an amount equal to the value of the goods or services for a short time. This practice produces trade credit, a significant source of asset financing. Of the $180.7 billion increase in liabilities of nonfinancial corporations (excluding farms) in 1979, 34% was provided by trade credit.[57]

Corporations set trade credit and accounts receivable collection policies in order to formalize an activity that has its roots in the early days of American commerce. During the colonial period, geographically disparate buyers and sellers met infrequently to settle accounts. American businesses have continued to grant trade credit over time, although technological advances have since bridged the communications gaps between buyers and sellers.

Trade credit is a fact of life for businesses domestically and overseas, but its primary justification is to remain competitive. On the surface, manipulating credit terms is a handy way to price products in response to economic upturns or downturns. For instance, lengthening a credit period is economically equivalent to lowering the price of the product. A recent survey, however, found that credit managers did not believe that either tightening or liberalizing credit terms would affect sales. The survey concluded:

> In the majority of firms, credit policy is determined not through active management initiative but rather through defensive acceptance of competitors' policies. . . .Terms are changed only as larger firms (or market leaders)— for reasons unexplained—change their policies.[58]

Credit Terms

All credit transactions consist of the "credit period" and the "credit arrangement form." Many times, provisions for a cash discount and a cash discount period are included. Usually, the credit period extends from the date of an invoice to the date on which payment is required, typically, 30 days hence. The credit period can also begin before goods are shipped, or on the shipping or receiving date. The credit period may be set to run from a given day within the month to a corresponding day in the next month. Credit terms sometimes account for seasonal sales peaks common to certain industries. For example, suppliers may allow retailers generous credit periods so that payments can easily be made when Christmas cashflows materialize.[59]

The standard credit period, 30 days, is expressed as: *net 30*. This means payment is due 30 days from the date the credit period starts. Many companies, however, take at least 45 days to pay their trade bills, in effect stretching the uses for cash as much as possible. During economic downturns, payments are extended even further. Credit managers realize that customers depend on trade credit as a form of short-term financing which, during an economic contraction, may be expensive or, simply, unavailable. Nonetheless, paying late is an abuse of the implicit agreement between buyer and seller. But credit managers are often reluctant to strictly enforce credit terms or penalize offenders because they fear customers will take their business elsewhere. Sometimes, credit managers lack the systems for tracking and communicating with habitual delinquents. Poorly administered credit terms create uncertainty for the cash manager who must forecast receivables and produce a cash plan. Also, corporations do not exhibit payment behavior found among consumers. Consumers are conditioned to expect dire consequences when they skip a few payments to the local department store.

Another form of common credit policy abuse involves expired discounts. A credit term may be expressed as: *2/10, net 30*. This means that a two percent discount is allowed if the customer pays his bill 10 days after the credit period has begun. The 10 days comprise the discount period. Accounts payables clerks routinely deduct the two percent from the face amount of the invoice although payment is made after ten days. Erratic mail times can delay payments and result in expired discount periods. We will see below how using postmarks to determine when bills are paid complicates the credit manager's task of monitoring discounted payments.

The credit arrangement form refers to the type of account involved in the credit transaction. In this country, most credit transactions are on an "open book account." This means that the seller creates an invoice which is sent to the buyer. The seller then enters the transaction into his accounts receivable ledger. In the course of global trade, credit arrangements are formalized with trade acceptances wherein drafts are drawn by sellers on buyers. When banks guarantee draft payments on behalf of buyers, the transaction is known as a banker's acceptance.

COMMERCIAL TRANSACTIONS

Payments represent only a portion of the activity that surrounds commercial transactions. Costs involved in making and receiving payments amount to only 10 percent of the overall cost of a business transaction.[60] While cash managers are concerned with controlling cashflows and the value of funds delayed in the mail, at the company, or at the bank, the lifecycle of transactions and the systems that route them cannot be ignored. Between the time that a customer places an order and the time that payment is received for goods or services, responsibility for the transaction falls into many hands. Manufacturing, marketing, sales, order-taking, shipping, credit, billing, receivables, and payables are all functions in addition to cash management that participate in a commercial transaction.

Many of these functions formalize their roles with policies. Sometimes intracorporate policy formulation is coordinated; sometimes it is not. When policies are coordinated, separate functions consider how their actions affect overall corporate profitability. For example, the marketing department may want to expand the customer base by offering liberal credit terms with a new product. This plan might bring in a new class of customers, those who represent a high credit risk. In a coordinated policies environment, the marketing department would consider that its plan may increase collection expenses out of proportion with increased sales. High-risk customers further add uncertainty to the cash manager's forecasts. At a company where priorities are set in a vacuum, the marketing department might be adamant about its primary objective: expanding the customer base.

It is important that the cash manager investigate how transactions flow through the firm. The cash manager's perspective is one that focuses on the time value of money; delays in invoicing and internal mail procedures appear to him as unnecessary time lapses that thwart his receipt of usable funds. One treasurer at a large household goods supplier took this integrated-systems approach when he implemented the use of automated clearing house (ACH) debits to electronically draw down the accounts of distributors. He found that he could persuade other managers in his company to combine the functions of order processing, shipping, and ACH debit tape preparation. When customers called in their orders, clerks keyed-in order data along with the customer account and payment and bank location information. The system was designed to automatically produce a magnetic tape overnight which was delivered to the corporation's bank the next day. The bank used the tape to initiate the ACH debits. The result was that good funds became available to the corporation two days after an order was placed.

Obviously, the treasurer in the above case worked with the credit manager when terms of sale were decided. What may not be so obvious is that the household goods supplier had the necessary clout to get its customers to agree to give up good funds two days after order placement. The customers in this case were given a financial incentive, a hefty discount, to compensate for the loss of disbursement float they enjoyed under the old system of mailing in checks for payment 20 days after they placed an order.

Negotiated Settlement

The example above shows how innovative firms can use alternative credit terms and payment mechanisms to negotiate settlements. Clearly, the competitive environment in a given industry dictates how successful a seller can be at the bargaining table. Buyers are not likely to relinquish substantial levels of disbursement float, discounts notwithstanding, if they can easily switch to another supplier. However, when the business environment does support a move to innovative payment negotiations, the seller can often successfully demonstrate value to the buyer. The seller can measure for himself, and suggest to the customer, the net present value of cashflows occurring with alternative credit policies. The net present value of cashflows considers the axiom that money has a time value. This means that a company which is owed, say, $100,000 in 20 days has to figure the opportunity cost, at its annual borrowing rate, of sacrificing use of those funds for that period of time. (Students of finance can refer to standard texts for net present value formulas.)

Consider a small tool manufacturer who supplies a large car manufacturer. The large customer takes 60 days to pay its small bills. The small supplier badly needs the money in sooner; when he has to borrow from the bank to cover shortfalls, he pays four percentage points above prime. (The smaller the firm, the lesser the clout at the bank, and the higher the borrowing cost.) The small firm decides that it will negotiate with the large customer for faster payment. This small company has to figure, first, what the net present value of current cashflows are by deducting transaction expenses and the opportunity cost of overdue payments from the face amount on the invoice. The small supplier can then offer the large buyer a discount for sooner payment that will result in an accelerated cash inflow that is economically no worse than the net present value of cash inflows under the current system. The small firm will try to settle on a discount that is actually slightly less than a discount that brings in economically equivalent cash inflows. The key to this negotiation is that the small firm demonstrates to the large buyer that the discount produces a payment—cash outflow—that is economically preferable to current payment behavior.

Postmarks and Deposit Dates

Another type of negotiated settlement may change discount terms so that a postmark on the envelope containing a check is not the basis for deciding whether a buyer qualifies for a discount. Many credit managers are under the impression that the Uniform Commercial Code requires that the postmark determine when a payment has been made on a timely basis. Research indicates that the widespread use of postmarks for this purpose stems mostly from tradition, not from a Uniform Commercial Code edict.[61] The practice has its legal foundation in contract law and judicial interpretation at the state level.

Although presently in the minority, some corporations are offering enhanced credit terms in return for funds becoming available in the seller's bank account within a stated discount period. The method of payment can be a preauthorized draft or an ACH debit initiated by the seller just prior to the expiration of the discount period. The date on which funds arrive at the bank, not a postmark, determines a payment's timeliness. The discount period might be lengthened from 10 to 14 days and be stated as: *2% 14 good funds, net 30*. The lengthened discount period compensates the buyer for lost disbursement benefits associated with postmarked-based credit terms and checks. Here, the seller reduces the uncertainty and delays associated with postmarks and the postal system operations, respectively. Larry Marks, formerly executive vice president at Phoenix-Hecht, in speeches reminds cash managers that postmarks and postal system procedures can be error-prone. The "good funds" credit policy also addresses a cash management dilemma: no system now exists for automatically and economically capturing postmark dates on envelopes, a failing that makes monitoring unearned discounts very difficult. By initiating the preauthorized payment, with a paper draft or an electronic debit, the cash manager at the collecting corporation gains critical control over the transaction. He can better forecast cash inflows and reduce collection costs.

By changing the discount factor (another example of negotiated settlement) corporations can compensate customers for paying electronically and assuring that good funds get into the seller's account before the discount period expires. Such an alternative credit term might be expressed as: *3% 7 good funds, net 30*. Again, payment timing is determined by receipt of good funds at the bank. This policy compensates buyers for the loss of disbursement float—the sum of checks outstanding—commonly experienced with paper payments. The buyer also incurs less transaction expenses: the costs of printing, mailing, reconciling, and storing checks. The rising costs of paper will, no doubt, play a large role in corporate decisions to switch to electronic mechanisms such as the ACH. A benefit to the seller is control: electronic payments represent good funds and eliminate the worry that payments may have been made with bad checks. As well, collection float is dealt a heavy blow.

The good funds term, used for either discount or net purposes, can discourage one form of credit policy abuse: remote mailing. Used to extend disbursement float, remote mailing depends on obscure post office locations from which corporations mail payments. Using remote post offices does not merely slow down receipts; when postmark data is the basis for qualifying for a discount or simply meeting net credit terms, this practice delivers the seller a double whammy. Remote mailing is very aggressive cash management from a disbursement standpoint, and, although inane, it is now being discussed in cash management circles as a way to combat Federal Reserve float reduction schemes. One large corporation headquartered in San Francisco is now using remote mailing. Its checks are printed and mailed in North Carolina. It is ironic that some firms that are now trying to get their customers to convert to good funds credit terms are the same companies considering using computers to design optimal remote mailing systems.

Industry analysts believe that negotiating with customers for electronic payments will dominate cash management discussions in the 1980s. The reason for the move toward electronic trade payments is the desire for cost-effective and reliable payment mechanisms. A contributing factor is, simply, that our culture has entered "The Information Age," the logical evolution of a postindustrial society. There is a wholesale automation of business systems now underway at American companies. Mini- and microcomputers are being installed to assist all corporate functions. They will help streamline the flow of commercial transactions.

The object of automation is to eliminate systems redundancy and the mountains of paperwork which, in the past, have routed transactions from the order processing department all the way to the bank for settlement. Dr. Bernell K. Stone, the noted cash management educator, believes that we are headed toward a business environment in which cash-cycle management will depend on electronic processing of commercial transactions. This view holds that the cash manager's special knowledge of payment systems, and the systems themselves that feed the cash manager daily balance information, will be crucial information turnstyles. Over the past several years, many cash managers have had to develop their own information management systems, independent of corporate data processing functions. As a result, valuable data on commercial transactions now enter the cash management department from external sources, and corporate accounting managers are now eager to have those data flows integrated into corporatewide systems. This process, information integration, will become the primary concern of cash managers in the 1980s.

Eventually, electronic business data interchange will be accomplished using standards now being formulated by the American National Standards Institute X-12 Committee. If that effort succeeds, customers will someday place orders using desktop computers which automatically prompt the flow of information to various departmental data bases at both buying and selling corporations. However, this scenario is not expected to be commonplace until the end of the decade. In the meantime, the National Automated Clearing House Association is working on standard formats which will soon facilitate electronic corporate-to-corporate trade payments through the ACH.

When we try to imagine how the flow of commercial transactions will be accomplished in the future, we quickly sense that serious thought has to be given to integrated system design. If a clerk at a purchasing company is automatically prompting the selling company to begin the ACH debit process, coordination among the purchasing, accounting, and cash management departments at the buying corporation is critical. In many cases, the cash manager will be responsible for informing other corporate managers about the operation status of electronic payment mechanisms. This cash manager, therefore, will need perspective on the validity of other departmental concerns.

It is easy to discuss the benefits of converting the customer base to electronic payments and negotiated credit terms. It is another matter entirely to implement this complex plan. Cash managers may encounter resistance from credit managers who are by nature a conservative lot. Furthermore, there are legal questions to be answered. The Robinson-Patman Act requires that credit terms be administered consistently and fairly across all customer classes. Firms are not permitted to give preferential treatment to a single customer or group of customers unless they can show that those customers represent a different cost of manufacturing or delivery. Better customers cannot be allowed to pay on terms of their own choosing.[62] The marketing department managers will have their own special concerns; for instance, how do credit policies affect sales?

A move to good funds credit terms across all company divisions or within certain subsidiaries is probably best introduced over a period of time by offering customers two sets of terms: one set for those who would continue to pay by check and the other set for those willing to pay electronically. It may be convenient to introduce alternative credit terms along with a price increase. Customers who agree to pay in good funds may be protected from the price hike. Ostensibly, this would not constitute preferential treatment to a certain class of customers, since the company could show that the cost of the service delivery is different between those who pay electronically and those who pay by check.

The costs of paper-based trade payments are rising at the same time that technological innovations offer cash managers cost-effective and reliable payment systems. Sellers are trying to convince buyers that disbursement float benefits can be traded off for better credit terms when payment timeliness is determined by the date good funds arrive in the seller's bank account. Preauthorized debits initiated by the seller using the traditional paper draft or the ACH are probable payment choices in a negotiated settlement. Indications are, however, that the thrust of this new trend centers on the electronic alternative, the ACH. When cost-justified, wires may be used to satisfy good funds credit terms.

Corporations are embracing computer technology on many functional levels. The successfully automated business systems of the 1980s will be those that take a comprehensive approach to integrated information flows and a projected need for systems capacity. The cash manager's perspective on this evolution will be important to many corporate departments. As the cash manager becomes increasingly aware of corporatewide information flows, he may find himself educating other managers about the value of data that eventually become financial assets.

The effects of alternative credit terms on cash management are important. In some firms, the impetus to change old habits will have to come from the treasury area. Therefore, cash managers not yet familiar with company credit policies can benefit by investigating current practices and researching how alternative policies using electronic trade payments are working at other corporations. A company whose customers pay electronically gains critical cashflow control, reduced collection float and lower handling costs. It is up to market leaders to set the pace in their industries.

LOCKBOXES

We saw in Chapter 1 that the cash manager's objective is to control the flow of corporate funds and optimize its earnings potential. He designs cash management strategies in order to accelerate cash receipts, on the collection side, and plan and slow payments, on the disbursement side. He maintains short-term forecasts, anticipating his daily cash position, which is verified continuously by analyzing bank balance reports. The cash manager creates and controls the cash reservoir which he strategically deploys to best serve corporate profit-making goals.

Accelerating cash receipts is the focal point of the cash manager's collection task. He is concerned with the mechanics of transforming receipts from credit and noncredit sales into usable funds. Credit sales typically involve checks mailed to a corporation in payment for goods or services. Noncredit sales involve payment for goods or services through checks, cash, and other forms of payment exchanged by seller and buyer at a branch office, sales outlet, or other arm of the company. The cash manager's job is to manipulate the flow of these receipts so that funds are available for company use as quickly as possible. He sees to it that checks paid to his corporation are deposited into banking networks for clearance with minimum time lapses. Once checks are cleared, or once the bank grants availability on checks, the cash manager has "collected balances" to work with. He also supervises the transfer of cleared checks and cash deposits from regional depository banks into his lead concentration bank where the corporate cash reservoir is maintained more efficiently and profitably.

From the concentration account, the cash manager funds disbursements or corporate borrowing requirements, or he invests in the money market. Regional depository banks may be either banks strategically located to intercept mailed checks (lockbox banks) or outlying banks that function as the deposit focus for company sales offices (field deposit banks). The cash manager monitors the average balances that must be kept on deposit at regional depositories to compensate those banks for their services. Where appropriate, the cash manager assures that fee payments for bank services are accurate.

Most large American corporations use lockbox banks to accelerate the flow of checks from credit sales. But a lockbox is not an actual receptical secured with a brass latch locked into place. A lockbox is really a process: a bank agrees to go to its local post office regularly, on behalf of the corporation, pick up mail, and haul it back to the bank where a sea of clerks perform the task of remittance processing. Depending on the type of lockbox service, bank staffers typically open envelopes, encode and balance checks and invoices, microfilm checks, deposit checks into the clearing stream, and produce account receivables data that can be delivered or transmitted to the company. The company can have envelopes, invoices, photocopies of check, exception remittances, and any correspondence forwarded to its office while the checks are already on the road to clearance. We will see below the technologies used in lockbox processing.

Lockbox Benefits

Corporations use lockboxes as an acceleration device. Lockboxes reduce collection float, comprised of mail float, processing float, and clearing float. Float refers to the cost (or benefit) associated with cashflow delays. Cash managers attempt to reduce collection float and extend disbursement float. Lockboxes also provide systems efficiency.

Mail Float.   Many corporations with a national customer base establish lockbox locations near customer clusters to reduce the time it takes for mail to travel to a depository bank. For example, a San Francisco company may have a Philadelphia lockbox to which customers in the surrounding region mail monthly remittances. Thus, the company receives its mail sooner; if the company simply had all its checks mailed to San Francisco, it might experience an onerous two-day wait for those funds while checks amble through the postal system from one coast to the other. The Philadelphia lockbox should receive company mail and be able to process receipts within one day of mailing. Large banks with sufficient lockbox volume often have unique zip codes assigned by the postal system specifically for lockbox mail. In this manner, bank couriers retrieve lockbox items, already segregated from other bank mail.

Processing Float.   A lockbox operation can prove much more efficient than corporate remittance processing on several counts. Bank staffers and managers are trained to concentrate on remittance processing as their primary objective. In some corporations, clerical personnel are shifted from one task to another as workloads warrant. While many corporations process remittances only during typical workday hours, many lockbox operations run on multishift bases. Some lockboxes even run on weekends, attempting to move the flow of paper continuously, although check deposits can only be posted to demand deposit systems on banking days.

The most important lockbox feature that addresses processing delays concerns priorities. The cash manager's goals can be different from the credit manager's goals: the cash manager desires available funds as soon as possible, whereas the credit manager strives for fast and accurate updating of accounts receivables files. As a result, remittance processing performed internally by a corporation may be geared to the credit manager's objectives; thus, workflows would emphasize bookkeeping and documentation, while actual check deposits might be held until the afternoon trip to the bank. By having a bank process remittances instead, cash managers utilize a system that emphasizes getting checks deposited into the clearing stream as quickly as possible. Moreover, in conjunction with bank lockbox processing, accounts receivables data can be tabulated and formatted for transmission to the corporate credit department, albeit *after the checks have been deposited.* Cash managers can automatically receive lockbox deposit information the same day that the lockbox work is performed.

Clearing Float. Lockboxes help corporations reduce clearing float, that is, delays associated with the time it takes to move checks through payment mechanisms and present them for settlement to the banks on which they were drawn. The checks that have to be shipped to a payor bank for collection are called transit items. Most checks handled by a local or regional lockbox should become usable funds in one day. Checks drawn on the lockbox bank, called "on-us items," represent usable funds on the same day that they are received into the lockbox. Because lockboxes are strategically located near customer bases, many of the transit items flowing into them are drawn on banks also located in the customer zone. The San Francisco company that has its lockbox placed in Philadelphia will likely receive into that lockbox checks drawn on East Coast banks, unless its customers practice remote disbursing. It takes the San Francisco company less time to collect East Coast checks from an East Coast lockbox than it would take if the checks had to be routed from a West Coast depository back to East Coast payor banks. By virtue of their location, then, lockbox banks can cut into clearing float and speed the process of transforming checks into available balances. The process of reducing clearing float is known as gaining faster availability on deposited items.

Faster availability is also possible when lockboxes are "emptied" and checks are deposited for the corporation many times a day. On average, large lockbox banks pick up mail from the post office from 15 to 20 times a day. Checks are kept moving toward clearance. Corporations that do not use lockboxes may open mail and get to the bank only once a day, often too late to receive optimum availability.

Furthermore, lockbox operations can be geared to coincide with bank deposit deadlines. For instance, mail can be picked up from the post office in the early hours of the morning, processed and checks routed to the appropriate payment mechanism by midmorning. Presumably, lockbox scheduling can take advantage of any early direct send. (Checks drawn on other banks are shipped to the drawee's Fed for collection, directly to another bank, or to a check clearing house in the drawee's area.) Often, deposit deadlines for lockbox items are later than over-the-counter deposit deadlines. Therefore, lockbox items have a better chance of making deposit cutoffs and getting into the daily clearing stream faster, than do over-the-counter deposits.

System Efficiency. Since banks provide lockbox work for more than one customer, obviously, economies of scale let them afford the necessary expensive hardware. From a corporate perspective, lockboxes are efficient not only when they relieve the company of internal overhead—a savings traded off by lockbox charges—but also when lockboxes reduce systems redundancy. If a corporation can receive magnetic tapes containing accounts receivable data, produced as a by-product of the lockbox function, then accounts receivables files may be automatically updated. The tape can be physically delivered to the corporation or the data can be transmitted over phone lines directly to the company central computer. The use of such technology in recent years has addressed the problem of companies having to wait for invoices mailed to the corporate credit department by lockbox personnel.

Lockbox processing represents efficient systems design because it allows checks to be deposited without upsetting the flow of paper that accompanies customer payments. Companies that perform manual accounts receivables updating can request that checks be photocopied before being deposited. The photocopies can then be returned to the company along with envelopes, invoices, or any customer correspondences.

Lockbox Operations

Banks usually differentiate between retail and wholesale lockboxes. Retail lockboxes typically process a high volume of items, say, 20,000 per month, that have small average dollar values, under $1000. Insurance premiums, mortgage loans, and installment loans, along with rent, utility, dues, and charge card payments are characteristic of a retail lockbox. Payments are often made by individuals to businesses. Retail lockboxes do not normally require customized processing because of the standardization of transactions and billing forms.

Wholesale lockboxes, on the other hand, usually process a lower volume of items that have large average dollar values. A lockbox that handles checks averaging at least a $1000 value is often termed wholesale. These types of remittances generally represent trade payables between corporations and require a more specialized processing approach since invoices do not always accompany payments, and since there is less standardization of transactions, billing forms, and remittance envelopes.[63] Wholesale accounts come in many varieties, such as single check and single invoice, multiple check and single invoice, or multiple invoice and single check.[64]

In recent years, as corporations have increasingly demanded specialized services for wholesale lockboxes, often involving direct interfaces between lockbox receipts and automated accounts receivable systems, banks devised automated data capture technology which requires some degree of standardization among customer data elements. Even though customized processing provides advantages to corporations, it results in higher processing costs and longer processing times. Standardization in wholesale lockboxes, similar to that found among retail processes, can help to mitigate high costs, but there is a trade-off: companies have to become more flexible in their desires for specialized information.

We will now look at different types of wholesale lockbox processes; there is a wide variety, but most services can be placed in three main classes:

1 Photocopy with manual update of accounts receivables data.
2 Data transmission involving key entry.
3 Data transmission involving machine-readable documents.

Photocopy.   With this system, a check amount is compared with an invoice amount; payee and check date are verified. Unless the comparison indicates a problem, the check is photocopied and promptly entered into the clearing stream, while the invoice, photocopy, and envelope are stored for later transmittal to the company. The check copies are totaled to balance against a tape developed by the check encoding function which has recorded the check amount. The bank keeps a microfilm copy of the check.

The purpose of this system is to provide the corporate customer with the original envelope, check photocopy, and, when one exists, the invoice for manual updating of the accounts receivable files. Since the checks and invoices are separated early in the process, the probability for error is high. Significant balancing problems are often encountered with this method because it is almost entirely a manual process. The processing costs charged by the bank tend to be directly proportional to the volume because of the manual effort involved. Since the information required by corporations can vary, and processing steps are often dissimilar, training of new personnel is a burden. Low-skill-level staff usually perform this type of processing.[65]

Data Transmission: Key Entry.   In this process, after initial verification of check and invoice data, the check is released into the clearing stream. There, after check amount and date are manually encoded, other check data can be automatically scanned or key-entered on magnetic tape or some other computer-readable storage device for later transmission to the company. This information is taken from the check's MICR (magnetic ink character recognition) line; it can include serial number, payor bank transit/routing number, account number, and dollar amount. Invoice and, possibly, envelope postmark data are key-entered onto data storage equipment. This information may include customer billing account number, invoice or purchase order number, invoice amount, and processing date. Once merged with the check MICR data, this information is later transmitted to the company for automatic updating of accounts receivables files.

Generally, a magnetic tape is sent to the corporation, although computer-to-computer teleprocessing via high-speed lines is also available. The invoice data entry performed by the bank, however, is manual, often expensive, and subject to human error.

Data Transmission: Machine-Readable Documents. While most uses of machine-readable invoices or remittance documents have been for retail lockbox applications, some industries have been successful in requiring their trade payments to be made using MICR or OCR (optical character recognition) remittance documents. All customer information, including dollar payment expected, is preencoded on the document and automatically read and stored on magnetic tape along with the check MICR data. All data captured is transmitted the same day to the corporate customer for automatic updating of accounts receivables files. The preencoding of documents reduces the amount of key entry done by the bank and, thus, greatly cuts down on error and expense. Using machine-readable invoices, however, may require companies to adhere to a degree of standardization in document design. This is sometimes a problem with companies that are reluctant to change the looks of invoices which project a time-tested image.

While data capture and transmission have received much attention in recent years, such highly specialized processing procedures, designed to improve the flow of receivables data, can impair funds availability and drive lockbox processing costs to an unjustifiable level. To combat this trend in wholesale lockbox processing, programs have been initiated to increase standardization to the level attained in retail remittance systems. These efforts have produced automated wholesale lockbox processing, which builds on the machine-readable document approach.[66]

Automated lockboxing uses computer and video or digital technology to capture check images for processing on video terminals. There, clerks prompted by the computer key-in payment amounts and any other special remittance information requested by a customer. Check, and possibly invoice, data are automatically read and stored with virtually no physical handling of documents. High-speed check encoding and sorting equipment and on-line photocopying are also important features of these systems. The key to automated lockboxing is that simultaneous to deposit processing, information needed to update accounts receivables files is produced. What is more, checks are entered into the clearing stream more quickly than in any other lockbox process. Accounts receivable data is easily collected for same-day delivery to the corporate customer via magnetic tape or data transmission. Hard-copy printouts are also available to corporations. (See Exhibits 6.1, 6.2, and 6.3.)

These automated lockbox systems enhance remittance processing and produce cost-efficiencies. Advantages include improved processing accuracy, faster cash availability, data base development, and accelerated accounts receivable information. This last feature is important to companies who may occasionally have to hold up shipments to key customers until payments have been received.

In 1981, Ingersoll-Rand, the giant in the heavy machinery industry, shifted 13 of its domestic divisions to automated lockboxes. The result: a 100% reduction in errors during the first month and speeded remittance data. Since then, other large and small companies (some with under $20 million in annual sales) either followed suit or began to consider this exciting new technology.[67]

Philadelphia National Bank was an early pioneer in the use of computer and video technology in lockbox operations; its CompuCash system was introduced in 1979 and has since been emulated. One key to the CompuCash system is that it eliminates most manual efforts after the mail has been sorted. Video images of checks and invoices are used to prepare accounts receivable data. It is this feature which enhances accuracy in remittance processing. The system is also capable of responding to additional customer needs, including research on previously processed checks. As of this writing, several other large banks have embraced check-imaging wholesale lockbox technology; they are as follow: Northern Trust, Security Pacific, First Interstate of California, Republic Bank-Dallas, and Harris Trust. Industry analysts expect that check imaging will be the driving force behind successful lockbox banks in the 1980s, since this tech-

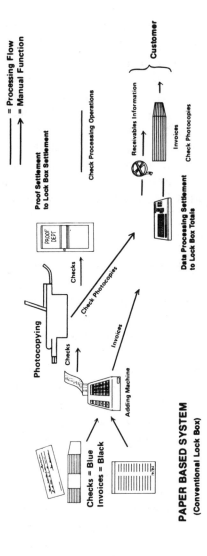

PNB Philadelphia National Bank

= Processing Flow
= Manual Function

Proof Settlement to Lock Box Settlement

Check Processing Operations

Checks

Photocopying

Check Photocopies

Invoices

Checks

Adding Machine

Checks = Blue
Invoices = Black

PAPER BASED SYSTEM
(Conventional Lock Box)

Receivables Information

Customer

Invoices
Check Photocopies

Data Processing Settlement to Lock Box Totals

In a paper-based system, checks, checks and invoices are reconciled and settled separately. This requires multiple operating departments to process payments; all of which interrupt the processing flow. In addition, accounts receivable information must be manually reconciled with lock box totals.

Exhibit 6.1. Graphic representation of traditional lockbox system. (*Reprinted courtesy of Philadelphia National Bank.*)

134

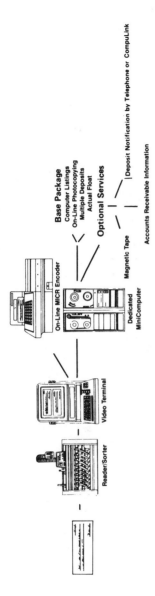

Philadelphia National Bank

Reader/Sorter

Video Terminal

On-Line MICR Encoder

Dedicated MiniComputer

Base Package
Computer Listings
On-Line Photocopying
Multiple Deposits
Actual Float

Optional Services

Magnetic Tape

Deposit Notification by Telephone or CompuLink

Accounts Receivable Information

FUNCTIONAL DESCRIPTION

The CompuCash system employs advanced technology to stream-line check processing and minimize the physical handling of items. Checks are taken from the envelopes and placed into the system's Reader/Sorter, where they are scanned at high speed. Simultaneously, a miniature TV camera captures a video image of each item. Operators at video terminals then use these images to process payments. During this phase, accounts receivable information can be entered into the system and checks can be automatically photocopied. The checks are encoded, audit trail endorsed, microfilmed and sorted by the on-line encoder. In addition to the basic package, CompuCash users can opt to receive customized receivables data via magnetic tape or transmission and/or deposit notification by telephone or PNB CompuLink.

Exhibit 6.2. Graphic representation of lockbox processing using video imaging technology. *(Reprinted courtesy of Philadelphia National Bank.)*

135

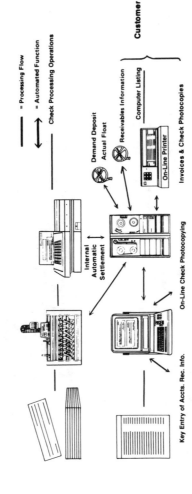

Philadelphia National Bank

— = Processing Flow

↕ = Automated Function

Check Processing Operations

Demand Deposit

Actual Float

Receivables Information

Computer Listing

On-Line Printer

Invoices & Check Photocopies

Customer

Internal Automatic Settlement

Key Entry of Accts. Rec. Info.

On-Line Check Photocopying

DATA-BASED SYSTEM
CompuCash Lock Box

CompuCash is a data-based system which is capable of providing *internal, automatic settlement* of both demand deposit account information and receivables data. More importantly, this information is readily accessible to users because it is stored within the CompuCash minicomputer.

Exhibit 6.3. Graphic representation of data-based lockbox system. *(Reprinted courtesy of Philadelphia National Bank.)*

nology greatly reduces what has become a business systems burden: human intervention. We are surprised, however, that there are, as yet, no robots working in bank lockbox departments.

Lockbox Costs

There are two types of costs associated with lockbox processing. First, there is a variable (per item) cost for each check processed in addition to the usual deposit charge. Second, there are fixed costs that reflect the lockbox rental, transfer costs (arising from the need to move money into the concentration bank), and, possibly, additional account charges for simply having a lockbox.[68] If automated procedures are involved, there may be additional charges for data capture, transmission, program maintenance, and telephone line usage. Lockbox pricing policies are diverse among commercial banks. Exhibit 6.4 shows the categories of service charges and the wide ranges for each.

Monthly Pricing Structure for Lockbox Services
(By Type of Service, By Number of Banks, By Deposit Size,
As a Percent of Total, In Mean Averages)

Lockbox Services	Under $500 Million	$500 Million- $1 Billion	$1 Billion- $3 Billion	$3 Billion- $5 Billion	Over $5 Billion
Demand deposits	.15	.1783	.1216	.1638	.3311
Account maintenance	3.33	2.375	4.32	3.30	3.50
Lockbox item charge	.2880	.1522	.1603	.1901	.1726
Minimum monthly charge					
First box	25.00	46.25	38.88	35.00	38.75
Additional boxes	0.00	25.00	16.66	25.00	32.50
Photocopy	.05	.1655	.0613	.0351	.0333
Rental charge	0.00	7.33	8.95	45.43	—

Exhibit 6.4. Monthly pricing structure for lockbox services, by type of service, number of banks, deposit size, as a percent of total, and in mean averages. (Source: *Status of Corporate Cash Management Systems,* Longport, New Jersey: R. T. March & Associates, March, 1980, p. 132.6.39.)

Lockbox System Design

In addition to incremental lockbox processing costs, cash managers designing check collection systems consider an optimal mix of lockbox locations that will intercept mailed receipts in various customer zones. Many banks and consultants have developed sophisticated optimization models that suggest the best locations and the number of lockbox sites appropriate for a corporation's customer bases. Lockbox studies examine existing corporate remittance patterns, mail times, and funds availability and devise solutions that represent a one-time improvement over current practices. Solutions may be found for a corporation that presently uses no lockboxes, or for a corporation that may need to add or delete lockbox locations due to changes in the customer base or product lines, or due to the effects of acquisitions.

Lockbox studies consider probable mail and availability times for corporate receipts sent to specific cities and banks therein. Most banks rely on one standard source, the Phoenix-Hecht mail-time data base, for mail-time statistics. Phoenix-Hecht measures average mail times from downtown central post offices serving a collection zone to downtown post office boxes in lockbox cities. (Since Phoenix-Hecht conducts its studies using downtown post office locations, as opposed to substations, their studies reflect mail times that are generally faster than that which corporations experience. But Phoenix-Hecht data reflects a common bias for all lockboxes, and, therefore, the use of the sample is justified.)[70]

Availability time reflects how long it takes a check to clear, or how long a bank says it takes a check to clear. Often, banks depend on published Federal Reserve availability schedules to depict the length of time that funds must be deferred—zero, one, or two days—before they can be deemed collected balances. However, many lockbox banks process checks via direct sends, which bypass their own Federal Reserve Bank by depositing the checks at the drawee bank, the drawee bank's Federal Reserve Bank, or a clearing house in the drawee bank area. Hence, there is an argument for the use of actual bank availability times rather than Federal Reserve numbers.[71] Dr. Steven Maier, Duke University professor and President of University Analytics, Inc., a leading lockbox location analysis firm, suggests that cash managers be cognizant of the important difference between Federal Reserve and actual bank availability measures: studies that do not account for actual bank collection performance may tend to recommend more lockboxes than are really needed.[72]

Cash managers have to study their current collection systems in order to predict potential benefits of a system design change. In so doing, they attempt to measure mail times for corporate remittances that are correct, on average, over the long run. Cash managers work with consultants, one of whom is probably a statistician; he assures that samples studied are valid and useful.

A cash manager may segregate and analyze all or a percentage of the typical large dollar remittances that make up mailed receipts. Perhaps he may also study 15% of the typical smaller dollar items in the receipt mix. A study can be based on items that represent one percent of the average dollar value of monthly receipts from a given customer zone. A common benchmark for sample size is 5000 items. However, the scope of the study often depends on corporate nuances; some companies want to study every single item they receive during one month. Generally, however, good studies attempt to produce meaningful solutions. A useful study accounts for seasonality patterns and may use samples taken during different months, say, February and August. Although such a range may extend the length of the study time, it is preferable to a study that is done during the Christmas season when mail times are erratic. Months that have four-day weekends are also bad times to conduct remittance analyses. Many firms study remittance patterns every two or three years; some companies have study cycles that range up to every five years.

A remittance study should first isolate desirable cities appropriate to the customer zone—locations with good mail service. This information comes from updated Phoenix-Hecht reports. The study then can look at a city's average, actual bank availability. In a given city, there may be three possible bank candidates; however, undertaking an analysis of the different check collection capabilities among the three banks may indicate only a one-half day float reduction improvement at the best bank.[73] Cash managers must decide whether the potential benefit justifies further analysis. Rather, a cash manager may choose the one of three banks with whom he already has an established credit relationship. Since lockbox accounts usually contain balances that are difficult to manage down to zero, it may be logical to use these balances to partially compensate the bank for credit services. Or a cash manager may pick one of the three banks based on its volume of direct sends—remember, a bank with an aggressive direct send program will probably be able to clear your checks faster than a bank with a passive approach in this regard. Of course, the bank with a good direct send program will not help you if its schedules for mail pick-ups and processing do not coincide with the direct send departures.

Dr. Maier, at the 1982 Annual National Corporate Cash Management Association Conference, drew attention to the fact that current lockbox studies assume that a corporation receives optimal processing priority at the lockbox bank. In reality, a company with a relatively small volume of lockbox items may not receive the same treatment that a huge lockbox customer enjoys. The bank may pick up the small-volume company's mail at midnight, hence improving its showing in the Phoenix-Hecht data base (during mail studies, banks time-stamp received items with a 24-hour clock). But, as a practical matter, this firm's lockbox is not promptly processed. This practice jeopardizes this firm's chances of getting its checks processed in time for early morning routing into the clearing stream.

Lockbox banks often claim that they can process a corporation's remittances in a two-hour time span. Whether they can and if they do is another matter entirely. Time lapses between when a bank picks up corporate mail and when checks are deposited into the firm's account are called bank processing float. Dr. Maier is now researching ways to measure bank processing float, a development which promises to close a loop in lockbox location analysis methodology. Cash managers undertaking lockbox studies should first request banks' responses to the Bank Administration Institute's model lockbox questionaire (included here as Appendix A). Then, they can easily compare different bank approaches to lockbox processing and customer service.[74]

Lockbox banking is one of the cash manager's most useful tools for accelerating cash receipts. We will see in Chapter 7 how cash managers track lockbox deposits with automated reporting systems and how funds are moved to concentration banks. We will also see how cash managers concentrate receipts from noncredit sales deposited by corporate field units into regional depository banks.

PREAUTHORIZED CHECKS

In addition to lockbox systems, cash managers use preauthorized checks to help accelerate receipts. A preauthorized check (PAC) is an unsigned demand deposit instrument, authorized to be drawn against a customer's checking account, often in payment of a continuing obligation of a fixed dollar amount. Used mostly to collect remittances from consumers, typical PAC applications include insurance and cable television bill payments, as well as leasing and mortgage company installments. PAC usage has expanded with the advent of budget payment plans by utility companies for their customers. PACs represent an alternative to retail lockboxes; they are appropriate for a company that has a large volume of low-dollar remittances.[75]

Because PACs are unsigned demand deposit instruments which a company issues to draw funds out of customer accounts, customers must sign written authorizations for this activity to take place. The corporation, in turn, provides the customers' banks with indemnification agreements, announcing the planned presentation of such unsigned instruments. Both authorization and indemnification agreements specify the amount and frequency of payments effected in this manner.[76] To initiate PACs, the corporation prepares a file of customers who have selected this payment method. The file contains all relevant data to produce the PACs: customer name, payment amount, payment date, bank name, customer checking account number, and the transit and routing numbers of the customer's bank. (The transit and routing number is assigned to each bank by the American Bankers Association National Numerical System; it identifies in which city, state, or territory a given bank is located.) Companies could prepare PACs from this information; however, they often use cash management banks who perform this function for them. The servicing bank prepares PAC based on the information supplied by the corporation and deposits the PACs into the check clearing system for collection.[77]

The method of maintaining customer payment files has been automated by many banks so as to increase the efficiency and cost-effectiveness of the service. The computer files provided by the corporation are updated continuously by the bank. Computer control reports, along with deposit and availability information for funds drawn, are both forwarded to the corporation.[78] For such a program to be effective in terms of improved availability and information flows, it must be able to support regular changes such as address and bank account changes and policy modifications. Most importantly, a bank must be able to print PACs on a timely basis and assure cash managers that expected funds have been retrieved.

PAC Benefits

PACs eliminate the mail and processing float that corporations incur when they have to wait for mailed payments and to process those remittances. With PACs, payment is received on the scheduled date without waiting for the return of an invoice or bill head accompanying a check. Check clearing float is also reduced since direct check production and deposit by the cash management bank often allows the bank to enter the checks into clearing mechanisms at earlier times; better availability is achieved because the remittance handling functions of lockbox processing are sidestepped.[79]

Another advantage to using PACs is that accounts receivable data is available before payment actually occurs. This allows for timely updating of receivables files and enhanced receipts forecasting. Automated PAC programs use high-speed check printer/encoders such as Troy systems, manufactured by Data Card Corporation. These systems let banks accept magnetic tapes, containing all payment information and run them on the printer/encoder equipment. PACs and management information reports are subsequently produced. These systems provide fast turnaround time from the receipt of the corporation's payment data to the deposit of the PACs in the corporation's account for clearance.

Efficient PAC programs depend on five key ingredients:

1   The corporation provides timely customer files and file updates to the cash management bank so that PACs can be produced for the specified due dates.
2   The bank, in turn, accepts payment files and file updates and translates the data into PACs in a timely manner.
3   The bank prints PACs rapidly and accurately for entry into check clearing mechanisms. Delays or errors in production retard funds availability and the verification flow of each receivables transaction.
4   The bank can obtain good availability on deposited items. Since the payments in PAC programs are typically consumer to business, PACs may be drawn on distant or dispersed locations. The bank must effectively collect such payments and, thus, provide the corporation with attractive funds availability.
5   The bank must be operationally savvy in this endeavor to achieve PAC program goals.

PAC Costs

Costs associated with PACs are lower than those experienced with lockbox processing. Administrative expenses such as invoice production, outgoing postage, and clerical handling are eliminated. Lockbox processing costs are also eliminated. Furthermore, the charge for PAC deposits is less than items deposited in a lockbox program where dollar amounts have to be encoded on each check; PACs, especially those produced in a totally automated environment, are fully MICR encoded. PAC price components may include the following: a monthly maintenance charge for the automated payments information file, depository account maintenance charges; deposited items charges, ledger entry charges for credit entries, and the cost of the actual check document. In total, PACs are less expensive than lockbox processing programs.[80]

PAC Acceptance

Because PAC programs involve highly specialized handling procedures, and because customer acceptance has been lackluster, service growth has been irregular. Customers dislike preauthorized payment plans because they fear losing control over their funds, and consumers especially distrust payment systems whose technology they cannot fully grasp. Corporate remitters do not like preauthorized payment plans which threaten to rob them of disbursement float without extending any concomitant benefit. Nonetheless, in certain business situations PACs are a useful device for cash managers who wish to accelerate receipts.

ACH COLLECTIONS

We have seen how cash managers use lockboxes and preauthorized checks to speed cash inflows. Now, we will look at how automated clearing houses (ACHs) are used to collect payments from customers. This method uses preauthorized electronic debits, herein called ACH debits. They are the modern successor to preauthorized checks and are most often used by certain insurance companies and utilities to collect fixed and variable payments. In Chapter 7, we will consider cash concentration and, also, how the automated clearing house system can be used to draw funds out of regional depository banks and pool them at the concentration bank. There, aggregate cash position management is most efficiently performed.

Before we discuss ACH collection, it is important to understand what the ACH is and how it works. Basically, an ACH is a computerized clearing facility that effects the paperless exchange of funds between banks. Funds transfer data are moved electronically. Because an ACH performs interbank funds transfers, it is the functional equivalent of a check clearing facility that processes checks. ACHs settle accounts among participating banks by transferring aggregate funds among accounts held at Federal Reserve Banks. Individual depositor accounts are settled by respective bank balance adjustments.[81]

The notable difference between check-based clearings and ACH transactions is that the ACH accomplishes funds transfers using an electronic medium. ACH transactions involve the following participants: an automated clearing house association (ACHA), the operator of the automated clearing house facility (usually the Federal Reserve), depository institutions that are members of the ACH, and corporations and consumers.

There are currently 32 ACH associations located across the nation. As of this writing, there are 40 ACH facilities, computer centers that process transactions. ACH associations are generally nonprofit organizations owned by banks in various regions. The National Automated Clearing House Association (NACHA), formed in 1974, governs interregional exchanges among local ACHs, just as the local associations promulgate rules which govern intraregional ACH transactions. The Federal Reserve District Banks operate most local ACHs, providing delivery, settlement, and processing (receiving, sorting, and reconciling) functions. The New York Clearing House Association operates the New York facility but depends on the Fed for settlement and delivery. Presently, several regional associations are considering using private data processing vendors for intraregional ACH processing.

There are two methods for transferring funds data between a bank and an ACH: courier delivery of batched entries on magnetic tape, and electronic wire transfer.[82] Most ACHs and banks exchange funds data by magnetic tape. When a bank receives funds transfer instructions from consumers or a corporation, it formats that information on tape and removes "on-us" entries, debit or credit transactions directed to accounts located within that bank. The bank then organizes a new file of transactions that go to other financial institutions. That information is on a tape which is delivered to the local ACH which is generally on the premises of the area Federal Reserve bank. There, the data is sorted by computer and tapes created for delivery to individual receiving institutions. The receiving banks run tapes on their own computers and, accordingly, debit or credit the accounts of their depositors. When an ACH entry is directed to a bank located in an area served by another ACH, the transfer information is sent electronically over the Federal Reserve Wire network to the appropriate ACH. There, a tape is prepared for delivery to the receiving bank.

Settlement for ACH transactions among banks is accomplished by adjusting balances held at the local Federal Reserve Bank. This takes place on the day after transaction initiation; hence, ACH transfers receive one-day funds availability. Funds transferred between Federal Reserve districts also receive one-day availability, regardless of the locations of the originating and receiving banks. Settlement again takes place on Fed books.

Using courier trucks to deliver batched entries on magnetic tape is not the most efficient way to transmit ACH transfer data. In the long run, the best way is to transmit the data directly by wire. If financial institutions have a direct communications link with the ACH, the two participants can communicate over telephone lines.[83] In 1979, the Federal Reserve Board developed guidelines for banks to establish direct data communications links with their ACHs. As technology becomes more accessible and useful to banks, we can expect that ACH transactions will be accomplished more often in this manner.[84]

Funds Flows

There are two types of entries that take place through the ACH: debits and credits. The flow of information in ACH transfers is always in one direction: from the originator to the receiver. The party wishing to transfer funds is the originator. In the case of ACH debits, a corporation issues instructions to its bank in machine-readable form, either on magnetic tape, diskette, or punched cards. This data tells the bank to prepare an ACH tape that will cause the customer (payor) account to be debited (drawn down) and the corporation (payee) account to be credited. In the case of

ACH credits, which we will discuss in Chapter 8, "Disbursing Cash," funds are distributed from the payor's account to the payee's account. Direct deposit of payroll through the ACH is an example of such a credit transaction. The originator in this case is the payor. Conversely, with ACH debit transactions, the originator is the payee, the collecting company. There are three pieces of information contained in any ACH transaction: (1) type of transaction, either debit or credit, (2) amount of transaction, and (3) effective (settlement) date. This latter piece of information adds a certainty to ACH transactions not found in the check-based payment system.[85] Cash managers know in advance that funds are available for use on a specific day, which aids the cash planning task.

Prenotification

Before a corporation can initiate ACH debits that will draw down customer accounts, it must first test the transactions by sending zero-value or "prenotification" transactions through the system 10 days prior to the first live transfers. (This test is required before any type of ACH transfer can take place.) The test verifies the accuracy of the information provided to the corporation by the customer and the customer's bank: account number and bank ABA identifying number, respectively. If the corporation receives no notice of rejection by the receiving bank, it may then initiate the ACH debits according to the information tested by the "prenote."

The corporation can continue to initiate debit entries under these terms until the customer revokes his authorization. With any ACH transaction, the receiver must sign an authorization for entries to be posted to his bank account. If the amount of the debit varies from the previous entry (for instance, a variable utility payment) the corporation must send the customer a written notification of the amount of the entry and the date it is scheduled for debiting. Moreover, the same direct notification procedure must be followed if the date of the debit is changed, even though the amount remains the same.[86]

Currently, ACH debits are mostly used by companies who want to effectively collect consumer payments that come due regularly. ACH debits work well for insurance and utility companies that handle a high volume of small payments. The advantages are as follows:

Invoicing float disappears (no bills to prepare).

Mail float is eliminated (payments are not mailed in).

Processing float is trimmed (no invoices to reconcile).

Clearing float is reduced (funds receive one-day availability nationwide).

Handling expense is lessened (ACH debits are less costly than preauthorized checks—no paper items have to be produced).

Accounts receivables files can be automatically updated.

Customers can be persuaded to participate in an ACH debit program by pointing out to them that ACH debits save the time and cost of mailing in remittances. Furthermore, the burden of bookkeeping is transferred to the bank and the collecting company. This can help forgetful consumers avoid late payment penalties. Corporate disadvantages do exist with ACH programs, however, including the need to maintain dual billing systems—one for electronic payors and one for traditional accounts. In addition, corporations may have to sacrifice using invoice mailings as an outlet for promotional materials. Primary problems with consumer acceptance include the fear that preauthorized payment plans rob the individual of check float and control over his bank account and funds.[87]

Corporate-to-corporate ACH applications are far less popular than the retail version. This is because payor corporations have been reluctant, historically, to sacrifice disbursement float. The oft-heard cash manager's lament, "I'll begin paying electronically when I'm paid electronically," exemplifies the traditional standoff. In the past, many cash managers felt that one of their primary corporate missions was to create disbursement float. For professional and economic reasons, this attitude is now beginning to change. Today, the cash manager's job increasingly calls for clever engineering of internal payment and collection systems. The cash manager must also supervise the management information produced by those systems. As well, the aggregate cost of paper payments is rising for both payor and payee. Some organizations are now experimenting with corporate-to-corporate payments using the ACH. But it will be some time before many corporations are positioned to go this route. For the cash manager who has just completed a complex and costly lockbox study, it may be difficult to ask senior management for the funds to research and develop an ACH debit program to collect remittances from corporate customers. Moreover, many corporations have decided to wait until the ACH system is perfected. For example, one system "bug" is the time-consuming and paper-based procedure for handling ACH return items. Paper return notices have been known to take several weeks to travel to where they can be reconciled, causing accounting and balance control headaches. The Fed has been working on this dilemma and, so far, has met with modest success.

These stumbling blocks notwithstanding, corporations *can* convince their trade customers to pay electronically, as we saw in our discussion of credit policies. Analysts expect this trend to continue and grow. The rising costs of paper and Fed plans to pass on the cost of its system float to banks, and ultimately check writers, will prompt many cash managers to consider ACH payments. On the retail side, the push toward electronic payments will no doubt be fueled by greater consumer awareness of the safety and efficiency of electronic banking. Although automated teller machines have existed since the 1960s, they are now just being embraced by consumers. With personal computers now entering homes at a rapid clip, we may find consumers more willing to experiment with electronic and home banking.

GIRO PAYMENTS

Another ACH technique for collecting consumer payments is the GIRO system. GIRO payments are credit transfers through the ACH. The system has its conceptual roots in Europe, where, in the 1600s, people began generating financial transactions through post offices. An electronic GIRO system involves consumers initiating funds transfers from their own bank accounts.[88] A payor instructs his bank to debit his account and pass a credit through the ACH to the bank account of the payee.

There are four initiation options available to the payor:

1 Standing Orders. A consumer has his bank automatically generate periodic payments of a constant amount such as rents, installment loans, and utility budget payments. The bank is given the necessary payee data when the standing order is arranged. This is stored, then included with each generated credit.

2 Telephone Instructions. A bank takes instructions to pay specific bills over the phone. This is done through a conversation with a bank employee or input directly to a bank computer via touchtone telephone. Again, payee data is kept on file.

3 Standardized Bills. A consumer signs and mails or delivers to his bank bills to be paid. This can be efficient when payee companies use some standard data line which can be optically scanned.

4 Automated Teller Machine (ATM). Using an ATM and a debit card, the consumer instructs his bank to pay specific bills. Payee data is stored on the bank computer.

Payee companies experience different degrees of reduced collection float depending on which of the above options the consumer uses. Standing orders eliminate all mail, processing, and check clearing float. They come close to affording companies the efficiency of the preauthorized debit technique. ATM payments also eliminate mail and check clearing float, although invoices still have to be generated. Telephone payments can also reduce costly collection float, but the consumer's bank may have to spend time formatting customer instructions onto an electronic medium before passing them through the ACH. The standardized bill option, while an improvement, still incurs mail and processing float.

Overall, GIRO payments afford better funds availability. Settlement for transactions is in usable funds on a specified date. This is an improvement over PAC plans wherein the availability for deposited items varies. Conversely, GIRO systems do not provide the payee company with the transaction control possible with PACs or ACH debits: the payor or his bank are active transaction participants.

GIRO payments improve information flows in receivables collection. Receivables file updating can be done automatically when data is captured and produced in machine-readable form. Although corporations do not enjoy the certainty of when payments will arrive, receivables posting is accelerated. Furthermore, GIRO payments can help corporations reduce the cost of collection services. Remittance and check handling may be totally eliminated, or at least greatly trimmed. Also, corporations can lessen dependence on decentralized lockbox networks and corresponding concentration efforts. Trade payments could be accomplished with GIRO techniques, although the same reasons for resisting corporate-to-corporate ACH debits may apply with this technique as well.[89]

GIRO Barriers

GIRO payments have yet to become widespread because of consumer fear and the perceived high cost to financial institutions. Also, many corporations refuse to accept GIRO payments which would require handling on an exception basis. This will hold true until automatic bank-corporate interfaces proliferate. Nonetheless, as more banks and merchants support GIRO payments in coming years, consumers will begin to perceive conveniences and corporations may then respond by experimenting with this form of electronic banking.[90]

7 Cash Concentration Systems

We have considered various ways that corporations attempt to speed the flow of remittances. Now, we will see what happens once funds are gathered at regional depository banks and converted to available balances: the money is moved to a concentration bank. From there, the cash manager makes investments, reduces debt, or funds disbursements. Cash concentration, then, involves transferring funds from one corporate account to another corporate account. It pools money that has been accumulated by the company's decentralized collection network of regional depository banks.

FIELD DEPOSITORY BANKS

A lockbox bank is one form of regional depository. The other, called a field deposit bank, accepts deposits from corporate field units, usually service stations, branches, catalog showrooms, warehouses, and so on. Often, deposits made by corporate field units are the result of noncredit sales: proceeds taken in over the counter. Selecting field deposit banks does not involve the same system design problems encountered with lockbox locations. Primarily, selection is based on a bank's proximity to the corporate field unit. However, Dr. Bernell K. Stone, in *The Financial*

Handbook, Fifth Edition, discussed certain tactical design issues associated with developing systems for concentrating receipts from field units. He stated:

These issues may be company or industry specific. They include:

Multiple Units at One Bank.   When more than one unit uses the same field deposit bank, should there be separate accounts and transfers out of those accounts, or should there be a single master account with zero-balance subaccounts?

Branch Banks.   Where branch banking is available, for instance, in California, should the company try to use branches of a major bank? The trade-offs are fewer accounts for transferring but, possibly, less convenient deposit locations.

Compensation for Field Banks.   What type of compensation method—fees, balances, or a combination—should be used to pay for charges at the field deposit bank level? Compensating balances are the norm, since it is difficult to remove all balances (sometimes, a portion of which is required anyway). Compensating field deposit banks totally in fees is almost always more costly than balance compensation.

Control.   Should the field deposit bank play a part in a firm's deposit reporting and deposit control? For instance, should a field bank call corporate headquarters if a deposit is not made by each unit within an account?

Deposit Information Gathering.   How should deposit information be gathered—phone calls or point-of-sale (POS) terminals? If phone calls are used, should calls go to a central company location, or should a third-party deposit information gathering service be used? When POS is available, it is generally preferable to phone calls. Deciding whether phone call data should be gathered by the company or by an outside service is a make-or-buy decision.

Deposit Information Gathering: Report Timing.   Most units report after the deposit is made, frequently, late in the day. Alternatives include more than one report per day or a midday report giving deposits (net receipts) for the afternoon and evening of the previous day and for the morning. The benefit is more information reported prior to transfer cutoff times, thus faster movement of funds out of field deposit banks.

Coin and Currency.   Arrangements must be made to provide coin and currency at some units. Frequency of replenishment and amount involves trade-offs in management costs and effort versus higher cash balances.

Armored Car Pickup.   If armored car pickup or delivery of cash is pertinent, the frequency and the time of day for both pickup and deposit are decisions that affect the cost of services and the amount of cash tied up.[91]

Deposits by a field unit can include both cash and checks. The field deposit bank performs necessary check collection functions for the field unit. In many cases, these checks are drawn on other local banks; local consumers write local checks. Sometimes, checks received by field units are drawn on faraway banks; hotel chains often accept out-of-state checks. Local checks can be collected in one day, but remote checks obviously take longer to clear and are frequently granted availability according to the local Fed schedules. Balances represented by such checks may not be usable for several days. Cash managers track the clearing float at the field bank level only when amounts are significant enough to warrant the effort.

CONCENTRATION BANK SELECTION

Concentration involves moving collected balances out of regional depositories—field deposit or lockbox banks—and pooling them at a concentration bank. A corporation may select one or several of its major credit banks as concentration points. This is done because adjustments to balances at concentration banks are often made by borrowing or lending. Thus, some administrative efficiency is achieved. Sometimes, concentration banks are chosen because they are near major money centers such as New York City where access to money markets is best. When divisional concentration is desired, cash managers frequently use multiple concentration points. Another, but now less common, reason for using several concentration points is regional gathering wherein two tiers of concentration banks exist to funnel money to a central account.

There has been a recent trend among cash managers, however, to streamline the number of concentration points in their systems. In part, this is possible because of advances in technology: reliable, same-day money transfers and good communications and information management capabilities can mitigate the importance of concentration bank location. Cash managers now carefully consider a concentration bank's operating efficiency with automatic depository transfer check preparation, accurate and timely wire transfers, ACH transfers, and interfaces to third-party data processing services.[92] We will see below how sophisticated uses of technology allow a cash manager to set up a system dependent on a single concentration point. This development helps reduce the cost and effort inherent in a large collection base.

CONCENTRATION TECHNIQUES

Three basic tools are used to move funds out of regional depositories and into concentration banks: (1) depository transfer checks (DTCs), (2) wire transfers, and (3) ACH cash concentration debits. We will see how each is used, depending on whether a system is based on field initiation or central initiation.

Field Initiation

Field initiation occurs when the money transfer is prompted at the local level by either the field unit manager, the field deposit bank, or the lockbox bank. Traditionally, the mainstay of field initiated concentration systems was the mailed DTC. DTCs represent a simple and relatively inexpensive method of transferring funds between locations.[93] A DTC is an unsigned check drawn on one corporate account and payable to the corporation at a concentration bank. DTCs are nonnegotiable, preprinted checks which need only the date and the amount filled in. Up until the mid-1970s, many corporations concentrated funds by having the field unit manager first make his daily deposit, then prepare a DTC in the exact amount of the deposit and mail it to a lockbox or concentration bank. The lockbox or concentration bank would then deposit the DTC into the company account where it would begin its journey through clearing mechanisms back to the field deposit bank for presentation. The corporate cash manager was regularly informed of deposit activity by the field unit manager.

Obviously, mailed DTCs initiated by field agents generate both mail and clearing float. It can take up to seven days for such DTCs to remove funds from field deposit banks. The built-in delay, in the past, gave the field depository plenty of time to collect checks that were part of the deposit. While this system sufficed in the 1970s, cash managers now will not tolerate having to wait that length of time for available funds at the concentration bank. Field deposit banks currently collect local checks in one or two days. In many cases, improved check collection performance is attributable to enhanced Fed operations. Therefore, mailed DTCs initiated by field unit managers are appropriate only when a corporation cares to let small balances build up at a remote field bank and offset activity charges incurred by the field unit. The mailed DTC technique may be appropriate when a degree of administrative autonomy is desired at the field level. However, in light of cash management objectives, this motivation is unsavory. Mailed DTCs are expensive and cumbersome, causing unnecessary delay in funds availability. For the most part, they have been abandoned.

Cash managers sometimes arrange for regional depository banks to initiate wire transfers, on a standing order basis, when available balances reach predetermined targets. This concentration method, using either the Fed Wire or Bank Wire systems, is useful when large balances regularly appear in field bank accounts. Commonly, this type of arrangement removes available funds from lockbox accounts. However, the corporate cash manager must perform a cost/benefit analysis in order to determine if the wire transfer is cost-justified. (Astute cash managers perform such studies when choosing any transfer device.) The cash manager compares the cost of the wire with the investment value of available balances.

When funds are wired from one bank to another, they are available for use at the receiving bank the same day. (Technically, Bank Wire transfers are settled by 9:00 A.M. the morning following wire execution.) If a cash manager can profit by investing pooled funds, relative to what he spends on the process of same-day transfer, then wires are justifiable. A typical wire could cost a total of $11.00. This includes charges levied by both the sending and receiving banks. For example, at a 12% cost of capital, the dollar amount of the transfer would have to be $33,000 or more to justify the transfer expense for one-day sooner funds availability.[94] Many times, how desperately a company needs cash helps decide whether the expense of a wire transfer is warranted. Cash managers also need to determine what is an optimum transfer frequency. Daily transfers for small amounts may be illogical; however, transfers two or three times per week may be reasonable. Wires can be initiated by field deposit banks or field managers, as well as by a lockbox bank. Corporate policy may dictate when such transfers should be made or how much money should be moved at a given time. ACH transactions are not initiated by field depositories.

Central Initiation

Central initiation occurs when a money transfer is initiated by the con- centration bank. Here, a system is needed for gathering deposit information from field unit managers or from field deposit or lockbox banks. There are two types of central initiation: company-managed and third-party as- sisted.[95] They differ in the manner that deposit data is collected.

Company-Managed Data Collection. In the case of company-managed central initiation, daily deposits are reported to a central corporate location. There, data is captured and then generated on magnetic tape, or other communication system, and subsequently sent or teleprocessed to the concentration bank. When the concentration bank receives the corporate data, it prepares and deposits DTCs into the corporation's account for each regional depository that holds funds to be concentrated. Often, high- speed, computerized equipment produces what is known as automated DTCs. While this activity is underway, checks are being collected by the field deposit or lockbox banks. Usually, the DTCs remove funds one or two days after deposit at regional depositories.

DTCs are usually collected through the Fed check collection system and are granted availability based on Fed schedules for presenting items between certain areas. Actual DTC availability, however, depends on how well the Fed system is working at a given point in time. As we saw in Chapter 4, the Fed transportation network can encounter delays due to bad weather or equipment failure. When this happens, credit may be given for a DTC at the concentration account before the funds are actually re- moved from regional banks. Cash managers enjoy dual balances when concentration machinery unwittingly creates money in two accounts at once!

A less common version of company-managed central initiation involves internal DTC preparation. Corporations produce DTCs after field units or lockbox banks have reported daily deposits. The DTCs are then phys- ically delivered to the concentration bank for deposit into the clearing process. For the most part, corporate DTC preparation is less efficient than having the concentration bank do the work. When companies create their own DTCs, they incur increased clerical costs, and when the number of reporting locations is high, companies risk processing delays and, hence, delayed funds availability. In addition, there may be inefficiencies because companies have to make DTC deposits by a certain bank cutoff time. This can mean that some locations, maybe those on the West Coast, will have deposits concentrated on a deferred basis. Because banks control their own deposit times, they can often process DTCs as late as 8:00 P.M. before having to close the day's books.[96]

In a company-managed system, the cash manager can also arrange to have the concentration bank initiate a wire transfer. Here, the concentration bank contacts the regional depository with wire instructions. When a wire is initiated by the receiving bank, it is called a "draw down."[97]

An alternative to DTCs and wires is the use of ACH cash concentration debits, sometimes known as electronic depository transfers. With this method, the concentration bank, instead of producing and depositing DTCs, creates and delivers a tape to its local ACH. This tape contains information on all the regional depository locations and the amounts to be debited electronically through the ACH network. Funds are available in the concentration account the day after the ACH transaction is initiated. (See Chapter 6 for a discussion of ACH operations.)

When ACH debits are used in a company-managed system, the corporation usually produces a magnetic tape containing all the reported deposit data. The tape is then delivered or electronically transmitted to the concentration bank which, in turn, initiates the ACH transactions. On a limited basis, some concentration banks will accept from a company a printout which lists concentration data.

The ACH cash concentration debit appeals to cash managers because it is less expensive than the typical DTC which, in turn, is much less expensive than a wire. Furthermore, ACH debits provide a one-day uniform availability, regardless of the location of depository banks. It is this uniform one-day availability feature which allows cash managers to locate concentration points anywhere convenient to them.[98] It also helps cash managers reduce the amount of concentration banks they need to pool funds from a nationwide collection base. One corporate treasurer who converted to ACH cash concentration debits found the process to be easy. After determining which field deposit banks could handle ACH debits— about 85% of them—he merely sent them a form letter authorizing them to accept the transactions. The remaining banks stayed on the paper DTCs system. His concentration bank managed the prenotification process which tests the transfer data accuracy.

A cash manager may worry that ACH debits could clear balances out of regional depositories too fast—before all local checks have been collected. If this happened, the company would be overdrawn. A steady diet of this could threaten the regional bank relationship. One possible result is that regional banks could require the company to increase its imprest balances (small balance cushions). Thus, if this result occurred, a key cash management objective would be sacrificed; why bother to accelerate cashflow if it costs more money to do so?

It is interesting, though, that the corporate treasurer mentioned above reported that he did not incur increased imprest balances, or balance deficiency charges, when he converted to ACH debits. In fact, some of his regional banks are manually debiting his accounts when they receive notification of the ACH debit transactions. At some field deposit banks, the corporation ends up being given credit for balances *longer* now that ACH cash concentration debits are removing funds. Why? Small, unsophisticated banks simply do not know what to do with ACH transaction notifications. We can expect dilemmas like this to continue at small field deposit banks, at least until more bankers are educated about handling ACH transactions.

Third-Party Data Collection.   Many large companies find managing their own deposit information reporting systems to be expensive and cumbersome. Instead, they rely on a third-party to gather and process daily deposit data. This is called, third-party assisted central initiation.[99] Like company-managed systems, the concentration bank initiates money transfers using either automated DTCs, draw downs (wires), or ACH cash concentration debits. The corporate cash manager receives deposit detail reports from the third-party data gatherer and the concentration bank. From these reports, he tracks funds movements and balances.

With this concentration technique, field unit managers or regional depositories make toll-free telephone calls to a data collection facility. POS terminals and telexes are also used. Usually, this facility is part of a nationwide data processing network operated by a bank or an independent service bureau. The nonbank vendors offering such deposit reporting services include:

National Data Corporation.

Interactive Data Corporation.

ADP Network Services, Inc.

First Data Resources, Inc.

Daily phone calls are the most common reporting medium. When the calls come into the facility, clerks enter the deposit amounts onto terminals. Each location is identified by a special number. At a specified cutoff time, the third-party transmits the information needed to concentrate funds over phone lines to the concentration bank. Functionally, third-party assisted central initiation is different from the company-managed version only in that daily deposit reports go to a central data collection facility not owned by the corporation. Companies with hundreds of locations reporting daily deposits find that using a third-party is much more efficient than doing the work themselves.

SYSTEM AUDITS

The cash manager who uses a third-party in his concentration system has to monitor how well the technique works. He has to intervene when field locations consistently fail to report on time. He may find that, indeed, the field agents are dutifully reporting but that the data collector is suffering from operational problems. He then needs to let the third-party know that he is evaluating its performance and, where appropriate, voice his complaints. The cash manager also has to monitor the concentration bank: are DTCs produced quickly enough to capture optimum availability schedules; are draw downs initiated according to a predetermined cash transfer schedule; are ACH debits handled correctly? Costs for cash transfers and the optimization of funds are also important considerations.

(Readers interested in mathematical programs used in conjunction with computers to solve cash transfer scheduling dilemmas can refer to work done by Drs. Bernell K. Stone and Ned C. Hill. Their 1979 *Working Paper No. MS-79-6* was an outgrowth of research supported by The First National Bank of Chicago.)

Balance Reporting

Large corporations often track daily concentration, depository and disbursement bank account activity with balance reporting systems. In the most sophisticated applications, cash managers use terminals to access

timeshared computers that relay daily bank balances and related transaction details. Before this technology became prevelant in the 1970s, cash
managers either called their banks or had their banks call them in order
to obtain current balance information.

Why monitor daily bank balances? As we will see in Chapter 8, cash
managers control disbursements by monitoring central bank accounts, not
by working solely from company books. This is so because company books
often reflect disbursements immediately, whereas bank accounts show
account debits only when checks have been presented for payment. The
difference in amounts represents the unavoidable float that accrues to
check-based disbursement accounts. By tracking actual daily bank balances, cash managers can best allocate cash where needed and find optimum uses for any excess. Monitoring balances tells cash managers *what*
money is *where*.

Balance reporting systems differ in the level of detail that they can
provide, as well as the time period for which past data are available, the
variety of reports, and their adaptability to user needs. A single bank
system provides reports only for accounts at that bank. A multibank system gives reports for as many banks the company can persuade to transmit
to the timeshared computer.[100] The BankLink Information System, li-
censed by Chemical Bank to other banks nationwide, is an example of a
multibank balance reporting network. Nonbank data processors, such as
National Data Corporation, also provide this type of communication system for corporate cash managers and treasurers.

These systems typically provide daily balance information (current collected and uncollected amounts) and average balance data (average available balance for the month, and possibly longer time periods, for instance,
year to date). Cash managers can also receive reports on how closely
balances are being maintained at predetermined targets and the average
balances needed to meet target levels for a certain time period, say, the
rest of a month. This lets cash managers know whether monthly compensation balance requirements are being met and/or whether transfers
in or out are necessary to optimize the use of company funds. Transfer
details can be summarized—for example, the number and amounts of DTC
deposits. Some banks can relay data on checks paid and include check
number, amount, and other information. Some systems also provide other
kinds of pertinent cash management information, including recent quotes
on money market instruments. Others allow cash managers to initiate wire
or DTC transfers directly from the computer terminals.

SUMMARY

Cash concentration allows the cash manager to pool corporate funds at a central account. From there, he can efficiently and productively deploy cashflows. Balance and deposit reporting systems are critical tools used by cash managers to monitor complex banking networks and allow the cash manager to perform aggregate cash position management: he either funds disbursements, reduces debt, or invests in the money market.

Cash acceleration and concentration systems are necessary because of the time value of money; idle funds are a cash management liability. Systems now used by large corporations for concentration are fairly well-defined. The technology exists to provide tighter cashflow control and management information. What cash managers look for in concentration banks and third-party data collectors is operational efficiency. As the Federal Reserve continues its efforts to reduce and charge for its system float, cash managers will turn increasingly to ACH debits to quickly and inexpensively concentrate company funds.

8 Disbursing Cash

Collecting and concentrating funds is only one side of the cash manager's task. In this chapter, we will consider strategies for cash disbursing. We will see that there is a lot more to disbursement than just paying bills. Picture an arch: the crux of cash management occurs at the keystone, where aggregate cashflows are balanced. Cash acceleration and concentration are tasks that feed the aggregate cash position; disbursement activities funnel funds where needed to keep the company strong and intact. The cash manager tries to hold together the company's short-term financial structure by optimizing the use of cash assets that make business enterprise possible. He does this by keeping funds productive. When not needed to pay bills or compensate banks, funds can be used to reduce debt or to make short-term investments. When necessary, the cash manager arranges for short-term debt. This way, a stable level of working capital is maintained and optimized.

Disbursement strategies aim to take advantage of the time value of money. Idle funds represent a sacrificed opportunity to earn interest or reduce borrowing costs. Therefore, cash managers set disbursement objectives that treat cash assets as commodities that return value to the firm. These include:

Centralized payment and balance information control.

Consistent, appropriate use of discounts.

Controlled disbursement funding.

Scheduled payments that avoid paying too soon.

Optimized use of disbursement system float.

System cost control.

We will see how cash managers have learned to optimize the use of cash outflows. We will also see that so-called "aggressive" disbursement strategies have incurred the wrath of the Federal Reserve. Much recent debate has centered on ethical questions surrounding optimizing funds at someone else's expense. We will look at these issues and the government's policy responses and suggest future implications for cash managers.

DISBURSEMENTS AND CORPORATE CULTURE

Disbursement systems are designed primarily to control and slow cash outflows; they set into place corporate policies that value the earning potential of cash. For instance, a corporate cash manager may computerize the scheduling of bill payments and automatic check preparation. In effect, this move takes payment discretion away from a risk-averse payables clerk and subordinates it to defined parameters. In this manner, the cash manager assures that bills are paid on time, but not too soon. The cash manager may also design a system that allows him to cover disbursement checks, not when they are written, but when they are presented at the bank for payment. *The Treasurer's Handbook* discusses the practice of matching disbursements with clearings and concludes:

> (There is a phenomenon) familiar to virtually all financial managers—actual cash balances in a (bank) disbursing account in excess of the book balances shown in the company's accounting records. The cash balances less (remittance) checks in collection are the funds actually available for use by the company. Using this float is entirely ethical and should not be confused with drawing checks for local payment on a deliberately remote bank in order to exploit collection times.[101]

Whether a disbursement system is abusive or not depends on its chief objective. If that objective is to exploit vendors by taking advantage of payment system inefficiencies, then we can infer perfidy. These arguments become complicated when corporate cash managers contend that their job is to optimize company cash. They sometimes feel that their role is to reap as much benefit as they can for their firms. They feel justified in using payments systems to their advantage until banking authorities create a zero-float world. Consider the case of the oil company that mails a payment for $1 million to a supplier. Through float extension techniques, that money can be kept in an interest earning capacity for as long as one week after mailing without jeopardizing the firm's trade relationship. The value to the oil company is obvious; now consider that this company makes, on average, $30 million in cash payments per day. Clearly, the cash manager would be remiss if he ignored the value of disbursement float. But who pays in the end? We will see when vendors and banks lose; and we will see when the American taxpayer ultimately pays for float.

Definitions of abuse notwithstanding, corporations have varied approaches to disbursement system policy. Some stress equitable dealings with banks and vendors. Other companies give their cash managers a license to milk every penny possible out of payment networks. Others focus on liquidity. In all, individual corporate culture determines how aggressive or conservative a company's cash management will be.

CENTRALIZED PAYMENT CONTROL

As we saw in Chapter 7, companies use decentralized collection networks to speed cash inflows. Conversely, systems that centralize payables can automatically control and slow payments. With payments centralized, the cash manager can evaluate the timing of bills coming due for the entire corporation and schedule them on a systemwide basis. This way, he can take the optimal economic time to settle obligations, and, in the meantime, keep funds productive. Centralized disbursements also permit more efficient monitoring of account balances and current float positions.[102]

By scheduling payments centrally, the cash manager assures that appropriate discounts are taken or that credit terms are met and late payment penalties avoided. A cash manager is a payment system expert; he is better equipped to supervise funds flows than a field unit manager swamped with administrative or marketing problems. The cash manager's priorities, then, are geared to cashflow planning and control. He is aware of the aggregate costs of missed discounts, whereas the branch manager may view one or two missed discounts as inconsequential. Furthermore, the cash manager is responsible for the aggregate liability of payments made too soon, whereas a field unit bookkeeper may be overly fastidious, paying bills the day they arrive.

Economies of scale are also important. From a central perch, the cash manager can rely on computerized reporting systems for managing dispersed bank accounts. He can concentrate funds and best allocate cash resources according to need. He can track available balances with balance reporting systems, and he can manage to have funds in several places at once. He can predict when disbursement checks to certain vendors are likely to clear and know when to cover them with funds clearing on the collections side. It is possible to have credit for a payment entered into a vendor's accounts receivable file while actual cash cover is made a few days later. Aware of historical payment system patterns, the cash manager knows to keep funds invested in highly liquid short-term securities until needed. He can invest his concentration bank balance for a short time although portions may already be earmarked to cover a disbursement check.[103] In effect, a good disbursement system allows the cash manager to pay a bill with invested funds, or from a concentration bank balance that does not really yet exist!

DISBURSEMENT FLOAT

What we just described is called "playing the float." We will now look at components of disbursement float and see how special disbursement tools and techniques are used in centralized payment systems to capture the time value of money. We can recall from earlier chapters that collection float is made up of mail float, processing float (either corporate or bank), and clearing float. We saw that as the cash manager attempts to speed receivables, collection float is a burden. Disbursement float, on the other hand, represents value to the cash manager. Therefore, he tries to increase it. He does this by looking for ways to maximize the value of each component of disbursement float.

In a centralized payments system, mail float can automatically occur when vendors nationwide are paid from one location. A cash manager in Seattle who disburses checks for trade payments due to vendors in Boston incurs several days more mail float than a Boston branch mailing would enjoy. A somewhat more assertive approach would involve the cash manager mailing bills from suburbs. One firm actually sends a clerk home early so that he can drop payments in an outlying suburban post office. This may delay funds one day. If qualification for discounts or simply meeting payment terms depends on postmarks, this stunt can doubly favor the paying company. It is not at all unusual for companies to grovel for a one-day disbursement float benefit; this should not be surprising given the enormous effort that goes into capturing fractions-of-day float reductions on the collections end of cash management.

Remote mailing involves having checks mailed from a location that is distant from the vendor. For example, a San Francisco company might mail payments from North Carolina to West Coast vendors. If those checks were drawn on East Coast banks, the remittances could conceivably cross the country two times before the vendor had actual use of the funds. While remote mailing is not widespread in cash management, it is performed— for the sole purpose of extending disbursement float.

Cash managers sometimes try to take advantage of processing float as well. If a vendor is not using a lockbox, the payee cash manager knows it and may attempt to foul up remittance processing. One tale that has made the rounds at cash management meetings concerns the payment addressed to a company president, marked "personal." When the president returned from a trip, there was the envelope on his desk. It contained a nice letter extolling the virtues of his firm's products. The president was so pleased that he saved the correspondence, hefty check included, to show off at the next board meeting. Self-respecting cash managers do not make such disbursement behavior a habit, but we can imagine that a cash manager strapped for money would resort to such a ploy.

It used to be thought possible to deliberately alter or mutilate checks so that they would be rejected by automatic sorting equipment found in bank lockbox shops. The idea was to punch tiny pinholes in a check's MICR line so that it could not be read automatically; a clerk would then have to set it aside for manual processing at a later time. However, new lockbox machinery allows for enhanced reject handling. The most time delay you could currently gain by mutilating checks is about ten minutes.

Where float optimization gets truly sophisticated is in the design of disbursement bank networks. Cash managers try to extend check clearing (availability) float. Additionally, they strive to take advantage of clearing system slippage. As we saw in earlier chapters, clearing float refers to the amount of time a payee must wait before deposited items become

usable funds. This mostly arises with transit items, checks drawn on banks
other than the depositing bank. Transit items have to be physically presented for payment. Availability schedules tell banks how long to defer
funds depending on the relative location of the paying bank. Check presentment is accomplished either through direct send clearing arrangements
operated by large commercial banks, or through Fed collection networks.

Sometimes, credit for transit checks is granted according to unrealistic
Fed or bank availability schedules, that is, before actual presentation. As
a matter of policy, the Fed traditionally absorbed the opportunity cost of
its unrealistic availability schedules (although this is soon to change). Early
crediting also takes place when bank or Fed collection systems foul up
or data bases have been improperly construed. These inefficiencies result
in clearing system slippage whose cost is not borne by vendors; the cost
is borne either by banks or the Fed (in which case, ultimately, taxpayers).
The sum of clearing float and clearing system slippage is called "presentation float." (See Exhibits 8.1 and 8.2.)[104]

Extending presentation float includes deciding where to locate disbursement accounts. First, most companies assign checks by class, based
on the zip code of the payee address. Check classes are then assigned to
disbursement bank accounts. (These accounts are not necessarily at remote
banks, but neither are they inevitably located across the street from vendor
headquarters.) These assignments, however, may not extend clearing float
when the payee uses a lockbox location near the payor. In that case,
disbursement studies, using computer models, analyze how long checks

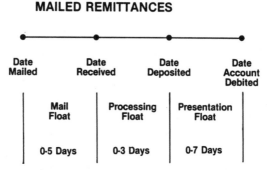

**DISBURSING SYSTEM FLOAT
MAILED REMITTANCES**

Exhibit 8.1. Depiction of potential time delays associated with mailed disbursements checks.
*(Reprinted courtesy of Dr. Steven Maier, University Analytics, Inc.: Duke University; and
Daniel Ferguson, The First National Bank of Chicago.)*

PRESENTATION FLOAT

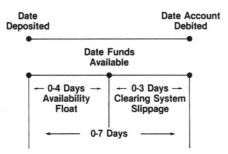

Exhibit 8.2. Components of presentation float associated with disbursement checks. *(Reprinted courtesy of Dr. Steven Maier, University Analytics, Inc.: Duke University; and Daniel Ferguson, The First National Bank of Chicago.)*

take to clear. Phoenix-Hecht, Inc. is a primary source of such studies. The disburser can then reassign checks among disbursement accounts to gain the most float advantage. Meanwhile, the collecting corporations may also be using computer models in lockbox location studies. The net effect? Computer wars with bank accounts chasing each other around the country.

To summarize, optimizing disbursement float includes designing payment plans that take advantage of these types of float: mail float (possibly five days), processing float, (possibly three days) and presentation float (possibly seven days). Some analysts would argue that systems designed deliberately to extend float at someone else's expense are, in short, abusive. No one, however, has proven that any such practices are illegal per se. We will now look at some common disbursement tools and techniques used by large American corporations. Whether these methods are employed with abuse as the goal really depends on the individual corporation's intention.

ZERO-BALANCE ACCOUNTS

The objectives of a firm's disbursement policy play a large role in bank account location. Some firms do not care to punish vendors by making them wait days for usable funds. Instead, they may place disbursement accounts where branch disbursing autonomy is desired and where, simultaneously, the corporate cash manager maintains funding control. In this case, zero-balance accounts are extremely useful. The company maintains zero balances in one or more accounts with a certain bank (sometimes its chief credit or concentration bank). These are subaccounts funded by a master account. The company instructs the bank to move funds between each subaccount and the master account so as to achieve a daily zero balance in each subaccount. The company's residual or deficient balance then resides in the master account.

The cash manager can control these accounts as if only one account existed. Tied into a balance reporting network, or notified by phone, the cash manager knows the daily funding requirement for the master account. The BankLink system and the NDC's Cash Management Exchange are examples of multibank balance reporting systems; individual banks also provide their own in-bank systems, such as Citibank's *CitiCash Manager* or Manufacturers Hanover Trust's *Transend*. The cash manager can receive details on each subaccount's activity as well as balance reports for the master account. Daily cash deficiencies in the master account are often funded by wire or by book transfers when the chief account and the master account are at the same bank. Also, the cash manager can arrange for automatic wire draw downs initiated by the disbursement bank and directed to the chief bank account where aggregate cash position is monitored.[105] When balance reporting and funding occur on a one-day lag basis, then a balance equivalent to an average day's disbursement amount is often required to prevent overdraft positions as well as compensate the bank for its services.

Zero-balance arrangements are popular because they allow a corporation to maintain centralized funding control and account management while at the same time they provide segregated payment activity. This segregation automatically produces audit trail and accounting integrity for special classes of disbursements such as payroll or tax bills. Separate statements and account reconciliation reports are available for each account in the system. Zero-balance accounts also allow satellite offices to keep disbursement authority. This is sometimes desirable given special relationships with suppliers who demand that bills be paid with local checks. In certain states, laws dictate that local vendors be paid with local checks. Zero-balance accounts can reside at banks also used for collection and/or concentration. When zero-balance accounts are located far away from vendors, the system takes advantage of clearing float at the payee's expense.

CONTROLLED DISBURSING ACCOUNTS

Controlled disbursing accounts are specially designed zero-balance accounts for corporate customers with significant cashflows. Some analysts distinguish between controlled disbursing accounts that are true zero-balance arrangements and those that contain some imprest balance for safety or compensation purposes. Controlled disbursing accounts are different from normal zero-balance accounts in that they are typically housed at branches or affiliates of major cash management banks. Often, the branch or affiliate location is *not* in a Federal Reserve city; they are out of the way, so to speak, and thus provide a special feature: this system identifies all checks presented against designated corporate accounts clearing through the day's final Federal Reserve and, if any, commercial bank direct send presentments. These final daily presentments of cash letters are typically before 9:00 A.M. Controlled disbursing banks often refuse to accept for same-day payment any correspondent cash letters arriving from the main bank processing center after the morning deadline. A few banks have followed the lead of Banker's Trust and refuse to grant same-day credit for on-us checks received through late-arriving correspondent bank cash letters or over-the-counter after 10:00 A.M.[106]

The purpose of all this is to be able to report to cash managers by mid- or late morning the amount of daily check presentments. Cash managers can thus be assured of daily funding requirements early enough to invest excess cash by 11:00 A.M., New York Time. This is when money market trading peaks. Using controlled disbursement accounts, they are certain that no later presentments will occur and cause a cash emergency.

Daniel M. Ferguson, Vice President at The First National Bank of Chicago, and Dr. Steven F. Maier from Duke University, both respected cash management thinkers, provide a definition of the purpose of controlled disbursement:

> The elimination of idle and unproductive balances from the company's bank accounts which would otherwise be tied up because of the uncertainty of when checks will be paid.[107]

From this statement, we can understand why corporations have embraced controlled disbursing as a technique for managing huge cashflows. The issue is control, knowing daily funding requirements. To cash managers disbursing millions daily, this information is vital to the smooth allocation of company cash. The key to controlled disbursement is that accounts located in Fed RCPC zones (see Chapter 4 for an explanation of Fed zones) generally receive their last daily Fed cash letters early enough in the morning for the bank to sort company checks and subsequently notify the cash manager of the funding need. This system is geared to corporate investment timing. Also, many of the controlled disbursing locations handle relatively small volumes of checks, thus facilitating corporate account identification.

Controlled Disbursing Statistics

According to a 1982 Phoenix-Hecht report, 80% of all banks surveyed were able to notify customers of daily disbursement totals by 11:30 A.M. East Coast Time. Sixty-four percent of the banks questioned stated that they were able to disclose 100% of daily disbursement totals when they made a first report to cash managers. Forty-five percent of the banks related the data by phone. Sixty-six percent refused correspondent direct sends at controlled disbursement sites. Sixty-one percent did not require that all controlled disbursement customers be credit worthy up to the bank's house limit. Seventy-eight percent said they did not mandate back-up lines of credit for all such customers. Sixty-six percent did not require controlled disbursers to purchase unrelated bank services. Sixty-eight percent did not ask that an imprest balance be maintained. Sixty-one percent who allowed funding through bank-initiated paper or electronic DTCs required customers to keep collected balances on hand equal to an average day's disbursement total. Of the banks who provided controlled disbursement through an affiliate or correspondent, 78% guaranteed funding from the flagship bank in the event of a funding failure.[108]

Why do banks seem confident that controlled disbursing does not threaten branch or affiliate safety? They are confident probably because funding is usually accomplished through same-day wire transfers. Other funding arrangements include book transfers, DTCs, electronic DTCs (ACH debits), the sale of investments (maturing repurchase agreements), loan takedowns, and transfers from lockbox deposits. When devices such as paper or electronic DTCs are used, there is at least a one-day funding availability lag, although ledger credit for a DTC of either variety, initiated by the disbursing bank, can be posted to the account. This may not be attractive to a bank worried about how its own return on assets stacks up since such an entry is properly designated as a nonearning asset. Generally, banks ask customers using these funding devices to maintain an average balance equal to one day's disbursement amount as a form of protection against overdraft. Maintaining a line of credit is an alternative which can be immediately activated should the company fail to cover. If customers consistently fail to cover controlled disbursements, banks may begin to return checks presented against those accounts. Since banks generally do not profit from controlled disbursement accounts, why do they bother? To capture corporate credit business or to acquiesce to demanding customers with clout.

REMOTE, CONTROLLED, AND REMOTE/CONTROLLED DISBURSING AND THE FED

Controlled disbursement arrangements are clearly intended to take advantage of Fed check presentment schedules to nonFed-city banks; the early and scarce physical check presentments make the plan work. While cash managers contend that the purpose of these accounts is cash control, in many instances, the early presentment cutoffs function to extend check clearing float: checks that do not make the early morning cash letters, presented directly or at the morning meeting of the local clearing house, are held for next-day payment. That is one more day that cash managers can keep funds invested. Any clearing system slippage that occurs is over and above this extension of clearing float. Many controlled disbursement sites are located in second-tier cities such as Savannah, in relation to Atlanta. However, when a controlled disbursement account is established in a very obscure place, like Grand Junction, Colorado, to pay a Los Angeles firm's Tallahassee vendor, we have remote/controlled disbursement. Any disbursement account, not necessarily one driven by same-day funding reports, that is strategically located to thwart check presentments is a remote disbursement plan. Criss-cross disbursements are one variety: West Coast vendors are paid with East Coast bank checks and vice versa. Ironically, it is possible for a check deposited in New York to clear more quickly to Los Angeles than to Chicago; big bank direct sends are the reason. (See Chapter 4 for a discussion of private clearing arrangements.)

In 1979, the Federal Reserve Board declared war on remote disbursing, convinced, as it was, that this practice caused significant levels of Fed float. (See Chapter 3 for a discussion of the Fed's war on float.) The Fed clamped down by pressuring banks to refuse to allow corporate remote disbursing. Remote banks in places like Missoula, Montana soon felt the brunt of Fed attention and began to require that corporations demonstrate that they had good business reasons for establishing these off-beat disbursing accounts. Some banks looked the other way while corporations merely opened post office boxes in their towns.

The Fed did not let up. Squeezed by Senator William Proxmire's Banking Committee, whose efforts eventually produced the 1980 Depository Institutions Deregulation and Monetary Control Act, the Fed was urged to either eradicate or charge for outrageous levels of Fed float. Some of this float was caused by Fed operational problems, which have since been addressed, and some was caused by Fed policies of granting credit for large dollar checks before their actual collection. Previously unwilling to change availability schedules for competitive reasons, the Fed turned its wrath on controlled disbursement practices.

In the summer of 1982, the Fed announced its now famous "nooner proposal," a plan to extend until noon the earliest final presentment time for Fed-city items. The Fed also released plans to phase in later presentment schedules for country and RCPC items, a move which would destroy controlled disbursement as we know it. Further, the Fed announced a plan to modify availability schedules that, in effect, would push the costs of clearing system slippage onto banks and, ultimately, corporations (see Chapter 5). The Fed proposed that banks be given the option, among others, of paying for float with balances held at Fed District banks.

On February 24, 1983, the Fed moved to 11:00 A.M. its final presentment times for checks drawn on Fed-city banks. On May 2, 1983, this deadline was extended to noon, local time, for all city items. In July, 1983, the Fed extended the noon deadline for all country and RCPC points with certain criteria as yet undecided. The Fed hopes to eradicate much of its system float with these measures. Side effects will include slightly faster check availabilies nationwide for items cleared through the Fed, an event which will cause corporations to consider changes to collection systems; it will be possible to receive about the same speed of check collection through Fed systems as is now possible through expensive private direct sends. All this implies less disbursement float available to cash managers.

If the Fed proceeds with its idea of instituting electronic check collection for large dollar checks, controlled disbursement arrangements will be doubly affected by checks clearing at unmanageable hours during the banking day and less float benefit. The electronic check collection plan would send debit information to paying banks over the Fed wire network before actual presentment of the paper items days later. There are, however, numerous legal and operational dilemmas surrounding electronic check collection that cause analysts to predict that it cannot be implemented as conceived.

Dr. Steven F. Maier proposes that controlled disbursement can survive Fed actions if conducted in what he calls "an insulated environment." He states:

> Contrary to common belief, banks may not need to know the exact dollar amount of checks being presented for payment against each corporate account in the early morning. All the corporation really cares about is knowing the amount it must fund that day. Basically, the bank can devise a way to estimate daily funding requirements. Assume that the bank only knows 80% of the actual check clearings by the time it must notify the cash manager. Let us suppose that this comes to $80,000 on Monday. The bank then asks the corporation to fund $100,000, with the bank estimating that the items yet received will total $20,000. By the close of Monday, the bank discovers that daily clearings only totaled $90,000. The bank then gives the corporation an earnings credit for the extra $10,000. On Tuesday, the bank asks for a funding of $200,000, then finds at day's end that the corporation is deficient by $15,000: $215,000 in checks were actually presented that day. The bank then makes a loan for $15,000, charging an agreed upon rate for overnight borrowing. Over time, the overestimates balance out with the underestimates, assuming an unbiased forecast. The earnings credit rate for excess balances will probably equal the rate for funds loaned. The corporation will perceive this insulated control disbursing account as no different in either cost or operating characteristics from the "actual amount notification system" in current use.[109]

Dr. Maier further suggests that controlled disbursing accounts can function well when funded by bank-initiated paper or electronic DTCs, later Fed presentments notwithstanding. Again, banks will have to forecast daily funding needs in order to notify cash managers early in the day of checks clearing. Safety net balances would most likely be required. Dr. Maier also believes that Fed plans to provide payor banks with MICR line check data several hours before actual delivery of the items will allow controlled disbursing to flourish. As of this writing, the Federal Reserve Bank of Cleveland is already engaged in such a pilot program. The idea is that the Fed will sort out those checks destined for specific controlled disbursing accounts at individual banks and format that information onto magnetic tapes which are then electronically transmitted to the disbursing institutions. These tapes are created for the sole purpose of allowing the banks to notify customers of checks that will be arriving for payment later in the day. In effect, this plan will make it easier for smaller, regional banks with capable account reconciliation programs and computer savvy to get into the controlled disbursing business. Of course, the Fed will charge a hefty fee for its services; only those banks who can make it worth their while will be tempted to take on controlled disbursing in this manner.

PAYABLE THROUGH DRAFTS

Payable Through Drafts (PTDs), as we saw in Chapter 1, are checks drawn on corporations, not banks. Although they look like normal checks, they are payable only when presented to the issuer. Banks, though, act as clearing agents for these instruments, receiving them from the Fed and passing them on to corporations. After a company has approved drafts, it instructs its bank to transfer funds from another account to the draft account. If the company fails to cover drafts on a certain day because the bank was late in getting the drafts to the company for same-day inspection, which in the past was a common occurrence, the bank must carry the drafts on its general ledger as "drafts in the process of collection" or some similarly entitled asset account. Provided the company maintained a deposit balance equal to the total of drafts carried in the bank's books in this manner, and the bank had in its draft agreement the option to charge the company's account for these drafts, their total value may be excluded from the bank's deposit liability for reserve and insurance computations.[110] This all means that drafts present banks with unique operational and accounting problems if the company does not keep a back-up draft balance. Generally, banks dislike drafts because they require special handling procedures, and can create float at a bank's expense. Nonetheless, it is recognized that drafts provide a needed disbursement option for some companies; banks often reluctantly concede.

Traditionally, cash managers attempted to extend disbursement float with PTDs. It was possible to gain an extra day's float when banks used slow, manual processing systems. Recently, though, large banks have developed automated float tracking systems and are able to charge firms for float caused by drafts. Additionally, many banks now require companies to maintain compensating balances for drafts. Aside from float extension, PTDs help cash managers solve certain legal or administrative dilemmas when inspection before payment is necessary. One example of this occurs with an insurance claim settlement in which the payee's endorsement constitutes a release of the issuing company from further liability. PTDs are also used to cover the expenses of outlying corporate field units when no local company bank accounts exist. Cash managers can pay field representatives this way when main office approval is after the fact. PDTs also protect against account overdrafts or embezzlement.[111]

ELECTRONIC DISBURSEMENTS

The most widespread use of electronic disbursements by corporations involves direct deposit of payroll through ACH credit transactions. (See Chapter 6 for a discussion of ACH operations and Chapter 4 for a look at corporate experiments with ACH payments.) Direct deposit of payroll, like other ACH transfers, has a value-dating capability which enables the employer to initiate transactions several days before the "value-date," that is, the day that the funds are to be credited to an employee's account. This value-dating capability aids the corporation in spreading out, over time, the activities of its payroll department.[112]

Companies often use direct deposit as an employee benefit. Employees enjoy convenience and do not have to worry about stolen checks. Companies hope that the goodwill generated offsets the loss of disbursement float experienced with such programs. Disbursement float may be sacrificed because ACH transactions draw down company payroll accounts on payday, whereas in traditional payroll check systems, a percentage of the workforce can be expected to delay cashing their checks for several days. Hence, funds (in check programs) are available for company use longer.

Another strong incentive for companies to convert to electronic direct deposits is the rising costs of paper-based plans. Xerox Corporation claims to have been able to offset lost float with administrative savings realized with its direct deposit program.[113] But other companies find prohibitive both the cost of converting payroll accounting systems and, possibly, having to maintain dual systems. According to a section of the Electronic Funds Transfer Act, companies can require employees to accept direct deposit, although the company cannot dictate where the employee must bank.[114] Some corporations are unwilling to risk trouble with unions by mandating direct deposit, so they must consider dual systems if they go the direct deposit route. Eugene Lendler, an electronic funds transfer consultant, suggests that cash managers concerned about potential union hostility to direct deposit merely point out to union leaders that corporations *make money* on check disbursement float. Lendler also believes that unions may be more amenable to direct deposit when they understand the concept of guaranteed availability of ACH transactions. To wit, a worker who waits until Monday to cash his paycheck could lose out if the company goes bankrupt over the weekend and its bank accounts are frozen.

As we saw in Chapter 6, corporations have yet to embrace the notion of paying each other electronically, although the concept of negotiating credit terms in an electronic payment environment is generating interest. The bottom-line, so to speak, is the rising cost of paper-based payments. Beyond spiraling expenses for paper, postage, and processing, corporations can expect higher banking costs in the near future. This is a result of the enactment of the 1980 Monetary Control Act (see Chapter 4) which allowed the Fed to charge explicitly for its services. As we have seen earlier, the Fed is also planning to pass on to banks, and ultimately corporations, its float. Combined with a trend among banks to revamp their cost accounting procedures and to unbundle services—price products individually—these events spell an increasing expense to corporations for using paper-based systems. When corporations no longer economically benefit from disbursement float, and when costs for paper systems finally become unjustifiable, more companies will turn to electronic payments through the ACH.

Additionally, as automated corporate systems for managing information flows become integrated, we can expect financial managers to become more comfortable with computers and take electronic payments more seriously. It is important to understand that many corporations do not want to incur the risk of experimentation when it comes to financial systems. It is one thing to introduce a bold new product; it is quite another to undo tried-and-true methods of managing company funds. Like any new endeavor, the ACH has encountered natural user resistance. Beyond that, some early operational mishaps fueled the fears of cynics. The Amway foul-up is now a legend: inadvertently, a concentration debit tape was run twice one evening and hundreds of "mom and pop" type distributors had funds removed from their bank accounts twice. It took months to untangle the mess of bounced checks. Since then, improved safety and control measures have been implemented with ACH processing procedures. But many cash managers still looking for an excuse to ignore ACH benefits continue to cite the Amway story.

Analysts now look toward certain study groups for a glimpse into the future, which will no doubt contain electronic payments. The National Automated Clearing House Association, soon to begin a corporate-to-corporate trade payment pilot, is one. The other is the American National Standards Institute X-12 Committee, which is formulating standards for electronic business data interchange. Meanwhile, EFT experts, among them George C. White, are carrying the crusade to corporate cash managers.

THE EQUITABLE LIFE ASSURANCE SOCIETY AND EFTs

The Equitable Life Assurance Society of the United States has taken the lead in electronic funds transfer (EFT) innovation among insurance industry giants. In the 1970s, the Equitable found that the enormous volume of receipts and disbursements it handled monthly was becoming burdensome. Taking a proactive approach to business system efficiency and cost, the Equitable decided to try out ACH debits for collecting premium payments. By 1982, the firm boasted of a $150,000 annual reduction in banking expenses and approximately $40,000 added to pretax investment income, achieved by converting preauthorized checks to electronic debits.

Also since the 1970s, The Equitable has implemented ACH applications for group annuity credits, direct deposit of payroll, electronic DTCs, check truncation, and telephone bill payments. In 1982 alone, The Equitable processed almost 6.5 million EFT transactions; a 45% increase over 1981 volume and a 128% increase over 1980 traffic. The Equitable reported that it saved $.03 on every electronic debit processed compared to the paper version. Every electronic credit saved The Equitable approximately $.16 compared to the cost of preparing and mailing a check. This figure includes the cost of float lost because payees receive funds availability on the transaction value-date.

Almost 23% of Equitable's recurring group annuity payments, due on the first of each month, are now paid electronically. Beyond the cost savings, the company cites the following benefits:

Gained competitive edge.

Eliminated uncertainty of the postal system and early mailings that are required to meet contractual obligations. With ACH credits, the Equitable assures that payments are made on the proper date, not too soon, not too late.

Eliminated negative float that sometimes occurred when annuitants received and cashed checks before the due date.

The Equitable's Assistant Vice President for Cash Management, Bruce W. Reitz, Jr., contends that lost disbursement float is offset by savings. He correctly assumes that bank charges for paper payments will rise as the Fed goes forward with its float reduction plans. Mr. Reitz's department is years ahead of other cash management operations that may have to react rather suddenly to upheavals in bank service charges.

The Equitable now pays over 21% of its employees with direct deposit through the ACH. While this program cannot be justified by cost-savings, the company feels it is a worthwhile employee benefit. One unquantifiable savings is the time that employees have to take off from their work to cash paychecks. Mr. Reitz notes that it is important that payee banks be capable of flagging and handling direct deposit accounts. Some banks, especially savings institutions, have been known to inefficiently credit employee accounts; furthermore, tellers mistakenly announce that the company did not get the money in on time. The Equitable has also been experimenting with a plan for truncating—stopping—payroll checks at the bank of first deposit and sending data through the ACH. The company hopes for cost-savings in the future with such programs. Additionally, the company is trying out telephone bill payments from customers; it believes the experience gained with this pilot will provide valuable insight when customer initiated payment plans (GIROs: see Chapter 6) become popular, as is expected, later on in this decade.[115]

The Equitable's EFT and cash management successes can be attributed to a corporate culture that supports innovation. Treasury team leaders, William Herzog and Ray McCron, have been responsible for putting together an operation that is a gleam in the eye of top management. The Equitable's approach to cash concentration involves four regional treasury centers that perform independent remittance processing and speed the flow of cash. The result is that the firm invests an average of $120 million daily. In fact, the concentration system worked so well by 1981 that The Equitable sought permission from the New York Insurance Commission to package and sell its processing muscle to other corporations. Robert Field, formerly with The Equitable and now a Chase Manhattan Bank vice president, helped develop a classy automated forecasting system that kept track of company cashflows and allocation needs.

A willingness to try electronic funds transfers, combined with a solid grasp of cash management techniques, can bring corporations many rewards, like those witnessed at The Equitable. Foresight is probably the key to success in this regard. All we have to do is look at the world of electronics quickly unfolding around us to realize that today's teenagers, addicted to computer games, will have no trouble accepting consumer electronic banking a few years down the road. Industries that have heavy retail customer bases are those that will turn quickly to electronics as the costs of paper transactions soar in the next few years.

9 Short-Term Cash Forecasting and Investing

The worst time to raise cash is when you need it most. It is an irony of life that banks do not like to lend to companies that cannot pay for services. The corporation that unwisely manages its levels of operating cash can appear healthy, show steady profits, and project a bright future but be illiquid—unable to meet its immediate obligations to suppliers, lenders, and the Internal Revenue Service, among others. That firm might need just a one-time infusion to "get it over the hump." Bankers know better. The company that cannot predict and plan its short-term cashflows simply does not have a handle on reality. Smart cash managers have learned to forecast cashflows for this reason.

PURPOSES OF CASH FORECASTING

The cash manager is concerned with the very near term: will the company be in an overdraft position in the next two weeks, or will $2 million be left unattended, earning zero interest for the next five days? While the monthly cash budget figures may indicate that cash inflows and cash outflows for the next 30 days will be equivalent—receipts equal disbursements—the cash manager knows to look closer. He inspects what will come in, what will go out, the scheduled dates for each and, more importantly, when will checks clear. As we have seen earlier, the cash manager must work from bank balances, as well as from company accounting records. If he fails to do this, company books may show that a large payment from a supplier has been recorded on the fifth of the month, but the bank balance will not show usable funds until, possibly, the tenth of the month. Throw in a bank holiday, a snowstorm, and the fact that the supplier is practicing remote disbursing and available funds may be delayed three more days. While the monthly, quarterly, or yearly budgets, prepared for accounting purposes, predict gross receipts and disbursements, they ignore the importance of the timing of cash transactions during a given period. The cash manager's daily forecast focus, however, is when receipts or disbursements cause bank balances to change.

Cash managers attempt to predict, then react to, future short-term cash positions: what will the available balances be daily, weekly, or monthly? He first collects information on planned receipts and disbursements three months out. He uses either nonstatistical or statistical modeling techniques for computing:

Receipts.   Cash sales, cash from accounts and notes receivable, sales of assets, investment proceeds, and entries of this nature.

Disbursements.   Payrolls, maturing debt, interest expense, large purchases, other expenses, taxes, and the like.

For the first month, the cash manager breaks down data into very detailed components. For instance, he may segregate transactions that behave differently: retail versus wholesale collections or different classes of trade payables.[116] This is an operational forecast from which he can analyze schedules for forecasted receipts and disbursements and then proportionally assign by day cashflows according to patterns of check clearings and presentations. He can also scale up or down this estimated distribution to account for variances he knows tend to show up. This activity provides a workable estimate of daily cash deficiencies or excesses. He will then be prepared to take action: either invest excesses temporarily or draw on a credit line to cover short-falls.

The forecasts for the second and third months do not require as much detail as the first month. Usually, the second and third month data are used as planning forecasts. They give the cash manager a more general idea of his cash requirements so that potential investments or cash needs can be anticipated. These forecasts should be updated weekly or biweekly to give the cash manager additional information and permit him to adjust his cash strategy to accommodate changing corporate requirements.[117] For instance, the cash manager at a hotel chain may see that sales forecasts from hotel managers in Florida indicate a big jump in revenues for an otherwise lackluster month. (In two months, the space shuttle is being launched with a noted celebrity as the first commercial passenger.) By looking ahead, the cash manager knows that he will have a large amount of extra cash on hand. He can then methodically decide the best use for that money.

TIME HORIZONS AND METHODOLOGY

Short-Term

Forecasting cash positions by day, weeks, and months is called short-term transaction planning. Here, the cash manager is primarily concerned with the next three months, with the first month broken down into an operational forecast that contains two-week components further detailed by expected daily transactions. The short-term forecast estimates the available bank balances in major accounts and allows for aggregate cash position management. The goals of short-term cash planning include:

Minimizing temporarily idle funds.

Avoiding over- or undercompensating banks with balances.

Matching the maturity schedules of very short-term investments with predicted funding requirements.

Being able to take advantage of cash discounts or reduced prices for supplies.

We will see below how forecasted receipts and disbursements data can be collected and put into a cash transaction framework useful to the cash manager.

Medium-Term

This is a planning forecast that typically extends up to one year and is broken down into months or quarters. Its focus is to provide input for making capital expenditure decisions, to evaluate the effects of alternative courses of action, and to monitor and react to shifts in sales projections and related trade credit changes. This forecast produces expected changes in accounting data. As such, it centers on the company's own books, rather than on bank balances. For example, a company may know that it intends to sell a piece of equipment or property in six months. Therefore, it will incorporate into the medium-term forecast the expected level of proceeds from this sale. Or a company may be able to prepare for seasonal cashflow fluctuations; more sales in a certain quarter can mean more tax liability.

The medium-term forecast is basically a control tool and keeps a corporation grounded in the financial realities of business enterprise. A market power play that promises a sensational profit picture can be quickly sobered up with the financial perspective that the medium-term forecast provides. Potential cashflow crises can be diagnosed and dealt with. This look ahead can also give the cash manager room to strategically plan short-term borrowing; he can shop for the best rates among his lending banks when he knows what he needs when, and how he can pay for it.

While the short-term transaction forecast considers receipts and disbursements and their relationships to bank balances, a common approach to formulating the medium-term forecast involves the *adjusted net income method*. Needed data come from accounting and budget sources and produce a balance sheet or funds statement forecast. Net income is predicted with noncash expenses, such as depreciation, added back in. From this total, changes in noncash items of the balance sheet are forecast, with cash assuming the form of the balancing item.[118] Because the adjusted net income method considers changes in company assets rather than daily cash transactions, it allows for a wide view of the financial health of the firm. For instance, an increase in accounts payable means an increase in a source of company funds for a certain accounting period. So, the medium-term forecast is used to predict the net income for an accounting period, one year or less, adjusted for depreciation. It depicts accounting events which will affect the level of cash available to operate the company.

It is important to realize that certain accounting data are forecasted—

for instance, sales figures. Sales may be forecast using the subjective method, trend forecasts, or causal means of estimation. Subjective sales forecasts are based on the forecaster's experience, knowledge of his industry, and sense of economic variables. It is a "gut feel," and surprisingly accurate. Trend forecasts, also known as "time series analyses," extrapolate past trends in order to produce a projection. Refinements of this technique can include adjustments for seasonal or cyclical variations. Causal sales forecasting methods try to identify the underlying determinants of sales in a formal statistical model. The forecaster examines a variety of numerical relationships from the past in order to formulate a causal model.[119] For an in-depth discussion of these topics, refer to *The Financial Handbook, Fifth Edition*.

Long-Term

Typically developed to look ahead for up to five years, the long-term forecast can be broken down by year, or two-year components detailed by quarters. The five-year time span is generally the maximum realistic forecast period due to the greater level of uncertainties involved. As a result, only a minimum level of detail is required.[120] The long-term forecast helps a company prepare for growth because it predicts long-term financing requirements in light of business goals. This forecast considers the state of the economy, money supply, and such factors as expected consumer habits. It allows for long-term policy formulation, as well as a protracted sense of financial health given simulated courses of action and funds flows. The adjusted net income method can be used to develop the long-term forecast.

APPROACHES TO FORECASTING

As stated earlier, the cash manager is primarily concerned with available cash positions in the immediate future. To predict these, he considers how much money the company will receive and how much it will disburse for, say, the coming three months. He then breaks the nearest month down into an operational forecast which predicts when receipts actually become usable funds at the bank and when disbursements are presented for payment at disbursing accounts.

A very simple forecast for the second or third month may look like this:

Starting cash balance:	$50,000
Cash inflows:	
accounts receivables	70,000
sales of fixed assets	10,000
Total cash inflow:	80,000
Cash outflows:	
payroll	30,000
vendor invoices	10,000
other expenses	15,000
taxes	25,000
Total cash outflows:	80,000
Ending cash balance:	$50,000

The operational forecast looks similar except that it shows projected cash inflows and outflows and beginning and ending cash balances for each day, possibly for a two-week span. The trick is to forecast each item so that actual cashflows are approximated. This involves relating expected receipts to increases in available balances and scheduled disbursements to decreases in available balances. For example, the cash manager may predict daily deposits based on field-unit sales forecasts. Knowledge of check availability schedules tells him when clearings will be consummated. This is a nonstatistical approach. A statistical approach can also be used to extrapolate future sales, based on historical trends and the assumption that business will continue as usual. The cash manager then relates this data to known check clearing patterns and arrives at estimated cashflows that will change bank balances.

It is much easier to forecast disbursements than receipts because the cash manager can rely on internal information and knowledge of payment policy in order to determine what needs to be paid when. He also has control: if he does not make a payment, then an outflow will not take place. Receipts flows, on the other hand, depend on outside persons taking action, including customers writing and mailing checks, or field units depositing daily proceeds. Very large corporations take a variety of approaches to developing the daily operational forecast, depending on the accounting structure of their organizations. These include:

Information Transformation. Scheduling cashflow implications according to internally available data, possibly invoices or purchase orders for disbursements and order entry or aged receivables data for receipts. Check clearing patterns may be garnered from bank availability schedules or account reconciliation programs.

Distribution. Spreading a total period's cashflow out over the days in that period according to a mathematical formula.

Combined Scheduling and Distribution. This done in accordance with a pattern of check clearing times.[121]

Trend Extrapolation. Assuming that past trends will continue, the future is predicted, often using formal statistical estimation that considers patterns, pattern changes, and disturbances caused by random influences.

Seasonality and Cyclical Change. Accounting for seasonal or cyclical fluctuations based on past variations, often using mathematical equations or models.

Drs. Bernell K. Stone and Thomas W. Miller, in *Daily Cash Forecasting: A Structuring Framework,* suggest a four-step approach to daily cash forecasting: problem structuring, approach selection, measurement modeling, and statistical technique selection. They discuss separating major from nonmajor cashflows, breaking nonmajor flows into components, and determining flow sequence detail and informations systems support. They differentiate between forecast and estimation modeling; and propose working backward from the forecast problem and company situation to arrive at the proper selection of techniques—for example, regression analysis or Box-Jenkins.[122]

Accurate cashflow forecasting hinges on the forecaster's ability to reduce the amount of observed error between forecast values and actual values that have occurred. Devising procedures for updating forecast models is crucial. This must be done on a regular basis or else forecast results will become increasingly irrelevant.[123]

CASH PLANNING

Determining how to adjust cash balances to an optimum level is called cash planning. To do this, the cash manager first computes an appropriate cash level, then figures how he will bring balances to this level. Developing the daily operational cash forecast provides data on how much cash will be in bank accounts and how much will be needed on given days. With this activity, the cash manager accommodates transaction flows. But he may also want to leave small amounts of contingency funds on hand. He may consider past deviations from target balances and leave enough to cover a typical but small spread. He also has to figure in levels of compensating balances, if any, and build them into his cash plan.

For each day in the cash plan, then, the cash manager computes an appropriate target for the opening balance by adding together the amount needed to cover daily cash transactions and the amounts needed for contingencies and compensation. If the daily opening balance is above the day's appropriate target, he then has an excess to use for investment, bank compensation, or debt reduction. If the daily opening balance is deficient, the cash manager knows to take action to prevent short-falls. He can perform the same analyses to determine optimum levels of cash balances on a monthly basis. Thus, for each day or month, the cash manager produces a cash plan which shows how the respective opening balances are adjusted by increases or decreases in short-term debt or investment.

CASH FORECASTING: THE LINK TO INVESTMENT STRATEGY

We have seen how the mechanics of cash management work to hasten the flow of cash receipts and control and to slow the flow of disbursements. We have described the cash forecasting function and have considered how cash managers prepare for changes to daily bank balances caused by expected cashflows. A cash management imperative is that idle excess balances represent an opportunity cost to the firm; ignoring investment possibilities, even for one day, is inconsistent with the objective of managing cash as an asset that must return value to the company. Our next logical focus is short-term investment strategies, their goals and guidelines. Various money market instruments and their characteristics will be reviewed.

It is important, first, to realize that maximizing the use of company funds depends on reliable forecasts of daily cash positions. The cash manager cannot effectively organize a short-term investing (or borrowing) plan unless he can accurately estimate his day's closing balance in time to enter the money market before noon New York Time, (a fact of life that puts a special burden on West Coast cash managers and banks.) Planning the day's investments begins first thing every morning. The cash manager relies on his operational forecast and reports on yesterday's final closing balance in order to estimate the day's closing balance. In effect, he predicts how much money he will have to invest, even for just one day, or how much he will have to borrow, even for just one day, in order to maintain liquidity and keep excess cash productive.

Since bank computers cannot finish posting a day's total debits and credits to a corporate account until the early hours of the next morning, the cash manager needs to forecast each day's closing balance so as to coordinate the investment function. But, he also needs to update the daily forecast with reports on yesterday's final closing ledger, and, possibly, collected balances. This fine-tunes the daily estimate. Some balance reporting systems are truly automated and work like this. The cash manager's computer is programmed to automatically telephone the concentration bank, or other data collector, and communicate directly with a computer there. The bank or vendor computer then transmits to the corporate computer data on final closing balances. This goes on around 6:00 A.M. When the cash manager arrives at the office, his computer has already printed out the balance reports. The use of sophisticated technology makes the cash manager's task easier but accurate forecasting is the backbone of short-term investing.

When we consider various money market instruments and how they are bought and sold, we will see that the margin of success in short-term investing often depends on timing and an ability to obtain the best possible rates on instruments approved by company guidelines. This implies that an effective investment strategy is not conducted in a crisis atmosphere. The cash manager who discovers at 2:00 P.M. an unexpected $2 million excess may have to scramble to place that money in an instrument that returns a decent yield and meets policy safety requirements. The cash manager who can predict the excess even one day before its arrival is in a better position to shop for the best rates on safe instruments.

Conversely, if the cash manager knows, from forecast reports, that he will be in a deficit cash position by the end of the day, he can prepare to raise funds, for instance, by issuing commercial paper, in an organized fashion. He can begin the placement process early in the day. If he has not started the placement effort by at least noon, his chances of securing borrowed funds at a reasonable cost diminish. Forecast reports also tell the cash manager how long a net excess or deficit cash position will last. Although there will be times when the cash forecast fails to predict a significant cashflow, the cash manager with a reliable forecast mechanism is bound to come out ahead over time.

SHORT-TERM PORTFOLIO MANAGEMENT

In most corporations, the cash management staff is responsible for short-term investing. One reason for this is that the cash manager has "hands-on" knowledge of the money market and its players. In connection with other tasks, the cash manager discerns which banks have sound management and competent personnel, as well as solid financial structure. Also in his capacity as manager of bank relationships and compensation, he is aware of short-term rate behavior. Furthermore, the cash manager is most suited to implement short-term investment strategies because he is the person most closely in tune with daily bank balance movements. While the accounting department is concerned with receipts and disbursements for financial reporting purposes, the cash manager considers when bank balances can be accessed for deployment. He also has information systems installed which deliver external data on company balances; sometimes, balance reporting systems have the ability to deliver current money market rates and allow the cash manager to initiate wire transfers. In essence, the cash manager is equipped, and psychologically geared, to react to fast-breaking investment opportunities. He and his staff are used to thinking in terms of very short time windows, days and hours. In the investment world, that is when profits are made, and fortunes lost.

The term "money market" refers to the marketplace where borrowers and lenders exchange short-term funds. As such, the money market does not exist in one unique location. Instead it is a complex of thousands of locations across the world where purchases and sales of short-term funds take place.[124] Most transactions are negotiated by telephone. The average transaction size is $100,000. If a corporation is purchasing or selling short-term securities, it can go directly to a transaction partner or work through an intermediary which may be a bank, government security dealer, or brokerage firm. Successful investing often depends on knowing who is willing to buy or sell a certain instrument at a given time. Cash managers who frequently participate in the money market know which banks, brokers, or dealers specialize in certain securities and which intermediaries are willing to work hard at hunting down desired instruments. Cash managers unfamiliar with the money market often ask their banks to help them find appropriate trading partners.

Short-term investing involves buying instruments whose lives extend one year or less. Because the cash manager generally forecasts only three months out, his investment horizon is generally 90 days. Suppose a cash manager buys a three-month Treasury bill on March 1. On April 1, his updated operational forecast reveals a need for cash in two weeks. To avoid a cash short-fall, the cash manager sells the Treasury bill in the secondary market through a bank, broker, or dealer. Most likely, he does not sacrifice any principal by selling the security before its maturing date.

Much investment activity centers on placing funds in interest-earning mediums for only a few days. Overnight investing, on a regular basis, can bring in earnings which justify the effort. When we consider the enormous energy that goes into speeding or slowing cashflows for mere portions of days, we realize that astute cash managers are those who leave work each day knowing that bank balances are minimal and all excess funds are busy earning interest, even if only for one day.

INVESTMENT RISKS AND RETURNS

It is a fact of life that few rewards, especially economic profits, are free. When we lend someone money and charge interest, in essence we are exchanging return for risk. Investors of all stripes know that risky investments, relative to other available options, can be expected to yield more return at maturity. The shakier the investment—the more risk that principal will be lost—the higher the stakes. Investment guidelines, which we will discuss later, are used to outline how much risk a cash manager can incur on behalf of his firm. For the most part, the cash manager is primarily concerned with preserving principal. Although he hopes for the best returns on short-term investments, he looks for instruments that are, above all, safe. Safe investments are those that carry no threat that principal will be lost. His job does not require that he gamble excessively for yield; his objective is only to keep excess funds productive.

Secondly, cash managers are responsible for keeping the company in a liquid position. If an unexpected need for cash should arise, the cash manager may need to sell investments before planned. Thus, an important criterion for a short-term investment strategy is instrument marketability. The cash manager would sooner sacrifice some degree of expected profit than be unable to meet obligations. When we review various instruments, we will see that Treasury bills are popular with cash managers because they can be easily sold—they have what is called "an active secondary market." In addition, the cash manager who sells a Treasury bill in the secondary market usually experiences little or no loss of capital. Treasury bills are safe, but low-yielding, compared to other short-term investments. However, investments that are not easy to liquidate command relatively higher yields in order to attract investors since, generally, any money market investment can be sold if enough price concession is given. There are several notorious exceptions to this rule of thumb; one is the 1970 failure of Penn Central. In that case, holders of commercial paper were stuck with illiquid assets.

Finally, yield—an investment's earning power expressed as an effective rate of return—completes the basis on which cash managers compare options. The risks associated with a certain investment determines its safety, marketability, and, hence, its yield. We will consider the nature of various investment risks to gain a sense of their effect on investment strategy.

Risks

Default Risk. Sometimes called financial risk, default risk is the threat that a debt issuer will fail to pay off the principal and interest on borrowed funds, and this must be considered by cash managers. Although no security is entirely default free, U.S. Treasury securities are generally defined as riskless in this sense because they are guaranteed by the U.S. government.

As such, Treasury bills and notes are often used as a standard for determining the risk premium of other short-term investments. To assist the cash manager in making short-term investments, other than in Treasury securities, the quality of corporate and municipal securities is graded by such investment rating services as Moody's and Standard & Poor's. Other money market instruments, such as bank certificates of deposit, are graded by certain large investors and market specialists, such as dealers and brokers.[125] Risk of default may be measured according to an issuer's financial stability, its handle on cashflows, and its management competency. Credit risk is the threat that the debt issuer cannot pay off all principal and interest at maturity.

Market Risk. Sometimes called interest rate risk, this is the threat that principal and/or return on a fixed-return security will be endangered if that investment vehicle has to be sold before maturity. This risk is a function of interest rate movements. Upon liquidation, some principal or return may have to be sacrificed when the market value of a fixed-return instrument is diminished because new securities entering the market command higher interest rates.

Lost Income Risk. During periods of high interest rates, the investor has the chance to "lock-in" high rates for long periods of time. Should the maturity of the investment be too short, the investor may find no vechicle available that offers the same high rate of return as that available on the original investment.[126]

Country Risk. Applicable to investments overseas, this is the threat that a foreign government will interfere with the movement or repatriation of U.S. dollars deposited in a bank located outside the United States. Foreign governmental instability or international hostilities contribute to sovereign risk, the threat that foreign deposits will be seized during a political upheaval.

MONEY MARKET INSTRUMENTS

Treasury Bills

Called "T bills," these are direct obligations of the U.S. government that are sold in minimum amounts of $10,000 and in multiples of $5000 above the minimum. They are sold on a discounted basis and calculated on actual days on a 360-day basis to pay par at maturity. Using readily available statistical tables, the cash manager converts the discount rate on T bills to the approximate yield of interest-bearing instruments. Because T bills are purchased at a discount and paid off at par, the lower the price, the higher the yield to the buyer or holder.

T bills come in several varieties: one that matures in 91 days (13 weeks) is called a three-month T bill; one that matures in 182 days (26 weeks) is called a six-month T bill; and one that matures in one year from issue (52 weeks) is called a "year" T bill. This terminology is used to describe T bills most recently issued. Once a new bill has been issued, the old bill is identified by its maturity date.[127]

Treasury bills are auctioned by the U.S. Treasury and both competitive and noncompetitive bids are accepted. A person who submits a noncompetitive bid is paid the average of all the competitive bids. Three-and six-month T bills are auctioned every Monday with settlement taking place the next Thursday. Every four weeks, an auction is held for year T bills. The year-bill auction is announced every fourth Friday (for exact dates, check with your local Federal Reserve Bank), auctioned the following Thursday and settled the next Thursday.[128] Procedures may vary among Federal Reserve Banks. T bills may be purchased without service charge from any of the 12 Federal Reserve District Banks or their branches. They are also available from the U.S. Treasury Department, Bureau of Public Debt. New T bills may be purchased through commercial banks or other financial intermediaries; there is usually a service charge attached to this effort. Previously issued T bills may be obtained privately or in the money market from a commercial bank or dealer. Interest earned from a T bill is exempt from local and state taxes, but it is subject to federal income tax.

After T bills are issued, a round lot trade in the secondary market is $5 million, but trades can be executed for as little as $10,000 at some concession to the round lot rate. Most institutions charge an odd lot fee for transactions less than $100,000.

T bills are issued in book entry form. An investor receives a statement of account, rather than an engraved certificate, as evidence of purchase. Ownership of bills is recorded in an established account at the Treasury, and statements are mailed four to six weeks after issue date. Accounts for book-entry T bills may be held in the names of fiduciaries or other entities. The investor pays the full face value of the T bill on auction date, and the Treasury mails a refund shortly thereafter for the amount of the difference between the face value and the issue price determined at the auction. Redemption of T bills recorded on Fed books is automatic at the maturity date, and the Treasury mails the investor a check. If the investment was made through a bank or dealer, payment is made in accordance with provisions stated by the investor on the purchase date. Sales of T bills before maturity are accomplished through Fed Wire transfers to commercial bank accounts held at the local Federal Reserve Bank.

Funds may be rolled over into a new T bill automatically at the maturity date as long as the investor requests this each time a bill matures. Proceeds of maturing bills can be rolled over on a noncompetitive bid basis into new bills that have an issue date corresponding to the maturity date of the old bills. One-year bills, at maturity, can be reinvested in either three-month, six-month, or one-year issues. Both the three-month and six-month bills can be reinvested into new three-month or six-month issues and may be rolled over into one-year bills when maturity dates coincide with new issue dates. The Treasury mails checks for discounts on the issue date of the new bills to pay the investor the difference between the face amounts of the maturing bills and the issue prices of the new bills.[129]

T bill yields become the base rate for all other money market instruments since there is no perceived risk associated with these government obligations. As the money market perceives a higher default or credit risk or less marketability for another investment vehicle of comparable maturity, its yield will be correspondingly higher. For instance, if a six-month T bill yields 10%, while a six-month domestic certificate of deposit yields 12%, the two percent differential reflects the higher risk or lower liquidity for the latter instrument. Cash managers find T bills to be handy short-term investment vehicles because they can schedule the maturity dates of weekly issues according to anticipated cash needs. Above all, T bills are the safest instruments in the money market, albeit the lowest yielding. The active secondary market for T bills gives corporate investors the confidence that invested funds can be accessed quickly and easily.

In addition to T bills, the Treasury sometimes issues shorter maturity bills on an as-needed basis. These are called cash management bills and usually have a minimum size of $1 million.[130] Of course, the Treasury issues longer-term securities: notes and bonds. Notes have a fixed maturity of not less than one year and not more than ten years from issue date. Bonds normally have a fixed maturity of more than ten years. For the most part, cash managers invest in T bills because they have short-term maturities.

Commercial Paper

Commercial paper issues are also money market instruments. These are unsecured promissory notes of corporations or financial companies that have extremely high credit ratings. The debt is issued to finance current transactions, providing needed short-term funds. Maturities on commercial paper can range from one to 270 days; however, the typical maturity period is between 15 and 45 days. Usually, commercial paper is issued in $100,000 minimums, although some borrowers will offer issues as small as $25,000. The average purchase size is often $1 million.

Commercial paper issued by a financial entity can be either bank or nonbank related. Bank-related commercial paper is issued by bank holding companies to support lending and leasing activities. Nonbank financial companies that issue commercial paper typically do so constantly to support consumer financing.

There are two kinds of commercial paper. Directly placed commercial paper is issued expressly by the corporation (or finance company or bank holding company) to the investor. The investor contacts an intermediary, generally a bank, that has been approved by the issuer to act in an agent capacity. Dealer placed commercial paper is marketed and distributed by a securities dealer who charges the issuer a commission. Dealer commissions are generally one eighth of one percent of the paper's face value.[131]

There is no secondary market for commercial paper, although many direct issuers have some form of prepayment option. Sometimes, dealers will buy back commercial paper at prevailing market rates. For the most part, commercial paper is held to maturity. Commercial paper is the only short-term instrument with a credit rating. Credit ratings are assigned by Moody's (P–1, P–2, P–3), Standard & Poor's (A–1, A–2, A–3) and Fitch Publishing Company (F–1, F–2, F–3). Commercial paper issues should have, at least, the second rating category to be seriously considered in the money market.[132] The rating agencies do not guarantee the accuracy of their reports, nor the creditworthiness of the issuer; they merely appraise the quality of specific debt issues. Of course, the rating agencies charge issuing companies for their services; these fees can range up to $35,000. Since the Penn Central Railroad failure in 1970, which left many investors with worthless paper, there has evolved the practice of backing commercial paper issues with bank lines of credit. In fact, to be given a rating these days, commercial paper issues have to have back-up credit lines. Institutional investors often conduct their own research on specific issues and look to the rating agencies to provide a bellwether of debt quality.

Repurchase Agreements

Repurchase agreements (repos) offer money market investors another outlet for short-term excess cash. In this arrangement, securities are sold under an agreement that the seller will repurchase the same securities at a given future time at the same price plus interest. These deals provide corporate investors with a way to earn interest on surplus funds for as little as one day. Repo deals are typically made for no longer than five days although, recently, there have been instances where repo maturities lasted up to one year. The interest rates on such transactions are negotiated between buyer and seller the day the deal is made. In effect, since securities are pledged as collateral within an exchange of funds, these transactions are collateralized loans of a fixed maturity at a fixed interest rate. Funds acquired through repo arrangements are available to the seller of securities, the borrower, the day the deal is struck.

Securities that are exchanged in repo agreements are usually U.S. government or agency issues. A trend in recent years, however, has been to use other items, such as bank certificates of deposit, corporate bonds, or gold as collateral.[133] This kind of collateral is considered less marketable than government issues; as such, interest rates are higher for this type of repo. Also, securities that have relatively long maturities, sometimes rendering them less marketable, command better yields than those with short maturities. Securities purchased in a repo deal often provide better rates than an investor can obtain in the outright purchase of the same securities. This rate differential protects the buyer in case the seller defaults on the repurchase and the securities have to be liquidated in the market.

Repos had enjoyed enormous popularity among corporate investors until 1982 when a New York bankruptcy court ruled that such arrangements represent collateralized loans, not securities purchases. If the ruling stands, it is possible that funds invested in repos could be tied up in bankruptcy proceedings for indefinite periods should a dealer issuing repos go bankrupt. The case in question involved the government securities dealer, Lombard Wall, that became insolvent overnight. Cash managers have reacted to this ruling by diversifying their repo investments among various dealers.[134] In the meantime, there are lobbying efforts underway for Congressional action that would mitigate the court ruling.

Borrowing through one-day repo arrangements provides securities dealers with a primary source of funds, used to finance trading positions. Commercial banks use repos to finance inventories of government securities. Banks enter into repo deals when one-day repo rates are below the Federal Funds rate (the overnight cost of funds exchanged among banks to meet Federal Reserve balance requirements).[135] The Federal Reserve System also participates actively in the repo market as a means of controlling the level of bank reserves and, hence, the money supply. Nonfinancial corporations, state and local governments, and insurance companies also borrow short-term in the repo market. These entities find repo rates to be lower than those on commercial paper debt issues and bank loans.

Repos are handy investments because the transaction terms can be construed to match a corporation's short-term excess cash position. While securities dealers typically require repo transactions to be at $1 million minimums, commercial banks may enter into a repo deal for as little as $100,000. Repos are generally purchased from large commercial banks although some small regional banks get into the repo market as a means of keeping corporate customers satisfied. Once a lender has exchanged funds for securities in a repo deal, he may then enter into a reverse repo transaction in which he temporarily sells the securities if he needs cash before the original repo matures.

Certificates of Deposit

Bank certificates of deposit are another popular short-term investment. Called CDs, these are time deposit obligations of banks. While most CDs are issued by large commercial banks, occasionally a savings and loan institution will issue them. CDs issued in bearer form, the most popular, are termed negotiable while those issued in registered form are considered nonnegotiable. Instruments of this nature issued by banks chartered in the U.S. are known as domestic CDs. Those issued by foreign banks or U.S. banks located overseas and denominated in dollars are Eurodollar CDs. Such obligations issued in the U.S. by branches of foreign banks are called Yankee CDs.

Domestic CDs.   The purchase minimum for domestic CDs is $100,000. Interest rates are negotiated between buyer and bank but are influenced by market trends. Rates may be either fixed or variable. There is a minimum 14-day maturity requirement, but most issues are for six months or less. Corporate investors are able to obtain CDs for precisely as long as they anticipate an excess cash position. CDs must be paid for with immediately available funds; they are likewise redeemed on their respective maturity dates.

Most domestic CDs are issued by large money center and regional banks. When issues are large, a bank may elect to work through a securities dealer located in New York City. A regional bank interested in selling CDs to a national as well as local constituency may issue the obligations through a New York correspondent. For the most part, investors in CDs tend to patronize the giant money center banks. They feel secure knowing that the bank behind the issue has a large asset structure.[136] This is compounded by the fact that FDIC insurance covers only the first $100,000. Therefore, because of high demand, the rates available on CDs issued by the large, well-known money center banks are generally slightly lower than rates offered by smaller regional banks.

There is a secondary market for CDs, and such trades are typically executed in round lots of $5 million. Sometimes dealers can effect secondary market trades for $1 million, although a five to ten basis-point concession is generally required. (There are 100 basis-points in a single percentage point of interest.) What determines the price of a CD sold in the secondary market is, as with other marketable instruments, the underlying creditworthiness of the issuer and the debt's maturity date. Moreover, CDs issued by the large money center banks for six months or less are more easily liquidated than CDs issued by small, unknown regional banks. While registered CDs are technically negotiable, there is, in fact, virtually no secondary market for these instruments because of the administrative steps necessary to effect ownership changes.

Eurodollar CDs.   As previously noted, Eurodollar CDs are dollar denominated deposit obligations issued by U.S. and foreign banks located overseas. Interest is paid at a set rate for a specific period of time. The market for these instruments is centered in London where the instruments are usually housed and dollar settlements are normally made. Settlement can also be made in New York. There is a $1 million minimum and a minimum 30-day maturity requirement. Interest payments are based on actual days on a 360-day basis.

Large multinational corporations that manage global investment portfolios are frequent buyers of Eurodollar CDs. As well, large domestic corporations and other institutional investors include Eurodollar CDs in their investment portfolios because these instruments typically provide slightly higher yields than domestic CDs. But international banks are, by far, the biggest customers for these instruments.

The rate spread is due to the nature of the Eurodollar market. It is a highly competitive arena that, compared to the U.S. banking system, is relatively free of interest rate restriction and regulation. Participating banks are not burdened by Federal Reserve balance requirements which, in this country, reduce the amount of investable funds that banks have at their disposal. International banks compete fiercely for funds in this area to support lending activity. The market's velocity, combined with the absence of intervening regulatory bodies, contribute to the perception that these instruments are riskier than their domestic counterparts. In addition, because there is no international monetary authority to rescue a failing bank, as the Federal Reserve might do if a U.S. bank were troubled, investors do not feel any ultimate security with Eurodollar CDs. Another applicable risk involves the fact that a U.S. bank holding company is not liable for the debts of its subsidiaries; if a London branch of a huge U.S. parent went under, the parent is not obligated to pay the subsidiary's debt. Investors discount this by assuming, correctly, that an internationally respected U.S. banking entity would not dare allow such a scenario to unfold. A final risk is the threat that a foreign government would interfere with the repatriation of the investment. Added together, these concerns make Eurodollar CDs less secure than domestic CDs. As a result, the yields are more attractive. This is an investment for savvy cash managers able to sort out the risks compared to the potential economic benefit.

There is an active secondary market for Eurodollar CDs with maturities six months or less. Round lot transactions typically trade at $5 million. While this secondary market is active, it is slightly thinner than the resale market for domestic CDs.

Another form of Eurodollar investment is the fixed-rate time deposit which represents an obligation of very large banks, both U.S. and foreign, located overseas. Typical investments are made at $1 million minimums for at least one day and the obligations reside in the bank's London branch. Since no debt instrument is issued, there is obviously no secondary market and, hence, no liquidity.[137]

Yankee CDs. Yankee CDs is the phrase that refers to interest-bearing obligations of non-U.S. banks issued in the United States by foreign banks. These are negotiable instruments issued in $1 million minimums for at least 30 days. Debtors are usually large banks from Western Europe or Japan; Yankee CDs are available from the New York branches or subsidiaries of these institutions. Risk associated with this type of debt is assessed according to the creditworthiness of the parent banking entity, its financial structure, and its strength. Investors, therefore, perceive Yankee CDs to be relatively more risky than other instruments. As such, they provide yields that are generally a bit higher than domestic CDs and Eurodollar CDs. Secondary market trades often involve $1 million minimums, but prices vary according to periodic supply and demand and the reputation of the originating bank.

Bankers' Acceptances. Another money market instrument is the Banker's Acceptance (BA). This instrument is a negotiable time draft, drawn on a bank, either U.S. or foreign, that the bank promises to honor at an agreed upon date in the future. The BA specifies an amount that both the bank and the buying party to a commercial transaction are obliged to pay later, although this device, in effect, replaces the buyer's credit with the bank's credit. BAs are used to facilitate international trade, but can be used domestically as well. For example, if a seller agrees to deliver goods to a buyer in six months, he can go to his bank, the buyer's bank or a bank familiar with the creditworthiness of the buyer, and ask the bank to "accept" the responsibility for honoring a time draft dated six months hence.

Once a BA has been stamped "accepted" by a bank, it may be sold in the money market at a discount. The seller may choose to do this if he needs cash immediately. The rate that the BA trades at depends on the credit of the bank on which it is drawn. The accepting bank may agree to buy the BA for its own account from the seller and, further, may rediscount the instrument and sell it to another investor. Upon maturity, whoever holds the BA presents it to the accepting bank for payment. The accepting bank collects the funds it is owed by the buyer.

BAs are mostly used in international trade where open book credit arrangements are not predominant. Credit risks and collection processes are hard to supervise in overseas trading, so sellers rely on banks as intermediaries in commercial transactions. Frequent BA investors include corporations, state and local governments, foreign and domestic banks, and money market mutual funds. Because the risk of BAs is measured according to the perceived quality of the accepting bank, they provide returns similar to CDs. The secondary market for BAs is also comparable to that for CDs: round lots trade between $1 million and $5 million and are available from large banks or New York dealers and brokers. Liquidity

in the secondary market is enhanced when the accepting bank is large
and well-known. Therefore, BAs sold by smaller, regional banks yield
higher resale rates.[138]

MONEY MARKET FUNDS IN A VOLATILE
INVESTMENT ERA

Money market mutual funds are not instruments but vehicles for entering
the money market. These are mutual funds which pool investor cash and
invest in diversified portfolios of money market instruments, primarily
commercial paper, CDs of all varieties, banker's acceptances, Treasury
bills and notes, and other government agency obligations and repurchase
agreements. By combining the assets of shareholders—investors—money
funds are able to seek the high yields offered by money market instruments
of large denominations which are beyond the reach of the average individual investor. Money funds derive their earnings in two ways: (1) from
the interest earned on portfolio securities, and (2) the change in the market
value of those same securities. Money funds determine each day the net
asset value per share and declare as dividends most of their investment
income. Fund expenses and management fees are accrued daily and fac-
tored into the daily net asset value per share calculation. Dividends and
gain distributions may be made in shares or in cash. There are no fees
charged for share purchase or redemption; for this reason, they are called
"no-load mutual funds." Transfer agents perform accounting and data
processing services for funds who are not equipped to do this in-house.
Money funds rely on banks—custodians—to hold investor deposits.
  In many ways, money fund accounts function like interest-earning
checking accounts. Money begins to earn interest the day a deposit is
registered. Shareholders can write checks at $500 minimums, to pay bills.
The shareholder enjoys disbursement float until the check clears back to
the custodian bank. The key historical difference between banks and
money funds, from an investor's perspective, was that the money funds
were able to capture extremely competitive yield advantages for shareholders at a time when banks were prevented by law from paying more
than passbook savings rates on demand deposits.
  The deregulation of the banking industry began in 1980, and slowly
banks have been freed from interest-rate ceilings on certain classes of

noncorporate deposits. In December 1982, the Depository Institutions Deregulation Committee authorized banks to pay unlimited interest rates on money market deposit accounts opened by individuals. These accounts have certain restrictions, including a maintained minimum balance of $2500. This has been a boon to small savers who desire the safety of FDIC insurance. (Money market fund investments are not insured.) Money market fund assets had peaked at $232.2 billion as of December 1, 1982; however, within one month after the new bank accounts had been authorized, money fund assets dropped over 13%. These regulatory upheavals have caused no end of consternation for money fund managers who are unsure what the future holds. Conversely, some innovative money fund organizations, including The Fidelity Group and The Dreyfus Corporation, have bought banks. Analysts expect a continuation of tactical moves by regulators, banks, and money funds as the process of bank deregulation unfolds.

As of this writing, there is debate over whether banks will be allowed, or willing, to offer competitive interest rates on corporate checking accounts. For the most part, corporate cash managers do not perceive a benefit in investing in bank checking accounts as a primary means of keeping excess cash productive. They are accustomed to the fiduciary responsibility implicit in their job descriptions and, unlike individual depositors, are not overly concerned with FDIC insurance that, in any case, covers only the first $100,000 of a bank depositor's assets. Cash managers have systems in place for managing aggregate cash positions and, therefore, are not interested in having to oversee hundreds of field bank accounts merely to earn an average rate on small balances. One cash management imperative is to reduce the number of bank accounts that have to be scrutinized. Banks are reluctant to offer interest on corporate checking accounts since such a move would invite unwieldy movements of corporate money. Corporate investments involve high stakes: typical investments range in the millions. It is unlikely that banks will rush to operate such potentially volatile transaction accounts.

Corporations have used money market funds to a limited extent as a means of "parking" excess cash until a suitable investment opportunity became available. Some corporations have used money funds as an alternative to remote or controlled disbursement accounts. Since money fund investments earn a market rate of return until the day that checks are presented for payment, they provide a handy disbursement service for companies too small to employ sophisticated forecasting, complicated funding, and aggressive investment techniques necessary to manage remote and controlled disbursement accounts. These small firms, along with certain nonprofit organizations, shift the administrative burden of investing onto the money funds they use.

Some cash managers and treasurers make a strong case for using a money fund as a portfolio manager when in-house staff are too busy or untrained in the art of money market investing. They have a point. Money fund portfolio managers are highly skilled and aware of the responsibility their shareholders place in their hands. Because money funds do not have FDIC insurance, the money fund industry is under enormous pressure to convince investors that money funds are safe. As such, portfolio managers are conditioned to perform well given the relatively conservative risk parameters outlined by their managements.

Cash managers interested in using money funds for disbursements must consider how well a particular fund is geared to perform this service. These are the things to look for:

Are money fund check formats consistent with current system checks?

Can facsimile signatures be used?

Are cancelled checks returned monthly or quarterly?

Can the money fund arrange for adequate stop payment procedures?

Are funds wired into the fund given same-day credit?

What is the daily cutoff for receiving credit on funds wired in?

How easily can money fund assets be liquidated: telephone redemptions with same-day wire transfers?

Do the instruments which the fund invests in meet corporate investment policy requirements?

How well has a certain fund performed historically compared to other money funds? (You can compare money fund performance by checking *Donoghue's Money Fund Report.*)

What minimum requirement does a fund place on the check writing feature?

Is a fund tied to a bank's automatic sweep program whereby daily excess funds are moved into a money fund account, thus relieving the cash manager of administrative supervision?

Is a particular fund geared to corporate or retail shareholders? (For instance, a money fund prepared to meet corporate needs will provide ACH cash concentration into a firm's money fund account. The Fidelity Group, in Boston, was a pioneer in this area.)

Is the custodian bank known for its operating skills?

What do other cash managers have to say about a certain fund?

While money funds are a fairly recent phenomenon, they have served investors well since their explosive growth in the past five years. It remains to be seen how the market for financial products will settle once the turbulent era of bank deregulation subsides. The world of money market investing is evolving rapidly as nonbank service providers encroach on a turf once reserved for banks. Indeed, the banking world has been turned upside down by firms such as Sears Roebuck that have begun to aggressively market a wide range of financial services. Conversely, as banks gain the authority to offer services once restricted to the securities industry, tactical competition among financial service providers will no doubt intensify.

INVESTMENT GUIDELINES

Corporations take a variety of approaches to investment policies. Some firms give the cash manager a loose reign on short-term investment decisions. Others carefully spell-out what types of investments can be made at certain maturities at what risk. Moreover, some policies restrict investments to portions of the excess cash pool. Policies often relate how a firm's senior management views the role of short-term investments. Is the treasury function seen as a profit center and evaluated as such? Or is the treasury designed as a service center that has as a supreme goal the safe-guarding of corporate financial assets? Is a firm willing to invest in its portfolio management staff, hiring skilled personnel to work solely on improving the return on short-term excess cash? Or does a company expect its cash manager to passively monitor the earning power of excess balances; maybe, a secretary is assigned to routinely arrange for repurchase agreements with the lead bank? In effect, is short-term investing seen as liquidity management or portfolio management?

A company that takes a liquidity management approach to its short-term investments focuses on the recording, control, and prediction of daily receipts and disbursements. Any excess cash is placed in simple overnight investments. On the other hand, a company with a true portfolio management approach to investing values the explicit income to be gained from sophisticated strategies. To some, sophisticated means having a dedicated microcomputer on hand that interfaces with external data bases such as money market rates, or that provides model-based decision support. At either end of the spectrum, investment guidelines define the cash manager's investment task. Guidelines prioritize company goals. For instance, a policy may dictate that securities cannot be sold before maturity. This restriction is intended to avoid book losses. It also restrains a cash manager from gambling on future interest rate movements and possibly profiting from clever hedges.

Policy guidelines may prohibit overseas investments where higher yields are found, or they may disallow purchases of domestic corporation preferred stock, even though risk-adjusted returns may exceed money market rates because 85% of such dividend income is free from Federal taxes to corporate shareholders.[139] Typically, guidelines indicate the type of securities to be purchased, and they may set a maximum dollar limit that can be invested in the securities of any one issue. In short, investment guidelines are formed based on the company's definition of allowable risk given sensitivity to instrument safety, marketability, and yield.

The most effective investment policies are those that allow cash managers some degree of flexibility while setting out clear parameters so that investments do not jeopardize company assets. When policies are too restrictive, they do not allow the cash manager to react to constantly shifting market conditions. This can severely diminish investment results. Nonexistent or unclear policies, on the other hand, may tempt a cash manager to get in over his head in a shaky deal for a mere 25 basis-point advantage. One way to assure that guidelines remain flexible and responsive to management goals is to schedule periodic reviews. Unfortunately, many firms simply dictate policy guidelines once, then forget about them. This results in a contemporary cash manager being stuck with risk parameters appropriate to the early 1970s; remember, that was when commercial paper was issued without back-up lines of credit. It was also before banker's acceptances were popular as a short-term investment.

Investment policies that work well provide cash managers and management with a valuable communication medium. The cash manager knows what authority has been given him and how his performance will be measured. When policies are reviewed at least annually, senior management is kept appraised of short-term investment earnings and how well the company fared given market conditions and definitions of prudence.

10 International Cash Management

In Europe, sales subsidiaries of a huge American manufacturer now purchase inventory from the parent for resale to local customers using a reinvoicing center located in Switzerland. The American firm thus centralizes exposure to a group of foreign currencies and takes advantage of lenient tax rules, writing off as much as 50% of annual inventory. Another corporation with overseas operations relies on its multilateral netting system to reduce the costs of purchasing foreign exchange and float associated with intracorporate transactions. Yet another American company with a plant in Venezuela depends on a team of runners to pick up remittance checks from customers and deposit them at the bank—the nation's mail system is one of the worst in the world.

This is a small glimpse at techniques used by cash managers to manage global liquidity. In this chapter, we will see how cash management among far-flung operations is performed. Although the objectives of global cash management are conceptually similar to the domestic counterpart, the nature of international banking and commerce is difficult to pigeonhole. In addition to striving for the most productive uses of corporate financial assets overseas, cash managers must contend with a patchwork of country regulations dictating how money can be repatriated to the parent, confusing bank practices, erratic qualities of funds transfer and postal systems, and volatile foriegn exchange rates. Another obstacle to smooth cash management in other countries involves the difficulty of enforcing credit and collection policies in foreign countries where inflation rates are so high that it makes economic sense for customers to finance their businesses by stretching payables for many months. Organizational development is also a problem: foreign subsidiary staff can be incorrigible when a hungry parent insists on having most excess cash upstreamed, leaving the local portfolio thin and unproductive.

Yet aside from such difficulties, international cash management, to many, represents an exciting and new field. To veterans, it is an arduous task whose rewards are often elusive but ultimately worthwhile. The large American banks at the forefront of global treasury consulting services—Bank of America, Citibank, Chase, Manufacturers Hanover Trust, and others—as well as huge European banks are eager to help American firms set up overseas. Cash managers who suddenly discover that they are responsible for designing an integrated global money management system turn to their banks for skill and experience. They soon discover that many of the tools used for domestic cash management have been fitted to foreign trade needs. In some locales, you can find automated balance reporting, same-day funds transfer, EFT, zero-balance accounts, lockboxes, and concentration points. Yet in other areas, typically struggling third world countries, banks seem doomed to operational inefficiency. If you are a cash manager bored with domestic duties, international responsibility can challenge your wits and capacity to learn new skills. Moreover, if your firm conducts business in countries that you would love to visit, hop aboard.

SPECIAL CONCERNS OF THE INTERNATIONAL CASH MANAGER

The most important fact of life for the international cash manager, whether from a giant multinational or a small specialty goods exporter, is that uniform banking and governmental and commercial practices are nonexistent. There is no watchful monetary authority that controls worldwide money supply like our own Federal Reserve System manages the American economy. There is no central payment system that acts as a bankers' bank; money is moved internationally using correspondent bank balances. Furthermore, there is a wide disparity from country to country concerning banking regulations. In some nations, the government has a heavy hand in deciding how American assets will be valued and profits returned home. The following difficulties contribute to the global cash manager's spheres of concern:

Organizational Development.
Country-specific economics and philosophy.
Foreign exchange exposure.
Funds transfer systems.

ORGANIZATIONAL DEVELOPMENT

Usually, a global cash management system does not appear overnight. American firms generally expand into overseas operations gradually, beginning with a few sales offices, then possibly establishing regional business offices. At some point, the treasury staff at headquarters realizes that a formal system, whether centralized or decentralized, is needed to integrate the flows of information and cash. A multinational may combine the strengths of centralized and decentralized control and formulate policy at headquarters, while local units supervise working capital, schedule financing, manage foreign exchange risk exposure, and invest excess cash. Of course, the local unit staff performs basic cash management: collecting cash receipts, controlling balances at a central bank account, planning disbursements, and forecasting.

Another approach calls for more centralized cash management planning, by far the most common organizational structure among American multinationals. For this to work, however, the senior treasury staff at headquarters has to have a keen sense of local market conditions. By assigning the responsibility for each region to a regional treasurer, senior treasury staff shares the task of keeping up with local bank relationships, securities markets, and currency movements. An adaptation of this may involve performance evaluation by budgets. Regional treasurers manage annual budget allocations while quarterly updates keep senior management in touch with local enterprise. A common problem arises when cash-rich subsidiaries or divisions are ordered to constantly fund cash-poor corporate brethren. The performers may resent it when they are not allowed to invest excess funds in money markets. The problem for senior management is to remind performers of corporatewide goals. This may be accomplished with clear growth incentives for local managers.

Another organizational problem involves credit and collection policies. Foreign subsidiary staff may be geared to sell company products and therefore may be reluctant to clamp down on hard-won clients who are slow to pay their bills. Stringent credit review policies are also hard to impose on a sales-oriented foreign staff. It is difficult for home office credit managers to control credit and collection risks at a distance. For some multinationals, the answer lies in formulating an international credit and collections manual that will educate and motivate local staff. While not inflexible, a good manual can suggest practical guidelines for conducting credit investigations, establishing credit limits, collecting receipts, determining appropriate bad debt write-offs, uniform aging and evaluation of accounts receivables, and system reporting. The international credit manager at headquarters can then review periodically how well local staff have implemented policies and adjust constraints to meet local operating conditions.[140]

COUNTRY SPECIFIC ECONOMICS AND POLITICS

Sometimes, cash managers new to the international scene experience a kind of culture shock when they realize the disparity between American business practices and those found in foreign societies. In fact, one Washington, D.C., outfit, Transemantics Inc., specializes in teaching American executives how to maneuver overseas. For instance, a manager headed for a stint in the Bangkok office can learn why business is best conducted there in soft-spoken tones. Whether an international cash manager is based at the home office, or is sent to run a regional treasury, he can benefit by researching the business nuances particular to countries where his firm operates. Of particular interest is how foreign cultures view American business prowess, whether they welcome it or fear it.

One way that an international cash manager guards corporate financial assets is to keep on top of foreign government attitude. The cash manager must constantly measure the threat that assets will be expropriated. This occurs when a host government either partially or totally confiscates corporate assets with or without compensation to the American firm.[141] A host government may perceive that an American company, through price manipulation, is thwarting that nation's ability to compete in national markets. Or a host government may be unhappy with an American company's reluctance to train and employ local personnel. The degree to which an American company upstreams operating profits via dividend payments and royalty or management fees is something that some host governments watch carefully and often regulate. But a government backed into a corner by its own troubled economy and political turmoil might move to expropriate or freeze American assets. Total expropriation happens when a government feels that it can get more mileage out of seizing plants brimming with American technology than it can sustain with continued friendly relationships with American corporations. The freezing of assets occurs when a foreign government restricts the use and movement of assets through discriminatory taxation, arbitrary manipulation of prices for raw materials, or placing ceilings on the amount of money that can be repatriated or the amount of finished goods available for export. The cash manager must monitor government attitudes and political situations which threaten American assets.

FOREIGN EXCHANGE EXPOSURE

The most widespread threat to the value of American financial assets overseas involves currency devaluation. In addition to restricting the repatriation of corporate cash, foreign nations may attempt to correct economic ills such as hyperinflation by devaluing their currencies in relation to other currencies worldwide. This results in the dilution of assets stuck in a country with a deflating value of money. Thus, a firm is exposed to the fluctuating real value of its expenses, revenues, and profits. This problem exists because a company must conduct trade in a foreign country using the medium of exchange—local currency—that is appropriate to that nation. For instance, you cannot use deutsche marks to buy goods in the United States because the medium of exchange here is dollars. You have to exchange the deutsche marks for dollars in the foreign exchange market before you can make your purchase.

A foreign exchange trader who buys and sells currencies for his own account and assumes exchange risk can accommodate the transaction. Traders, generally, are employed by large banks and other financial institutions. A broker, who acts merely as a matchmaker between persons wanting to exchange currencies, can also help. The transaction risk involved is that the value of foreign currencies can change in relation to each other. For example, when the dollar at a given point in time has become strong relative to another currency, it takes more of the other currency to match the purchasing power of the dollar. A foreign subsidiary or customer with a previous commitment to pay a U.S. supplier in dollars will be hurt by the dollar's strengthening because more of a foreign currency will be needed to pay the bill. The movement of the dollar's value in the foreign exchange market has, in effect, increased the cost of the purchase. On the other hand, the value of accounts receivables expected in dollars will have been enhanced. International cash managers attempt to predict rate fluctuations and the effects on current asset valuation. To avoid coming up short in the course of handling business receipts and disbursements, they often buy and sell forward contracts to protect the productivity of company cash. We will look at this below.

In the foreign exchange market, currencies, in the form of bank drafts, can be traded at rates that represent spot prices. A spot contract implies immediate exchange. In New York, immediate delivery is typically one business day for North American currencies (U.S. dollars, Canadian dollars, and Mexican pesos). Otherwise, two days is the norm. Same-day exchange and delivery of bank drafts is possible at a premium above standard quotations given by traders and reported in newspapers.

The forward exchange market involves contracts for the buying and selling of currency at some future date. Standard maturities are for one, two, three, six, and twelve months. A forward contract for any maturity may be negotiated but transactions costs may be relatively higher. For example, an American importer may purchase a forward contract when he expects to pay for goods delivered in 90 days. The payable is invoiced in Swiss francs. To avoid the risk that the Swiss franc may be revalued, which would result in the need for more dollars to purchase the same number of Swiss francs, the importer buys a forward contract for the required amount of Swiss francs at the current market rate. The Swiss francs will then be available at the agreed price in 90 days when the payment is due.[142] Readers may refer to the vast literature available on foreign exchange trading for an in-depth look at market dimensions and operations.

The Federal Reserve Bank of New York published in 1978 a valuable introduction to the subject, entitled *Foreign Exchange Markets in the United States* by Kubarych.[143]

Indeed, the volatility of exchange rates is one of the international cash manager's most pressing concerns: he faces two types of foreign exchange exposure stemming from translation and transaction risk. Translation exposure concerns long-term assets or liabilities denominated in foreign currencies that may be altered, in U.S. dollar terms, when exchange rates have fluctuated and a corporation must record consolidated accounting data. The corporation may realize either translation losses or gains. Transaction exposure concerns current assets and liabilities denominated in foreign currencies that may be altered, in U.S. dollar terms, as a result of the firm's having to make or receive a payment in the course of international trade. We will consider below how American companies use bilateral and multilateral netting systems and reinvoicing centers to reduce the amount of funds exposed to transaction risk.

Exchange Controls

Host governments in Latin America are notorious for imposing restrictions of how much local money American firms can exchange for dollars and send back to the U.S. parent in the form of dividends, fees, or interest and loan repayments. As a result of regionwide exchange controls, often limiting cross-border funds movements to 20% of a firm's registered capital base, money is blocked. To deal with this, corporations may invest in local financial instruments, such as certificates of deposit, government bonds, corporate securities, time deposits, or real estate. Given the recent turbulence of Latin American economies, local investments are a tricky business; it is difficult to predict any degree of financial stability in certain countries.

However, clever schemes exist for utilizing blocked funds. For instance, Company A, a large U.S. corporation, arranged a parallel loan with another U.S. firm, Company B. Company A's Colombian subsidiary, which had a large amount of blocked pesos, lent these pesos to the Colombian subsidiary of Company B at an attractive rate, relative to local interest rates. In return, the U.S. parent of Company B provided an equivalent loan in U.S. dollars to the parent of Company A at a very attractive rate.

Another firm has a cash-rich subsidiary that lends on the "street market," also known as the secondary market. This is an unregulated though legal extra-banking system popular in Latin America. Lenders include bank affiliates, industrial firms with blocked funds, local leasing and insurance companies, domestic brokers, and any other organizations desiring remunerative rates on peso holdings. Street market rates are adjusted to account for peso devaluation. Still other companies combat exchange controls and adjust for currency devaluation by overinvoicing exports to foreign subsidiaries. A recent approach is to sell "technology" to a local consulting firm that then sells it to subsidiaries. The consultant keeps a commission and returns the rest of the payments to the U.S. parents.[144]

FUNDS TRANSFER SYSTEMS

All U.S. dollar receipts and payments outside the United States, whether they involve trade, investment, Eurodollar, or foreign exchange transactions, are ultimately effected through the transfer of funds between bank accounts in the United States. Similarly, all German mark or French franc transactions are effected in Germany or France, respectively. Thus, every foreign exchange transaction involves at least two shifts of bank deposits in national currencies. If Barclays Bank buys German marks from Credit Lyonnais, Barclays will arrange for funds to be transferred from its correspondent account in New York to that of Credit Lyonnais. At the same time, in Frankfurt, funds will be transferred from a correspondent account of Credit Lyonnais to one of Barclays.[145]

For many years, funds transfer instructions were sent by cable. In response to cable messages, banks made the appropriate debits and credits to the accounts of their correspondents. In 1977, The Society for Worldwide Interbank Financial Telecommunication (SWIFT) began operations in Brussels. SWIFT is a computerized system for relaying payment instructions written in a standardized format among over 800 European, North American, and Latin American international banks. A SWIFT message can be sent from one bank to another in minutes. This technology is a boon to the cash manager who can be assured that funds transfer instructions will be carried out with one day. Under standard airmail procedures, funds transfers can take days. Telex messages can be effected in one business day, but they are costly compared to the efficient, electronic SWIFT.

CHIPS (Clearing House Interbank Payments System) is used by international banks in New York to settle dollar transactions. On October 1, 1981, CHIPS moved from next-day to same-day settlement, an event which drew lots of attention to this EFT network that now handles over $180 billion in average daily volume, which includes over 90% of all foreign exchange trades. CHIPS is owned by the New York Clearing House Association; its participants include 12 major New York banks, branches of foreign banks, and Edge Act subsidiaries of out-of-state banks. Edge Act companies are affiliates of American banks chartered to conduct international business transactions. Unlike SWIFT, which is a data transfer system for effecting debits or credits to correspondent bank accounts, CHIPS is a genuine funds transfer operation: CHIPS member banks receive payment instructions and credit from correspondents or corporate customers and then effect actual same-day funds transfer through the New York Clearing House Association computer, which debits and credits the appropriate Clearing House accounts of CHIPS member banks. Cash managers begin the credit transfer process on a given day by instructing their banks to initiate CHIPS payments on their behalf.

International commercial banking operations are based on correspondent bank relationships; funds transfers may be effected as described above: through cable, telex, or SWIFT messages which result in debits or credits being properly allocated among correspondents, or through CHIPS funds transfers. International banks provide corporate customers with a wide range of services, including investment, Eurodollar, and foreign exchange transactions; automated balance reporting (in some locales); loans, accepting drafts; providing credit data; and consulting of all varieties; in addition to basic cash management services such as lockboxes and concentration and zero-balance accounts. When setting up overseas, it is important that the cash manager research the operating ability of local banks. There is a wide disparity owing to the levels of technological expertise demonstrated among various nations.

The cash manager must investigate how funds are normally moved from one locale to another. He may find that, unless he specifies SWIFT data transfers, a local bank will rely on the traditional method of airmailing funds transfer instructions to a correspondent. This can take a minimum of three days; more often delays amount to a week of lost funds availability. If the local bank does not have a correspondent relationship with the bank of destination, another bank will have to serve as an intermediary. Much more time may be lost. Unlike the payments system that we often take for granted in the U.S., the world of international banking may seem strange when we consider how most European banks are compensated for services. They value date transactions. That is, when a company instructs a bank to initiate a payment, the bank typically debits the company account immediately but holds the funds for its own use for up to three days. The bank receiving the payment may also hold the money for a few days before crediting the transaction beneficiary.

Latin American banking practices are another story all together. There are no standardized intracountry check clearing times in many Latin American nations; availability on funds is often a matter of negotiation between company and bank. Furthermore, account analyses are generally unavailable. Companies have to use their own methods for tracking banking expenses. In Latin America, phone balance reporting is infrequently practical, so companies have to send messengers to pick up daily balance printouts from the banks. In Venezuela, the mail system is very poor, so corporations rely on runners to collect checks from customers. Once checks are deposited at a bank, if the bank of payment is located within the same city as the collecting bank, credit to the receiving firm is posted within 48 hours. Check collections involving banks outside major cities usually experience three day delays, that is, if the two banks share the benefit of communicating with computers. Otherwise, funds availability may be delayed for at least one week.[146]

CASH MANAGEMENT TECHNIQUES

One of the most widely used cash management techniques in Europe involves concentrating subsidiaries' cash at a single bank either within a country or on a regional level at a money center. Often, Europeanwide systems are established at a bank in London or Amsterdam. Asian systems are typically centered in Hong Kong or Singapore. Funds in the accounts of cash-rich subsidiaries are used to fund deficit subsidiaries. Funds may be allocated by a special bank procedure in which credit balances are used to offset overdrafts at the end of each day. Or more complex schemes using zero-balance accounts may be used. Excess funds are reported daily to the company. Generally, amounts over target are invested.

International lockboxes are used to intercept a U.S. company's foreign payments. Payments denominated in a foreign currency are settled in the country where the currency is legal tender. This avoids cross-border check clearing. Besides mail delays, cross-border checks involve lengthy collection delays and costs reaching to as much as one percent of the face value of the check. An international bank can have one of its branches intercept and collect checks for a cash manager, then report transaction data back to the company. U.S. dollar checks may be sent back to the U.S. by courier.[147]

Although not a new concept, intracompany netting has gained wide popularity among U.S. cash managers seeking to defray the high costs of foreign exchange, time delays, and opportunity costs associated with intracompany, cross-border transactions. Bilateral netting provides that one subsidiary's receivables are another's payables. It is the off-setting of trade-related claims and liabilities between kindred companies in two countries. The key is that only net amounts owed need to be transferred. Multilateral netting is simply the netting concept extended to a system that involves related companies in many countries. One of the benefits of netting schemes is that, overall, a multinational has a smaller volume of funds that have to be transferred globally, hence lower currency exchange expense; in addition, there are the benefits of administrative efficiency, enhanced parent control of foreign operations due to improved transaction reporting, and the reduction of lost funds availability that occurs with bank value dating.

Reinvoicing centers are another device gaining attention among international cash managers. A reinvoicing center is an entity set up by a multinational for the purpose of buying from the group's manufacturing subsidiaries in the currency of the production units and reselling to the sales subsidiaries in the currency of the ultimate purchaser. For example, a German manufacturing subsidiary that normally exported directly to the French sales subsidiary and invoiced it in French francs, would instead sell the inventory to the reinvoicing center, that would, in turn, sell to the French subsidiary for French francs. The physical goods would still be shipped directly from Germany to France, although the title would pass through the center. To determine the price in deutsche marks, applied to what was originally a French franc sale, the center would use an intracompany parity rate, which would be changed only occasionally to reflect major shifts in exchange rates. The benefits to reinvoicing are automatically centralized foreign exchange risk, an ability to maximize after-tax returns (given exchange control regulations) and to minimize the after-tax cost of borrowing, and enhanced data control on cross-border transactions. Like netting plans, the ability to set up reinvoicing centers depends heavily on government regulations in specific countries.[148] Some countries ban either scheme outright. Other nations, such as Switzerland, are prime locations for reinvoicing centers.

SUMMARY

Global cash management is a complex but challenging endeavor. The international cash manager can do much to help his firm operate overseas where banking, commercial, and government practices are often unwieldy. A firm's foreign financial assets are precious, but they need a watchful guardian in light of quickly evolving trade conditions. We have tried to describe here some of the realities of international payment systems; however, a comprehensive discussion of the myriad rules and strategies employed by U.S. multinationals is beyond the scope of this book. There is a great deal of literature available on a wide assortment of international finance for interested readers. One source, Business International, Inc., located in New York City, regularly publishes in-depth survey reports on international cash management.

Appendix

THE CENTER FOR CASH MANAGEMENT STUDIES

BANK ADMINISTRATION INSTITUTE
60 GOULD CENTER / ROLLING MEADOWS, ILLINOIS 60008 / (312) 228-6200

MODEL LOCKBOX QUESTIONNAIRE

Attached is the final version of the Model Lockbox Questionnaire. This questionnaire is the result of initial work done by a project task force chaired by Shirley J. Gilmer, Vice President of RepublicBank Dallas, and incorporates suggested changes and comments received from many bankers as well as members of regional cash management associations and the National Corporate Cash Management Association.

The purpose of the Model Questionnaire is to provide a useful tool to enable lockbox banks to establish a comprehensive set of answers to lockbox questionnaires sent by corporations, leading to greater efficiencies in the many banks that frequently receive questionnaires. For the corporate cash manager, the questionnaire will provide a model from which to select appropriate questions, and will help to insure that a meaningful comparison can be made of lockbox questionnaire responses received from different banks.

> I. Mail Processing
> II. Lockbox Processing
> III. Check Processing and Funds Availability
> IV. Automated Lockbox Via Data Transmission
> V. Deposit and Balance Reporting
> VI. Pricing and Account Analysis

Reprinted here courtesy of the Bank Administration Institute

MODEL LOCKBOX QUESTIONNAIRE

FINAL VERSION

SEPTEMBER 7, 1982

Mail Processing

1. Describe the flow and processing of mail in your city's main mail facility. Please indicate the Post Office's processing hours during the week and on weekends, separately.

2. Does your bank have a unique Zip Code assigned for receipt of Wholesale and/or Retail Lockbox items? (Specify whether the unique Zip Code is for wholesale mail only, retail mail only, the entire bank, wholesale and retail items, or bank building tenants.)

3. Please list your bank's schedule for post office pickups of Lockbox mail for weekdays, weekends, and holidays.

4. What is the average length of time between the pickup of items at the Post Office and delivery to your bank? Is the courier an outside service or internally managed? If internally managed, is it under lockbox management?

5. Where is mail that is picked up at the Post Office delivered to your bank? If not directly to your Lockbox Department, by what method, and how often, is it delivered to the Lockbox Department? What is the length of time between bank arrival and lockbox arrival?

6. What degree of sorting is performed by the Post Office? By your bank, i.e., who performs the fine sort to the individual lockboxes?

7. If you sort yourself, please describe the type and speed of the sorting equipment.

8. Please provide copies of the last Phoenix-Hecht mail study reflecting your bank's "current" smoothed mail time averages for all of the Phoenix-Hecht mailing locations.

9. Using your most recent Phoenix-Hecht Mail Arrival Study or an internal bank analysis, please complete the table below by indicating the percentage of Lockbox mail received for each pickup and the corresponding deposit cutoff for that pickup. Please indicate the time of day used to start calculating the cumulative percentages received. Please state which study (P/H or internal) was used to determine these figures.

% of Mail Available for Each Pickup Time	Pickup Time	Cumulative %	Deposit Time

Lockbox Processing

1. What are the monthly volumes and percentages for your retail and your wholesale lockboxes (items, dollars, number of lockboxes, and number of customers)? Please exclude concentration accounts.

2. How many full-time employees are directly assigned to your Lockbox operation? Please break out the total by Supervision, Administration, and Production.

3. How many part-time employees supplement the full-time staff during peak periods? What is your source of part-time employees?

4. What is the average seniority of the clerks in your Lockbox Department? What is the seniority of the supervisors and managers?

5. What is your Lockbox Department's processing schedule? This should include active and inactive hours for weekends and weekdays.

6. If checks are processed during the weekend period or holidays, is the output (details of payment received) distributed to the lockbox customer that day or the next business day?

7. Please provide us with a list of bank holidays. Does your bank process lockbox activity on these days?

8. Do you offer multiple deposits as a feature of your lockbox service? What are the deposit times and how are they determined? Can you combine multiple deposits to a single credit for statement purposes?

9. What is the latest mail pickup to be included for ledger credit on a same-day basis?

10. What steps are taken to insure that optimum availability of funds is achieved for lockbox deposits? Is there priority handling of items for certain lockbox customers (i.e., large monthly dollar volume customers)?

11. Are large dollar items separated and handled faster or differently? Over what dollar size? Is this done automatically or manually, and when?

12. What special arrangements are made to handle lockbox items during peak volume periods?

13. Do you process and deposit all payments same day received? If not, what percentage of items is carried over?

14. Please provide a description of the major components of your Lockbox Department's processing procedures. This should include the overall method of processing (assembly line, group, individual) and the specific processing procedures for a standard wholesale lockbox.

15. What type of reproduction equipment does your bank use? Please send a sample photocopy.

16. Please describe your procedures for processing foreign checks received in the lockbox. What float period is assigned foreign items? Are procedures/float assignments different for Canadian or Mexican items?

17. By what methods can you deliver the hard copy of lockbox remittance detail? Does your bank use U.S. Postal Service Express Mail Service or other similar courier services? If so, can you give representative rates and times for various delivery options?

18. Describe your quality control system for items within your Lockbox Department.

19. How do you define a processing error and what is your error rate per 1,000 wholesale items processed?

20. Is there a formal procedure for responding to adjustment inquiries from lockbox customers? If yes, please explain and include time frame. In the event of an error, who would we contact at the bank?

21. Do you maintain affiliations with a bank (or banks) in other cities or states which would provide lockbox processing? What benefits would accrue from these arrangements?

22. Please provide the names and telephone numbers of three of your present lockbox customers as references, and the appropriate individual to contact.

23. Do you require a Lockbox Agreement? If so, please include a copy.

Check Processing and Funds Availability

1. Please describe the major components of the Check Processing Department's procedures and how it interfaces with the Lockbox Department, highlighting the complete flow of checks. Which department MICR encodes checks processed by lockbox?

2. How do you compute the availability which is passed on to the customer? Is float calculated on each check processed, is a float factor assigned to each account on the basis of recent experience with the customer's receipts, or is the float factor used for all the bank's customers based on a bank average? If a float factor is used, how often is it re-evaluated?

3. During what hours and days does your Proof Transit Department operate? If your Lockbox and Proof Transit departments work on weekends, are those remittance items processed also cleared during the weekend? How is availability determined for items processed on weekends and holidays and when will ledger credit be given?

4. If you determine availability by individual check endpoint, please provide your bank's latest availability schedule. Do your customers have different availability schedules from which to choose? Also, are there distinctions for large and small dollar checks? If yes, what constitutes the dollar thresholds?

5. What is the settlement hour for your local clearing house? Is there more than one clearinghouse meeting? What is the latest pickup time from the Post Office box for presentation of that day's clearing house meeting? Do local clearing house checks receive any special handling in order for them to be presented at the meeting hour?

6. Please list the member banks of your clearing house association, by meeting.

7. Does your bank make direct sendings to correspondent banks, Federal Reserve Banks, or Regional Check Processing Centers? Please list your direct send endpoints.

8. Are direct sends made on Saturday and/or Sunday?

9. How frequently is your check collection pattern reviewed and updated? Is this done on a bankwide basis or are lockbox deposits analyzed separately? How is this analysis performed?

10. Can your bank provide an availability analysis for lockbox items/deposits? If so, how frequently is this analysis performed? Is there a charge for this service? Please include a copy of this report, if available.

Automated Lockbox Via Data Transmission

1. Please describe your data transmission services for capture and transmission of remittance detail such as account or invoice number, MICR line or other number combinations for automatic posting of accounts receivable records. How do you capture data? Keystroke or MICR read? Do you have optical scan? How many accounts of each type of data capture method do you have?

2. Do you use BAI formats?

3. Will you provide a special format?

4. Please describe any special equipment used for data transmission. Do you provide CPU to CPU transmissions?

5. How many customers do you provide data transmission via tape? Via CPU to CPU?

6. How soon after the day's final deposit cutoff can remittance detail be transmitted?

7. Please provide us with three customers currently utilizing your data transmission service and the appropriate individual to contact for reference purposes.

8. Do you provide data consolidation/pooling service for your customers multi-lockbox systems? How many customers do you have on this service?

Deposit and Balance Reporting

1. For a given day's activity, at what time of day can you inform the lockbox customer or his designate of the total amount that will be credited to his account? What impact will this time have on the deposit schedule? What options are available for reporting deposit information?

2. Does your bank have the capability to provide same day float information for lockbox deposits? If yes, can this information be provided at the same time as the credit information? Please explain if available at a time different than credit information.

3. Does your bank use a packaged third-party automated balance reporting system or has your bank developed its own automated balance reporting system? If so, please briefly explain how your system works and include any written material on the subject.

4. If your bank provides a terminal based balance reporting system, do you input lockbox information? If so, when is the information available (i.e., on-line, same day, next day, etc.)?

Pricing and Analysis
----

1. Does your bank publish a fee schedule with definitions of all your
   bank's activities and services? For how long are these prices
   guaranteed? If yes, please forward a current copy. If no, please
   provide prices for the following listing of basic services.

   a. Lockbox Rental Charge
   b. Lockbox Maintenance (Fixed)
   c. Per Item Processing, Including a Photocopy, Attaching Checks to
      Remittance Statements, etc.
   d. Notification to Customer of Daily Deposit
   e. Wire Transfer (Outgoing)
   f. Wire Transfer (Incoming)
   g. Account Maintenance
   h. Deposit Ticket
   i. Item Deposited
   j. Item Paid
   k. Return Item
   l. Stop Payment
   m. Data Transmission
   n. Data Consolidation/Pooling

2. Do you routinely provide a monthly account analysis? Please provide
   a sample analysis statement. How soon is the analysis available after
   month end?

3. How is your earnings credit determined, adjusted, and applied? Please
   include in your explanation the impact of your reserve requirement and
   a listing of your earnings credit for the last twelve months.

4. Can funds on deposit as compensating balances under a financing
   agreement (line of credit, etc.) be used to offset lockbox charges?
   If yes, what percentage can be applied?

5. What time frame does your bank use when reviewing balances for deficiency
   or excess (rolling 12 month average, calendar year, etc.)?

6. Do you accept fees as compensation for your lockbox services? Is the
   customer given the option of compensating your bank on either a fee
   or balance basis? Is the price the same for either option? Are fees
   paid by invoice or by direct charge?

7. If there is an adjustment made to our bank statement, what procedure
   is used to assure a corresponding adjustment to our analysis? How is
   adjustment handled if analysis has already been issued?

References

CHAPTER 1

1. Suzanne Wittebort, "The Frantic New Pace of Cash Management," *Institutional Investor,* June 1981, p. 181.

2. James F. Lordan, *The Banking Side of Corporate Cash Management,* Boston: Financial Publishing Company, 1973, p. 34.

3. David Dewan, *Managing Corporate Cash,* New York: American Management Association Extension Institute, 1976, p. 14.

4. Wittebort, p. 191.

5. Wittebort, p. 179.

6. Lordan, p. 3

7. Lordan, p. 31.

8. Paul J. Beehler, *Contemporary Cash Management: Principles, Practices, Perspective,* New York: Wiley, 1978, p. 117.

9. Alfred DeSalvo, "Cash Management Converts Dollars Into Working Assets," *Harvard Business Review,* May–June 1972, p. 98.

10. Allen J. Grieve, "Cash Collection/Concentration Services: The Current Impact and Future Prospects of Automated Clearing House Applications," Unpublished doctoral dissertation, The Stonier Graduate School of Banking, p. 53.

11. Lordan, p. 37.

CHAPTER 2

12. R. Wayne Mondy, Robert E. Holmes, and Edwin B. Flippo, *Management: Concepts and Practices,* Boston: Allyn & Bacon, 1980, p. 7.

13. Charles H. Ludlow, "Managing Working Capital," in *The Treasurer's Handbook,* ed. J. Fred Weston and Maurice B. Goudzwaard, Homewood, IL: Dow Jones-Irwin, 1976, p. 438.

14. William E. Donoghue and David C. Jones, "Evaluating The Cash Manager: Calculation of Net Yield on Cash and Near-Cash Assets," *The Journal of Financial Planning,* Spring 1977, p. 47.

15. Robert A. McDaniel, *Cash Management Consulting Newsletter,* December 1978, p. 1.

16. Lawrence J. Gitman, *Principles of Managerial Finance,* 2nd ed., New York: Harper & Row, 1979, p. 220.

17. Coopers & Lybrand Newsletter, January 1982, p. 1.

18. *Greenwich Research Associates, Cash Management Report To Participants,* Greenwich CT: Greenwich Research Associates, Inc., 1981, p. 9.

CHAPTER 3

19. Lordan, p. 6.

20. Lordan, p. 8.

21. William E. Donoghue, *Cash Management Manual,* Holliston MA: P and S Publications, 1978, p. I.4.3.

22. Grieve, p. 4.

23. Grieve, p. 4.

24. Beehler, p. 266.

25. Grieve, p. 6.

26. Grieve, p. 6.

27. Grieve, p. 8.

28. Donoghue, *Cash Management Manual,* p. I.4.5.

29. Lordan, p. 49.

30. Donoghue, *Cash Management Manual,* p. I.4.6.

31. Donoghue, *Cash Management Manual,* p. I.4.7.

32. G. J. Santoni and Courtenay C. Stone, "What Really Happened To Interest Rates?: A Longer Run Analysis," *Federal Reserve Bank of St. Louis Review,* 63, No. 9, November 1981, pp. 1–14.

33. Donoghue, *Cash Management Manual,* p. I.4.10.

34. Peter Koenig, "How Competition Is Sharpening Cash Management," *Institutional Investor,* June 1982, pp. 221–234.

CHAPTER 4

35. U.S., General Accounting Office, *The Federal Reserve Should Move Faster To Eliminate Subsidy of Check Clearing Operations,* Washington, D.C.: GGD-82-22, May 1982, p. 42.

36. U.S., General Accounting Office, pp. 42–43.

37. American Bankers Association, *Electronic Check Collection,* Washington, D.C., July 1981, p. 4.

38. Beehler, p. 276.

39. *Corporate EFT Report: Electronic Funds Transfer News for Bankers and Cash Managers,* New York: Pace Communication, II, No. 18, June 23, 1982, pp. 1–3.

40. Beehler, p. 273.

41. George C. White, "Electronic Banking A Cost-saving Alternative For Many Corporations," *Westchester Business Journal,* February 24, 1981.

42. George C. White, "EFT Opportunities for the Innovative Corporation," *The Journal of Cash Management,* II, No. 2, June 1982, pp. 42–48.

43. White, *The Journal of Cash Management.* pp. 42–48.

44. Lordan, p. 33.

CHAPTER 5

45. *The Cash Manager Newsletter,* Holliston, MA: P and S Publications, IV, No. 4, April 1982, p. 3.

46. Craig F. Sullivan, "Reviewing Bank Account Analysis: Ramada's Approach," *The Journal of Cash Management,* II, No. 4, November 1982, pp. 24–30.

47. *Cash Management Brochure,* Chicago, IL: The First National Bank of Chicago, 1976, p. 6.

48. James F. Lordan, "Cash Management: The Corporate-Bank Relationship," *The Magazine of Bank Administration,* February 1975, p. 15.

49. Beehler, p. 26.

50. Stuart A. Abramovitz, "Management and Control of Banking Expenses," *The Cash Manager Newsletter,* IV, No. 5, May 1981, p. 1.

51. Ned C. Hill, William L. Sartoris, and Sue L. Visscher, "The Effective Cost of Bank Credit Line Borrowing," Paper Presented at the National Corporate Cash Management Association Annual Conference, Atlanta, GA, November 7–9, 1982.

52. Abramovitz, p. 3.

53. Craig F. Sullivan, "Consolidating Corporate Funds Using Electronic Depository Transfers," Paper Presented at the Corporate Electronic Banking Conference sponsored by White Papers, Inc., October 14–15, 1982. Also, Sullivan, "Reviewing Bank Account Analysis: Ramada's Approach."

54. Beehler, p. 30

55. *The Leahy Financial Newsletter,* Fullerton, CA, II, No. 4, April 1979, p. 2.

56. Buddy Letourneau, (Charlotte, NC: North Carolina National Bank) Letter to the National Corporate Cash Management Association Annual Conference, Atlanta, GA, November 7–9, 1982.

CHAPTER 6

57. Robert W. Johnson, "Management of Accounts Receivable and Payable," in *The Financial Handbook* ed. Edward I. Altman, New York: Wiley, 1981, p. 28–25.

58. Ned C. Hill, "Factors Influencing Credit Policy: A Survey," *The Journal of Cash Management,* I, No. 2, December 1981, pp. 39–41.

59. Robert W. Johnson, *The Financial Handbook,* p. 28–25.

60. *The Cash Manager Newsletter,* V, No. 12, December 1982, p. 5.

61. Theodore O. Johnson, "Credit Terms Policy and Corporate Payment Practices," *The Journal of Cash Management,* II, No. 3 p. 15.

62. Theodore O. Johnson, p. 18.

63. Grieve, p. 22.

64. "Automated Wholesale Corporate Lockboxes Accelerate Corporate Cash Flow," *Cashflow,* January–February 1982, p. 40.

65. Beehler, p. 80.

66. Grieve, p. 23.

67. "Automated Corporate Lockboxes Accelerate Corporate Cashflow," *Cashflow,* January–February 1982, p. 42.

68. Bernell K. Stone, "Cash Management," in *The Financial Handbook* ed. Edward I. Altman, New York: Wiley, 1981, p. 27–12.

69. Grieve, p. 28.

70. Stone, p. 27–14.

71. Stone, p. 27–14.

72. Steven F. Maier, "Collection System Design," Paper Presented at the National Corporate Cash Management Association Annual Conference, Atlanta, GA, November 7–9, 1982.

73. Steven F. Maier, "Collection System Design."

74. Steven F. Maier, "Collection System Design."

75. Grieve, p. 30.

76. Grieve, p. 30.

77. Beehler, p. 43.

78. Beehler, p. 44.

79. Grieve, p. 31.

80. Grieve, p. 33.

81. Norman Penney and Donald I. Baker, *The Law of Electronic Funds Transfer,* Boston, MA: Warren, Gorham & Lamont, 1980, p. 3–2.

82. Penney and Baker, p. 3–3.

83. Penney and Baker, p. 3–3.

84. Penney and Baker, p. 3–19.

85. Grieve, p. 50.

86. Penney and Baker, p. 4–6.

87. Penney and Baker, p. 4–7.

88. Penney and Baker, p. 5–41.

89. Grieve, pp. 57–59.

90. Penney and Baker, p. 5–46.

CHAPTER 7

91. Stone, p. 27–10.

92. Stone, p. 27–26.

93. Beehler. p. 48.

94. Sullivan, "Reviewing Bank Account Analysis: Ramada's Approach."

95. Stone, p. 27–21.

96. Beehler, p. 51.

97. Stone, p. 27–21.

98. Sullivan, "Reviewing Bank Account Analysis: Ramada's Approach."

99. Stone, p. 27–21.

100. Stone, p. 27–7.

101. Frederick W. Searby, "Cash Management: Helping Meet The Capital Crisis," in *The Treasurer's Handbook* ed. J. Fred Weston and Maurice B. Goudzwaard, Homewood, IL: Dow Jones-Irwin, 1976, p. 451.

102. Beehler, p. 56.

103. Beehler, p. 57.

104. Daniel M. Ferguson and Steven F. Maier, "Disbursement System Design for the 1980s," Paper Presented at the National Corporate Cash Management Association Annual Conference, New York, NY, October 25–26, 1981.

105. Stone, p. 27–8.

106. *The Leahy Financial Newsletter,* V, No. 3, March 1982. p. 2.

107. Ferguson and Maier.

108. *Disbursement Practices,* Chicago, IL: Phoenix-Hecht, 1982.

109. Steven F. Maier, "Insulated Controlled Disbursing: A Technique For Coping With Noon Presentment and Other Possible Check System Changes, *The Journal of Cash Management,* 2, No. 4, 1982, p. 35.

110. Lordan, p. 34.

111. Lordan, p. 39.

112. Penney and Baker, p. 5–32.

113. Penney and Baker, p. 5–33.

114. Penney and Baker, p. 5–37.

115. Bruce Reitz, "The New Checkless Society: Electronic Funds Transfer," *ICP Interface,* Autumn, 1982, p. 11.

CHAPTER 9

116. Donoghue, *Cash Management Manual,* p. II.3.5.

117. Alan H. Foster, "Cash Forecasting and Short-term Investing," in *The Treasurer's Handbook,* ed. J. Fred Weston and Maurice B. Goudzwaard, Homewood, IL: Dow-Jones-Irwin, 1976, p. 438.

118. Foster, p. 255.

119. George G. C. Parker, "Financial Forecasting," in *The Financial Handbook,* ed. Edward I. Altman, New York: Wiley, 1981, p. 26–6.

120. Foster, 253.

121. Bernell K. Stone and Tom W. Miller, "Daily Cash Forecasting: A Structuring Framework," *The Journal of Cash Management,* I, No. 1. p. 42–43.

122. Stone and Miller, pp. 43–44.
123. David Wismer, "Daily Cash Forecasting," *The Cash Manager Newsletter,* V, No. 1, January 1982, p. 1.
124. Joseph Bench, "Money and Capital Markets: Institutional Framework and Federal Reserve Control," in *The Financial Handbook* ed. Edward I. Altman, New York: Wiley, 1981, p. 1–19.
125. Foster, p. 259.
126. Bench, p. 1–12.
127. Tildon W. Smith, "Short-term Money Markets and Instruments," in *The Financial Handbook,* ed. Edward I. Altman, New York: Wiley, 1981, p. 25–7.
128. Smith, p. 10–7.
129. James F. Tucker, "Buying Federal Reserve Securities at Federal Reserve Banks," *Federal Reserve Bank of Richmond,* May 1982, p. 4.
130. Smith, p. 10–7.
131. Robert T. March, *The Investment Side of Cash Management,* Longport, N.J.: R.T. March and Associates, March 1982, p. 85.
132. Smith, p. 10–6.
133. Smith, p. 10–11.
134. "Perspectives," *Cashflow,* December 1982, p. 48.
135. Smith, P. 10–12.
136. March, p. 99.
137. Smith, p. 10–5.
138. Smith, p. 10–6.
139. *The Cash Manager Newsletter,* V, No. 9, September 1982, p. 6.

CHAPTER 10

140. "Global Cash Management: Corporate Strategies and Systems," *Special Report,* New York: Business International, 1982, pp. 28–29.
141. Beehler, p. 220.
142. Beehler, p. 248.
143. Richard M. Levich, "Exchange Rates and Currency Exposure," in *The Financial Handbook,* ed. Edward I. Altman, New York: Wiley, 1981, p. 12–4.
144. Louis J. Celi, "Cash Management at a Latin American Tempo," *The Cash Manager Newsletter,* III, No. 12, p. 1.

145. Ian N. Giddy, "International Commercial Banking," in *The Financial Handbook,* New York: Wiley, 1981, p. 14–31.

146. "Global Cash Management," p. 65.

147. H. Clay Simpson, Jr., "International Corporate Cash Management," *The Journal of Cash Management,* II, No. 1, p. 40.

148. "Global Cash Management," p. 128.

Bibliography

BOOKS AND MONOGRAPHS

ACH Operations Handbook. Washington, D.C.: National Automated Clearing House Association, 1981.

Automated Clearing Houses: An In-Depth Analysis. Atlanta, GA: Atlanta Payments Project, 1974.

Automated Clearing House File Specifications. Washington, D.C.: National Automated Clearing House Association, 1975.

The Banker's EFT Handbook. Washington, D.C.: American Bankers Association, 1975.

Beehler, Paul J. *Contemporary Cash Management: Principles, Practices, Perspectives.* New York: Wiley, 1978.

Cash Management. Chicago: Phoenix-Hecht, Inc., 1980.

Cash Management. Chicago: First National Bank of Chicago, 1976.

Cash Management for Bankers. Chicago: Phoenix-Hecht Cash Management Services, Inc., 1980.

The Consequences of Electronic Funds Transfer. Cambridge, Mass.: Arthur D. Little, Inc., 1975.

Compton, Eric N. *Inside Commercial Banking.* New York: Wiley, 1980.

A Costing Manual: Justification for Full ACH Participation. Washington: National Automated Clearing House Association (American Bankers Association), 1982.

Dingledy, E. "EFTs: Implications of Explicit Fed and Bank Service Pricing." In Kenneth L. Parkinson, Ed., *Cash Management Strategies and Systems for the 1980's.* White Plains, N.Y.: MDS Publications, 1981. pp. 159–170.

Donoghue, William E. *The Cash Management Manual.* Holliston, Mass.: Cash Management Institute, 1977.

Electronic Money and the Payments Mechanism. Boston: Federal Reserve Bank of Boston, 1980.

The Federal Reserve System: Purposes and Functions. Washington, D.C.: Board of Governors of the Federal Reserve System, 1974.

Fisher, D. I. *Cash Management.* New York: The Conference Board, 1973.

Goodman, S. *Cash Management for Small and Medium-Sized Companies.* New York: Prentice-Hall, 1972.

Hill, R. W., Jr. *Cash Management Techniques.* New York: American Management Associations, 1970.

Hunt, Alfred L. *Corporate Cash Management Including Electronic Funds Transfer.* New York: AMACOM, 1978.

Lordan, J. F. *The Banking Side of Corporate Cash Management.* Boston: Financial Publishing Company, 1973.

Martin, Claude R., Jr. *An Introduction To Electronic Funds Transfer Systems.* New York: AMACOM, 1978.

Operating Guidelines of the National Automated Clearing House Association. Washington, D.C.: National Automated Clearing House Association, June 1979.

Operating Rules of the National Automated Clearing House Association. Washington, D.C.: National Automated Clearing House Association, June 1979.

Penney, Norman and Donald I. Baker. *The Law of Electronic Fund Transfer Systems.* Boston: Warren, Gorham & Lamont, 1980.

Robertson, Robert R. "Developing Corporate Services." In William H. Baugh and Charles E. Walker, Eds., *The Banker's Handbook.* Homewood, Ill.: Dow Jones-Irwin, 1978. pp. 961–972.

Shain, John H. *An Approach to Analyzing the Potential Impact of Pricing Federal Reserve Services.* Wayne, Penn.: Littlewood, Shain & Company, 1979.

Status of Corporate Cash Management Systems. Longport, N.J.: R. T. March & Associates, March 1980.

Sure Pay Marketing/Education Manual. Washington, D.C.: National Automated Clearing House Association, December 1976.

The Systems Approach to Cash Management. White Plains, N.Y.: Marshall D. Sokol Associates, Inc., 1981.

Index